W9-BTQ-263

THE
Antitrust
Religion

THE
Antitrust
Religion

EDWIN S. ROCKEFELLER

CATO INSTITUTE
WASHINGTON, D.C.

Library of Congress Cataloging-in-Publication Data

Rockefeller, Edwin S.
    Antitrust religion / Edwin S. Rockefeller.
        p. cm.
    Includes bibliographical references and index.
    ISBN 978-1-933995-09-0 (alk. paper)
        1. Antitrust law. 2. Price fixing. I. Title.

    K3850.R63 2007
    343'.0721—dc22

                                                          2007031026

Cover design by Jon Meyers.

Printed in the United States of America.

CATO INSTITUTE
1000 Massachusetts Ave., N.W.
Washington, D.C. 20001
www.cato.org

For MWR

Contents

ACKNOWLEDGMENT   ix

INTRODUCTION   1

1. WHAT IS "ANTITRUST"?   3

2. THE ANTITRUST COMMUNITY   15

3. FROM "TRUST-BUSTING" TO THE PRESENT   27

4. THE MAGIC OF "MARKET POWER"   39

5. MONOPOLIZATION   47

6. MERGERS   63

7. "TYING" AND "EXCLUSIVE" DEALING   75

8. PRICE FIXING   87

9. IN CONCLUSION   99

NOTES   105

INDEX   119

Acknowledgment

Robert A. Levy, Senior Fellow of the Cato Institute, provided substantial editorial assistance. His help is gratefully acknowledged.

Introduction

We aspire to a government of laws, not of men. The rule of law implies ascertainable, coherent rules for guiding and judging behavior. It is the thesis of this book that antitrust law is not consistent with our aspiration for a rule of law. There is no such thing as antitrust law. Antitrust is a religion. Antitrust enforcement is arbitrary, political regulation of commercial activity, not enforcement of a coherent set of rules adopted by Congress.

Thurman Arnold, assistant attorney general for antitrust in the New Deal, described the origin of and need for the religion of antitrust in the following manner:

> Historians now point out that Theodore Roosevelt never accomplished anything with his trust busting. Of course he didn't. The crusade was not a practical one. It was part of a moral conflict and no preacher ever succeeded in abolishing any form of sin. Had there been no conflict—had society been able to operate in an era of growing specialization without these organizations—it would have been easy enough to kill them by practical means. A few well-directed provisions putting a discriminatory tax on large organizations would have done the trick, provided some other form of organization were growing at the same time to fill the practical need. Since the organizations were demanded, attempts to stop their growth necessarily became purely ceremonial. . . . The actual result of the antitrust laws was to promote the growth of great industrial organizations by deflecting the attack on them into purely moral and ceremonial channels.[1]

This book's thesis will be developed first by defining antitrust as a religious faith with an existence independent of the antitrust statutes. Chapter 2 describes the development of a cult of professional followers who serve as a priesthood to carry out the ceremonial function of antitrust. Chapter 3 contains a brief history of attempts at reform. Chapter 4 discusses the central element of antitrust faith—"market

1

power"—an imaginary, hypothetical concept borrowed from economic theory and used by the antitrust community as though it describes something that actually exists when, in fact, the concept of market power is based on false assumptions about a future that cannot be known. Chapters 5 through 8 describe activities attacking supposed evils identified by the antitrust religion and point out the inconsistency of those activities with our aspirations for a society ruled by laws and not men. The final chapter draws the tentative conclusion that educating society about the unsoundness of the basic elements of the antitrust faith might lead to meaningful change.

1. What Is "Antitrust"?

Quasi-religious Faith Distinct from the Antitrust Statutes

Section 4 of the Clayton Act of 1914 provides that any person "injured in his business or property by reason of anything forbidden in the antitrust laws" may sue for three times his damages plus costs and "a reasonable attorney's fee." Section 1 of the Clayton Act defines the term "antitrust laws" as including the Sherman Act of 1890 and the Clayton Act. These are referred to in this book as "the antitrust statutes." Definitions are important for making sense of the subject. The antitrust literature provides little help. Most of it perpetuates confusion. Consider the following example from a basic textbook used at the Harvard Law School:

> Antitrust law implicitly but clearly takes a particular stance toward the economic problems to which it applies. On one hand, its very enactment indicates that Congress rejected the belief that market forces are sufficiently strong, self-correcting, and well-directed to guarantee the results that perfect competition would bring. On the other hand, antitrust's domain is intrinsically limited.[1]

What are the authors talking about? Antitrust law? Antitrust? The antitrust statutes? Do they recognize any difference among those three terms? There are two antitrust statutes, the Sherman Act and the Clayton Act, adopted by Congress and found in the U.S. Code. You can look them up. The quoted passage does not refer to those statutes but begins with the undefined term "antitrust law," which implies a coherent set of rules that "takes a particular stance." The student is told that enactment of "antitrust law" shows that Congress rejected a belief that the market is self-correcting. But Congress did not enact "antitrust law." It enacted two antitrust statutes, one in 1890 and another in 1914. What beliefs Congress entertained or rejected at either of those times is debatable.

Next the student is introduced to an additional undefined term—"antitrust." "Antitrust" has a "domain." Authors Phillip Areeda and Louis Kaplow began with an imagined concept of "antitrust law" and then shifted to a discussion of "antitrust," something different from "antitrust law" and even more distant from the antitrust statutes. Antitrust has an existence outside of the antitrust statutes. Antitrust not only exists but also does things. It is a formidable actor. The professors describe it thus:

> Antitrust supplements or, perhaps, defines the rules of the game by which competition takes place. It thus assumes that market forces—guided by the limitations imposed by antitrust law—will produce good results or at least better results than any of the alternatives that largely abandon reliance on market forces. Therefore, the perfect competition model can be viewed as a central target, the results of which antitrust seeks, but the conditions for which antitrust does not take for granted. Antitrust thus looks to perfect competition for guidance, but the analysis inevitably emphasizes the myriad and complex imperfections of actual markets.[2]

Antitrust "supplements" or "defines." The professors are not sure which. Antitrust "assumes" things. Antitrust "seeks results" but "does not take things for granted." Antitrust "looks to perfect competition for guidance" to supplement the guidance that it has received from antitrust law's limitations. Having extracted from the antitrust statutes an imagined concept of "antitrust law" and having pulled out of that hat a rabbit called "antitrust," the professors conclude by telling us what "the analysis" emphasizes. The student might wonder: where did "the analysis" come from? The antitrust statutes? Antitrust law? Antitrust? Whose analysis is it? Why is it "the" analysis?

Antitrust is not defined in any of the provisions of the antitrust statutes. It can't be translated into foreign languages. Antitrust was not enacted. It is not a coherent set of rules. You can't look it up. Experts are required to interpret it. Much of it is in the eye of the professor. In their casebook, Eleanor Fox and Lawrence Sullivan write of "the central concern of antitrust" and its "several goals" and that "antitrust regulates economic structure and economic conduct through law."[3] They also tell us when a court decision is "a defeat for antitrust."[4] Timothy J. Muris, while chairman of the Federal

Trade Commission, observed that there is much to do "to assure that antitrust avoids the mistakes of its past."[5]

Antitrust can't be amended, reformed, or repealed. It is an intuitive mix of law, economics, and politics; a mystical collection of aspirations, beliefs, suspicions, presumptions, and predictions. Antitrust is a quasi-religious faith independent of the provisions of the antitrust statutes.

Antitrust has many doctrines that are analyzed endlessly in lectures, seminars, articles, and court opinions. The antitrust faith is based on four elements that are seldom mentioned but will be discussed in subsequent chapters of this book. They are as follows: (1) a belief in the legend of Standard Oil, (2) fear of corporate consolidation, (3) a belief in the magic of "market power," and (4) faith that government can protect us from those evils.

Vague Statutes—Unaccountable Discretion

The antitrust statutes give to those in positions of power wide discretion to interfere with commercial activity and freedom of contract. Three provisions illustrate the point, two from the Sherman Act of 1890 and one from the Clayton Act of 1914.

Section 1 of the Sherman Act designated as a federal crime "every contract, combination in the form of trust or otherwise, or conspiracy, in restraint of trade or commerce among the several States, or with foreign nations." That declaration of Congress would have outlawed any contract in interstate commerce, because every contract restrains some trade. (If I contract to sell you a wristwatch, I am restrained from selling the watch to someone else. You, in turn, are restrained from buying another product with the money that you paid to me.) To avoid that truism, the judiciary invented the so-called rule of reason, amending the prohibition by Congress of *every* contract in restraint of trade to prohibit only those contracts found by the courts to "unreasonably" restrain trade. As a result, unless the restraint is one that the Supreme Court has presumed to be unreasonable— such as the so-called per se offenses discussed later—it may be impossible to tell whether a contract is unlawful without a lengthy trial. Justice Louis Brandeis suggested that the trial should proceed along the following lines:

> The true test of legality is whether the restraint imposed is such as merely regulates and perhaps thereby promotes

competition or whether it is such as may suppress or even destroy competition. To determine that question the Court must ordinarily consider the facts peculiar to the business to which the restraint is applied; its condition before and after the restraint was imposed; the nature of the restraint and its effect, actual or probable. The history of the restraint, the evil believed to exist, the reason for adopting the particular remedy, the purpose or end sought to be attained, are all relevant facts. This is not because a good intention will save an otherwise objectionable regulation or the reverse; but because knowledge of intent may help the Court to interpret facts and to predict consequences.[6]

In other words, everything is relevant but nothing is determinative. An absolute prohibition by the legislature was turned into a delegation of discretion to jurors and judges to approve or disapprove contracts after a lengthy inquiry as to whether or not they restrain trade "unreasonably."

Section 2 of the Sherman Act made it a crime "to monopolize" or "attempt to monopolize" any part of the trade or commerce among the several states or with foreign nations. No one knows what those words mean. Over the past century, judges and commentators, such as Areeda and Kaplow, have developed a vocabulary for talking about the subject, but no meaningful rules have emerged. Court declarations perpetuate ambiguity. According to the Supreme Court:

> The offense of monopoly under section 2 of the Sherman Act has two elements: (1) the possession of monopoly power in the relevant market and (2) the willful acquisition or maintenance of that power as distinguished from growth or development as a consequence of a superior product, business acumen, or historic accident.[7]

In 1918 Justice Brandeis attempted to distinguish between contracts that promote competition and those that suppress or destroy competition but was unable to do so. Similarly, in 1966 the Court sought to differentiate between willful acquisition of monopoly power and being an effective competitor but was unable to state any rule for doing so. The result has been to leave to judges, juries, and officials at the Justice Department and FTC power to make arbitrary decisions on a subjective basis.

Most government activity under the antitrust statutes finds its support in section 7 of the Clayton Act, which prohibits corporate acquisitions "where . . . the effect of such acquisition may be substantially to lessen competition, or to tend to create a monopoly." Yet we have no workable definition of what constitutes "competition" and no way to measure it. Applying section 7, the Supreme Court under Chief Justice Earl Warren essentially declared all corporate mergers unlawful. Expressing concern with industrial "concentration" and desiring to protect "small business" from more efficient competitors, the Court during the 1960s decided every case in the government's favor. First came the *Brown Shoe* case,[8] which involved the acquisition by Brown (primarily a shoe manufacturer) of Kinney (primarily a shoe retailer). The Court held the merger illegal under section 7 in two ways: first, as a horizontal merger and, second, as a vertical merger. Both companies made shoes. Brown made roughly 4.0 percent and Kinney made roughly 0.5 percent of the nation's shoes. Merger of the two manufacturers, said to be "horizontal" because it involved two companies directly competing with each other, was found illegal. The Court also held the merger of Brown and Kinney illegal as a "vertical" merger—i.e., one involving two companies that had a supplier-customer relationship—because Brown, selling 4.0 percent of the nation's shoes, merged with Kinney, a retailer that accounted for 1.2 percent of U.S. retail shoe sales. The vertical merger of the supplier Brown with its customer Kinney was said to "foreclose" a share of the retail market otherwise open to manufacturer-competitors of Brown.

Four years later, in the *Von's Grocery* case,[9] the Court concluded that section 7 prohibited the merger of two grocery chains because the merger would result in ownership by a single firm of 1.4 percent of the grocery stores in the Los Angeles metropolitan area, accounting for 7.5 percent of the area's grocery sales.

Mergers neither horizontal nor vertical—where the merged firms were not competing and did not have a supplier-customer relationship—were given the sinister-sounding name of "conglomerate" mergers. The Court upheld government action to prevent conglomerate mergers on theories that they raise "barriers to entry," eliminate "potential competition," or create opportunities for "reciprocal dealing." Mergers that created "competitive advantages" were condemned for doing so. Economic efficiency created through

7

merger not only didn't serve as a defense but also became a basis for a conclusion of illegality.

By the late 1960s the operative question became not whether a merger was illegal but whether the government would oppose it. In 1968 the Justice Department published Merger Guidelines that were more permissive than Supreme Court rulings such as those in the *Brown Shoe* case.[10] The result has been to transfer to government attorneys the arbitrary power to decide whether or not a merger will be allowed or prohibited, guided only by an irrational fear of corporate consolidation. Moreover, since 1976 all corporate mergers above a certain size have had to be reported to the government in advance.[11] According to the Commentary on the Horizontal Merger Guidelines published by the FTC and the Justice Department, "For more than 95% of the transactions reported . . . the Agencies promptly determine . . . that a substantial lessening of competition is unlikely."[12] During fiscal 2005, notices of 1,695 proposed mergers were filed. The FTC challenged 14, and the Justice Department challenged 4, a total of 18 out of 1,695, or 1.06 percent.[13] There is no way to tell which mergers will be allowed and which will not. The process will be examined in more detail in Chapter 6.

No Clear Rules—Arbitrary Decisions

Lacking any coherent, ascertainable rules in the written antitrust statutes, judges and other government officials make arbitrary decisions using antitrust doctrines based on a faith not easily overcome by reason, logic, or empirical data. There is no need to explain decisions not made. A contract, a "monopoly," or a merger permitted requires no explanation. Most corporate mergers reviewed by the government are cleared without question or explanation. Only attacks call for justification. If the decisionmaker wishes to disapprove, the language of antitrust is there to justify the disapproval. Metaphorical labels such as "the market" are used as though they are factual descriptions. Antitrust doctrine containing a prohibition is recited. The disapproval has been rationalized.

The success of Microsoft Corp. came at the expense of some of Microsoft's competitors—losers in the marketplace who sought government action against a winner. Interest was first aroused at the FTC, where two commissioners favored action, two favored doing nothing, and the fifth declined to participate. The assistant attorney general at the time was an activist new to the job. She took over the matter and persuaded Microsoft to make some changes in its method of doing business. That agreement was presented to a district court for adoption as a consent decree without any findings of fact. The district judge to whom the case was assigned had read some books about computers. On the basis of such reading he rejected the decree as inadequate.[14] A reviewing court of appeals said it was the job of the attorney general, not a district judge, to decide the adequacy of such decrees.[15] The appeals court sent the matter back to a different district judge.[16] That judge later denied a contempt petition, issued a preliminary injunction, and referred the case to a special master,[17] a decision reversed by the court of appeals.[18] Meanwhile, the Justice Department began an entirely new, somewhat broader, proceeding that resulted in a district court's issuance of 400 or so "findings of fact"[19] and then a memorandum and order, in which the judge confessed an inability to determine what to do because of divergent opinions about the future.[20] He concluded that "plaintiffs won the case, and for that reason alone have some entitlement to a remedy of their choice," including breaking up the defendant.[21] That remedy should be adopted, he said, because it was urged by government officials "in conjunction with multiple consultants," and such officials are expected to act in the public interest, whereas the defendant is not.[22] That order was vacated by the court of appeals.[23] The court recited prevailing doctrines of market definition and power, which contain assumptions about a future that no one can know but could be applied to the Microsoft case because of the phraseology of the district judge's findings of "fact."[24] Assisted by some notions about "short term" and "long term" and some fine distinctions between "procompetitive" and "anticompetitive" conduct, the Court labeled Microsoft, like the legendary Standard Oil, a monopolizer and as such prohibited by section 2 of the Sherman Act.[25] The Justice Department abandoned any further attempt to break up the company but did insist on several regulatory restrictions to protect complaining competitors.[26]

Futility of Reform

Attempts at reform or repeal of the antitrust statutes are futile as long as faith in Antitrust with a capital "A" is preserved. Provisions of the antitrust statutes contain words without definition, but, except when amended by Congress, at least the words are fixed. One can look them up and write them down. Antitrust, the mystique, is a different matter. One cannot look it up. Joel Klein, while serving as assistant attorney general in charge of the Justice Department's antitrust division, described the antitrust laws as "common law statutes." He said to a meeting of antitrust lawyers, "You know, so much of litigation in the Supreme Court, or whatever, will be on what exactly are the words of the statute. But in antitrust it really is much more dynamic."[27]

The antitrust lawyer must learn a special vocabulary not found in the U.S. Code. Observable phenomena are described by metaphors, which are not scientific labels of real-world data but artificial concepts, like "market" and "market power." Antitrust experts speak a sort of poetry. Journalists and politicians take it as a description of reality. The public is confused. Antitrust concepts give a sinister characterization to the ordinary phenomena to which they are applied. "Oligopoly" is a good example. People who are learned in antitrust vocabulary know that an oligopoly is simply any number of sellers more than one—a common situation, but it sounds to the average citizen like a nasty condition and cause for concern.

Fashions in antitrust concepts change even when the statutory words don't. Some terms achieve acceptance for a time but then lose their appeal and are abandoned. "Reciprocity" is a good example. At one time the FTC chairman saw reciprocity as an evil of great potential, warning that it "could result in closed-circuit markets from which medium or small factors are excluded" and, "thus oligopoly would be magnified in a sort of circular integration fashion . . . foreclosing the opportunities of firms without substantial market power to gain access to the inner circle of firms."[28] At about the same time, the head of the Justice Department's antitrust division stated that "there is a legitimate basis for attacking reciprocity, not only under section 1 of the Sherman Act . . . but also under section 2 . . . as an unlawful attempt to monopolize."[29] Some hand wringing occurred, but the attack never came. Eventually, it became clear to everyone that the nation is not in any danger if businesspeople tell each other: "I'll buy from you if you buy from me." Also, the word got around that it isn't a very effective way to do business anyway, so we just don't hear much about it anymore.

"Conglomerates" had a longer run as antitrust witches. Having succeeded in obtaining Supreme Court declarations that virtually

10

all mergers of competitors as well as those of customers and suppliers are prohibited by section 7 of the Clayton Act, the government harassed "conglomerates." In addition to court proceedings to prevent corporate acquisitions by conglomerates, both the FTC and the Justice Department conducted highly visible investigations of those that merely existed. The campaign was eventually abandoned. Many of the most feared "conglomerates" later shed their acquisitions or went out of business altogether without any help from government.

A key concept that currently has a firm grip on the imagination of the antitrust community is the concept of "market power" (see chapter 4). "Market power" is an imaginary concept borrowed from theoretical economics. It incorporates assumptions and predictions but is used by the antitrust community as though it describes facts subject to proof.

Antitrust as faith endures not because it has a fixed basis in science or reason but because it does not. Faith in antitrust allows the pursuit of mutually exclusive goals. It serves the human desire for both justice and "fairness." The attempt to rationalize antitrust as consumer welfare economics has eliminated some of the glaring irrationality of interpretations of the antitrust statutes. Antitrust doctrines have been tidied up, but no amount of economic theory can resolve the basic conflict inherent in the human desire for both efficiency and fairness—goals that are often incompatible. The antitrust religion allows the pursuit of both goals simultaneously. It also avoids facing three real issues: (1) how to state a normative rule that distinguishes between contracts that unreasonably restrain trade and those that do not; (2) how to distinguish between willful acquisition of "monopoly power" and being an effective competitor; and (3) how to tell whether a merger may substantially lessen competition.

The generality and ambiguity of the antitrust statutes allow arbitrary decisions disguised as findings of fact. Market efficiency requires no government interference on its behalf. Fairness does. Antitrust allows the decisionmaker freedom to intervene on the side of fairness when he wishes to do so. The decision is not dictated by any objective measurement but by labeling as findings of fact theoretical concepts such as "the market" and "market power." Unstated assumptions and predictions are incorporated into conclusions stated as facts, and then doctrines dictate the result. To maintain an appearance of a rule of law, the decisionmaker portrays the process as a factual inquiry followed by findings of fact to which rules are then applied. Actually, the result is dictated by the assumptions and predictions. Where one comes out is determined by where one starts in. Assumptions and predictions cannot be proven. They are subjective judgments in which the decisionmaker's personal sense of fairness cannot be ruled out.

Change through Rejection of the Faith

Faith in antitrust—as a policy and as an enforcement mechanism—overcomes reason based on either theory or evidence. In 1978, using economic theory, then-professor Robert Bork made obvious the paradox of the pursuit in the name of antitrust of the mutually exclusive goals of protectionism and a free market.[30] Adjustments in antitrust doctrines have occurred, but the statutes remain unamended, and Supreme Court precedents remain available to state attorneys general, private plaintiffs, and federal authorities whenever they choose to be "vigorous" about enforcement.

In 1976 Richard Posner, while a University of Chicago Law School professor, recommended repeal of all antitrust statutes except section 1 of the Sherman Act.[31] In 1986 professor D. T. Armentano concluded that "antitrust law" has lost "its claim to legitimacy" and explained why.[32] Several years ago Robert Crandall and Clifford Winston of the Brookings Institution assessed the evidence on whether antitrust policy improves consumer welfare. They concluded that there is no evidence that it does.[33]

There is little reason to believe that evidence, or the lack of it, any more than economic theory, can counteract the nation's commitment to faith-based antitrust. As Armentano pointed out, the benefits of antitrust regulation are substantial—especially to the antitrust community. Yet that group's indifference or even opposition to change is not the primary obstacle to repeal of the antitrust statutes. The primary obstacle to repeal is the depth of the nation's faith in antitrust. That faith is held not only by those who profit from antitrust enforcement but also by those for whom it is a costly nuisance. The antitrust statutes will not be repealed or significantly amended as long as faith in antitrust retains its grip on the psyche of journalists, academics, and policymakers.

It is possible that the public could be educated to understand what is really going on and to understand that the basic elements of the antitrust faith are unsound. We do not need to fear corporate consolidation. The imagined magic of market power is just that—imagined. We do not need government protection against imaginary evils. Unfortunately, none of those in a position to discover and publicize the error of the beliefs supporting the antitrust faith has any incentive or inclination to do so. Their activities are described in the next chapter.

2. The Antitrust Community

The antitrust faith is preserved by a cult of professional followers who call themselves "the antitrust community." Basic elements of the antitrust faith have been part of the American psyche since the "trust-busting" era of Theodore Roosevelt, but it was not until the 1950s that a cadre of professionals devoted to promotion of antitrust took shape. President Eisenhower's attorney general, Herbert Brownell, appointed a National Committee to Study the Antitrust Laws. In 1955 that group published a report that became a handbook for aspiring antitrust lawyers. The group's members and consultants formed a nucleus of the antitrust community-to-be.

In 1953 the incoming Eisenhower administration replaced Herbert Bergson as assistant attorney general in charge of the antitrust division. Bergson then opened an office for the private practice of law in Washington, and promptly took on representation of corporate clients, including those seeking merger clearances from the antitrust division. Having just left that office, his qualifications for such representation were unmatched. But Brownell indicted Bergson under a law that prohibits representing someone with a claim against the government within two years of leaving government employment. A district judge dismissed the indictment, concluding that a claim means a demand for money or property, not the seeking of merger clearances.[1] The indictment may have gilded rather than tarnished Bergson's attractiveness to corporate clients with antitrust problems. Within five years he had built a premier practice and was elected chairman of the American Bar Association's antitrust law section, which he had helped organize in 1952.

Although the antitrust community is a welcoming group and its members enjoy a feeling of kinship, one cannot become a member of it overnight. It takes about six months to become familiar with the territory and comfortable with the language. The veteran has little advantage over the novice, since neither can predict results, but the practitioner has to speak the language. The subject is not complex, merely confusing to outsiders. As has been said about coaching football, one must be smart enough to be good at it and dumb enough to take it seriously. There are three steps in the process of joining the antitrust community. The required skills can be acquired in law school or by reading or listening to continuing legal education lectures. First, one must become familiar with a few statutory provisions and be able to recall them at any time. Second, one must learn to recognize a few terms not found in the statutes, such as "per se" and "rule of reason" and a few case names, like *Illinois Brick* and *Noerr-Pennington* so as not to be one-upped by other initiates, who like to use case names as shorthand for the doctrines they contain. Third, one must pick up a few terms from microeconomic theory.

The third step is a critical one—learning to speak a vocabulary of meaningless or ambiguous terms with authority. One must learn to use metaphors like "market" and "barrier to entry" as though they have meaning that one fully understands. That skill comes through practice with actual situations where decisions are being made—in government or private law practice—learning through experience at the expense of the taxpayer or of the private client. Simple use of the terms is not enough. Statements must be made with sufficient pomp that it is difficult for the listener to avoid taking them seriously. And to be taken seriously one has to take oneself seriously. That skill is acquired not by listening but by talking when others are forced to listen. In that respect, there is no substitute for government service since the government antitrust official must be listened to no matter what is being said. In the antitrust community, just the right amount of self-righteousness must be displayed. Here, also, government experience is the best teacher.

There is an additional dimension to the value of government experience, particularly if it is recent. Today there are obstacles to making immediate use of government experience for the benefit of a private client the way Bergson did in the early 1950s, but if lawyers are to attract and hold clients with antitrust problems, it helps if clients think the lawyer has some better source of information than the newspapers. Appearance of proximity to the decisionmaker adds value to the lawyer's opinions. Much antitrust law practice consists of assessing and influencing the thinking of middle-level government officials on matters over which they have broad discretion.

The antitrust lawyer is selling access to and insight into the minds of those making subjective decisions off the record. In merger matters, that is almost the entire game. Statutory and case law, if applied vigorously, would stop virtually all corporate mergers, leaving only this question: will the government attack this one? Pinning the right descriptive metaphor on a set of facts determines the outcome.

No amount of study of written material can provide as much chance to avoid expensive miscalculations as a well-timed lunch, tennis game, or casual resort hotel conversation with a well-chosen official. It is not a matter of corruption but of access to decisionmakers and assessment of their thinking. As professor Spencer Waller, director of the Institute for Consumer Antitrust Studies at Loyola Chicago School of Law, has written, "Knowledge of the decisionmakers, familiarity with current enforcement policy, even if unpublished, and access to the agencies play a critical role in selling oneself as an expert."[2]

Development of the Antitrust Community

The antitrust community includes practicing lawyers, law professors, economists, and government officials who hold conferences and publish materials propounding antitrust doctrines. The antitrust community comes together in the American Bar Association's antitrust law section. Membership in the ABA is a prerequisite to enrollment in the antitrust section. Within 25 years of its 1952 beginnings, the section had grown to 11,000 members. Membership peaked in 1980 with a mailing list of about 13,000 dues payers. In recent years membership has remained at around 11,000, but participation by members in section activities has greatly increased. Current section dues are $50 per year. A promotional brochure promises "networking" with "a diverse group of thousands of professionals, including attorneys in private practice and government practice, corporate in-house counsel, international associates, judges, economists, and law students."

The antitrust section has a roster of officers elected each year, usually without opposition, and a council of 15 members with staggered three-year terms. The chairman of the Federal Trade Commission, the assistant attorney general for antitrust, and a federal judge are also ex officio members of the council. The section has 28 general committees, 6 administrative committees, 3 program committees, and 7 publication committees. There are also 11 special task forces.

During 2006 the section of antitrust law scheduled meetings in New York and Washington, as well as at Chateau Montebello in Montebello, Canada; the Savoy in London; Halekulani, Honolulu, Hawaii; St. Regis Monarch Beach Resort, Dana Point, California; and the Sanctuary, Kiawah Island, South Carolina. The largest gathering of the membership occurs during the annual spring meeting in Washington, timed for the cherry blossoms. At the 2006 meeting in late March, 2,200 members had preregistered before the meeting began. The fee was $725. Participants came from 43 states and 38 countries. For dinner, 118 tables seating 10 persons each were sold out. "Non-government" people paid $135 for a seat; "government, academic, and students" paid $95. Cocktails were provided at massive receptions sponsored by law firms.

As of June 30, 2005, the section's finance officer reported reserves of $7,320,980. Operations during fiscal year 2003–2004 produced net revenues of more than $900,000. The budget for 2006–2007 projected net revenues of $275,000. In return for paying dues, ABA members receive the *Antitrust* and *Antitrust Law Journal* three times a year and the opportunity to participate in section activities. They also receive discounts on publications sold by the section. Members prepare reviews, manuals, handbooks, guides, and monographs. Those are then sold to the general public for hundreds of thousands of dollars a year. *Antitrust Law Developments* (5th ed.), described in the publications catalog as a "must have" for the antitrust practitioner, is hardbound in two volumes totaling 2,000 pages and priced at $365. An annual supplement is available at $115. The publications catalog itself consists of 36 pages. Included are three merger books priced at $149.95 each. Two are second editions and the third is a third edition. A 171-page paper titled *Market Power Handbook* is available at $134. The 2006–2007 budget planned for gross revenues of $737,063 from publications.

Waller's overview of the situation follows:

> The antitrust world, to a large extent, is driven by the American Bar Association Antitrust Law Section and the antitrust partners of the large law firms which dominate the Section and handle the vast majority of large antitrust matters. The ABA Antitrust Section provides the most direct

opportunities to demonstrate that you are a member, and major player, in the antitrust club. . . . [ABA] socialization . . . provides . . . the language and acculturalization to work the halls of power and interact with practitioners of similar backgrounds who may be friends, foes, or the government decision-maker in any given matter, and who may surface in the same or different posture in the next matter.[3]

Members of the antitrust community aren't likely to offer any serious criticism of enforcement policy or to develop any constructive proposals for reform except as related to procedures or the elimination of statutory exemptions from the antitrust laws. Anyone dealing closely and continuously with antitrust is busy profiting from the status quo. The ABA antitrust section has become a cheerleader for whatever government activity is currently in fashion and its global extension. The section's long-range plan states that part of its "mission" is "enhancing its role as the preeminent source for analysis, debate and continuing legal education in the antitrust, competition law, competition policy and consumer protection fields." Its charter states that within its mandate is "the development of *active* antitrust enforcement" (emphasis added). In April 2002 that meant "support for full funding of the federal antitrust enforcement agencies."[4] No systematic review or evaluation of such activism is ever undertaken. The basic questions—for example, did this proceeding make any sense or accomplish anything?—are seldom asked at meetings or in publications of the section. Instead, officials responsible for continuation of fiascoes such as the Justice Department's fruitless campaign against IBM and the FTC's pursuit of an imaginary "shared monopoly" of ready-to-eat cereal manufacturers are given "achievement awards" for their contributions to the community.[5]

In 1958 a Committee on Antitrust Policy of the Twentieth Century Fund published a report based on a review of antitrust history in 20 industries, concluding the following:

By this time several hundred cases have ended in decrees of various sorts designed to bring about changes in market structures and business practices. Yet very little time and effort have been spent, either inside the government or out, in assessing the effects of these decrees on the behavior of firms or the status of competition in the affected industries.

> How differently do the firms encompassed act from the way
> they would if a case had never been brought? Is competition,
> in some meaningful sense of the word, noticeably improved?
> Almost no one has bothered to enquire.[6]

The Antitrust Modernization Commission Act of 2002 created a commission consisting of 12 distinguished members of the antitrust community and gave the commission $4 million over a period of three years to make recommendations about "issues and problems relating to the modernization of the antitrust laws."[7] The assistant attorney general for antitrust, having been asked to provide his views as to topics that the commission might study, suggested that the group "should consider engaging respected experts (including those who do not earn their living providing antitrust services) to design a rigorous study of the effects of antitrust enforcement." The commission emphatically rejected the suggestion. At a forum during the 2005 spring meeting of the antitrust section one commission member said that a study of empirical data as to what, if any, benefits result from antitrust activity would be too difficult because the data are not readily available, and the commission had better uses for its resources.

Those actively engaged in antitrust practice must talk as though there are ascertainable rules that make sense and do their best at "the relatively sterile function of weaving together old decisions in an attempt, usually futile, to design a legal fabric at once a little more appealing to their clients' needs and to the courts' tastes."[8] Members of the antitrust community, when advocating change, usually restrict themselves to "remedies" and procedures. They are reluctant to evaluate results or to analyze judicial attempts to state normative rules. They find it difficult to stand apart from existing doctrines that they are continually obliged to advocate.[9]

Law School Indoctrination in Elements of Antitrust

Antitrust, as distinguished from the antitrust statutes that anyone can look up in the U.S. Code, is a mystical collection of persistent beliefs, not necessarily based in either fact or law or subject to control by Congress. Those beliefs are kept alive and transmitted to new generations by members of the antitrust community at bar association conferences and in law schools. At an Antitrust Masters Course in Sea Island, Georgia, one prominent member of the antitrust community told would-be masters paying a substantial attendance fee that "it is important to go beyond a list of 'do's' and 'don'ts' and try to explain, on a deeper level, what the antitrust laws are all about."[10]

Antitrust masters must get beyond mere interpretation of legal requirements enacted by legislatures and administered by government officials because there are few fixed rules. They must sense at a "deeper level" the meaning of it all. The principal vehicle for transmission of this learning once was study of court opinions and casebooks containing them, but much court doctrine is now acknowledged by the antitrust community as out of date. "The traditional law school casebook misses the point of modern antitrust law and practice," writes Waller.[11]

Compilers of casebooks have had to recognize the futility of trying to portray antitrust as a unified coherent system of law. Some have turned their courses into history courses presenting endless unanswerable questions.[12] Some have attempted to distinguish themselves by "a balanced, diversified approach in presenting a wide spectrum of ideas regarding the goals and economic underpinnings of antitrust law" permitting the students "a larger perspective for individual choice."[13] One trio of professors has produced a casebook titled *Antitrust Law in Perspective: Cases, Concepts and Problems in Competition Policy*[14] in which they attempt to bring the student closer to reality. According to one book review, the authors "avoid formal categories" and "focus, instead, on economically based concepts." The book contains an introduction to the study of antitrust law with "three themes": (1) how antitrust is "evolving from the analysis of discrete categories of behavior toward reliance on a set of core concepts," (2) the "unfolding trend toward globalization of antitrust law," and (3) "skills demanded of the antitrust lawyer." The book is characterized as "a casebook for our time."[15]

A primary assumption behind years of antitrust teaching—that the antitrust laws provide a coherent, rational, and discoverable set of rules by which to evaluate behavior—can no longer be taken seriously. Yet that situation cannot be directly addressed. Antitrust law professors cannot admit that the antitrust community is administering a system of mere regulatory hunches by those who happen to be in decisionmaking positions, but that is the implicit thesis of the casebook for our time. To be an antitrust lawyer in our time, one must grasp "concepts" that are "evolving" to get to "a deeper level" of "what the antitrust laws are all about." To develop that skill, one must study handbooks, manuals, guides, monographs, and reviews. The student must go beyond "formal categories of behavior" and "focus" on "core concepts" to understand how anti-trust law is "evolving." Meetings must be attended and lectures listened to. Indoctrination by elders of the community must be absorbed.

Students of antitrust are taught to answer questions in a language of metaphors. The notion is conveyed that the word game students are trying to learn and the concepts they are struggling to grasp are scientific descriptions of real-world phenomena, not just metaphori-cal descriptions of an imagined one. Numbing students' minds begins by introducing the untranslatable word "antitrust," which has no fixed content. Where the word came from and its lack of definition are not discussed. Professors of antitrust law, such as those at Harvard quoted in chapter 1, are at ease with the regal personification of antitrust implied in terms like "antitrust's domain," "the task of antitrust," and "the targets of antitrust."[16] Such professors are able to work with the explicit personification of antitrust by the use of active verbs in phrases like "antitrust seeks" and "antitrust does not take for granted"[17]—implying that the pro-fessor is on speaking terms with the seeker or doer, and that someday the student may be, too.

Law school casebooks still present the material under a table of contents that suggests the subject matter can be organized into a coherent system of discoverable rules constraining the decision-maker, rather than only gaseous concepts that permit unpredictable results based on hunch or whim. Because "antitrust" has no fixed meaning, neither can "antitrust law." Repeated use of the terms "antitrust" and "antitrust law" gives students the feeling that the terms have a definite meaning when they do not. That is not explicitly acknowledged. Instead, students are told that antitrust "is a unique blend of intellectual theory, social policy, political economy, micro-economics and law."[18]

Sinister-Sounding Terms—Self-righteous Feelings

The antitrust community invents sinister-sounding terms for natu-ral phenomena and enjoys a feeling of self-righteousness in protect-ing the public from those evils. The antitrust process is said to be a "complex" one "by which the policymaker must select among competing policy values."[19] That makes policymakers of all those making antitrust decisions. An important part of the process is affixing to freely-arrived-at contracts between consenting adults labels that imply the use of force when none is involved. That is done by the use of misleading metaphors, such as "market power," "market control," and "market dominance." A firm that made 40 percent of the sales in some past period is said to "control" 40 percent of the market. A firm that sold more of something than any other seller is said to "dominate" the market. But control or dominance results from offering for sale something that people want to buy. People can't be forced to buy. There is no force involved. No one is controlled or dominated. In some cases the supposed antitrust victim is not the party supposedly controlled or dominated but might like to be— someone who may have been deprived of an opportunity to sell. For instance, as in "reciprocity" (I won't sell to you unless you buy from me) or "exclusive dealing" (I won't sell to you if you buy from anyone else). In other cases such as "tying" contracts (if you want to buy my machine, promise to buy my salt or ink or punch cards that go in it), the supposedly injured party may not have the machines to sell. In cases of "predatory pricing" (selling at prices lower than those at which competitors wish to sell) or "predatory buying or predatory bidding" (buying at prices higher than those at which competitors wish to buy), nothing predatory is occurring. People are simply making freely-arrived-at contracts of purchase and sale.

The multiple goals of antitrust provide psychic income to all participants by applying sinister-sounding labels to natural business activities. No matter whom antitrust community members are representing, they can feel that they are serving the public interest. On one side of the argument, lawyers are defending economic efficiency and consequent consumer welfare. On the other side of the argument, lawyers are defending the right of the little man to fundamental fairness, protecting him from being controlled, dominated, or excluded by forceful and predatory behavior. On either side, antitrust lawyers can feel that they are doing the right thing for others while doing well for themselves.

During the past 50 years antitrust lawyers, like most lawyers generally, have made a transition. Most formerly independent professionals chosen by clients for objective judgment, knowledge, and integrity have had to become self-promoting participants in institutional commercial operations sustained by expensive advertising and active business solicitation. In the early years, programs of the ABA section of antitrust law identified speakers only by their individual names; law firm names were never printed in the program. That has changed. Lawyers no longer practice law under their own names but under an established institutional trade name. No name is complete without an institutional affiliation. Some combine both law firm and academic connections, using one or the other as best suited for the occasion. For most, practicing law means serving as replaceable cogs in huge wheels grinding on at high hourly rates churning out memos, reports, briefs, and depositions for clients of "the firm." A few of the more independent-minded have become buccaneers who invent a class of supposed victims, elbow their way to the head of a parade of others doing the same, and then shake down defendants for huge settlements resulting in little, if any, benefit to the purported "clients" but handsome fees for the lawyers.

That transition may have been especially pronounced and visible in the antitrust community, but to make up for it, there are also special compensations beyond the money for antitrust lawyers. Litigating can be equally strenuous in any specialty, but it is less intellectually demanding to be an antitrust adviser than to be a tax lawyer. Tax lawyers can make mistakes. Since there is so little predictability in antitrust law, one can seldom appear to have been wrong. It is difficult to be an incompetent antitrust lawyer. Almost any minimally trained attorney can do the work; the challenge is to get business. Class-action lawyers create their own clients. Large law firms hang onto clients inherited or recruited across different lines of specialization under one tent. Risks of failure and personal responsibility are minimized.

One of the most satisfying compensations of being a member of the antitrust community is the feeling of camaraderie that comes with sharing a special language and being a member of a club not open to the general public. The community shares a desire to pass that camaraderie on to future generations. As one chairman of the antitrust section has stated, "While many organizations function principally for the benefit of their members, the Section has always recognized a broader mission."[20] The section's mission statement includes, among other things, "Making known to a diverse group of law students and young lawyers the opportunities for satisfying and rewarding careers in the practice of antitrust law, and encouraging them to consider pursuing such opportunities." One chairman of the section has referred to "spreading the antitrust gospel."[21] It is difficult to imagine an organization of tax lawyers talking that way.

Spreading the gospel is not confined to the continental United States. In somewhat the same pattern as the attorney general's National Committee to Study the Antitrust Laws during the Eisenhower administration, an International Competition Policy Advisory Committee created during the Clinton administration published a weighty report and served as a springboard for members of the U.S. antitrust community to advance their careers doing missionary work abroad.[22] An International Competition Network has been organized. Its fifth annual conference, held in Cape Town, South Africa, in May 2006, was reported to have attracted "nearly 300 representatives from about 70 antitrust agencies."[23] The fourth annual conference, held in Bonn, Germany, in June 2005, was attended by "more than 400 representatives of 80 competition agencies and competition experts from international organizations and the legal, business, consumer, and academic communities."[24]

In support of proposed appropriations for fiscal year 2007, the FTC chairperson asserted that her commission "plays a leading role in key multilateral fora" (sic) promoting "cooperation and convergence toward best practices with competition and consumer protection agencies around the world."[25] Participation in activities of this sort provides members of the antitrust community opportunities for foreign travel, for business development, and for reinforced feelings of self-righteous satisfaction with "spreading the antitrust gospel."[26]

3. From "Trust-Busting" to the Present

There is no consistent U.S. policy toward competition. The antitrust community is *pro*-competition, not just *anti*-trust. Antitrust believers see competition as the basis of the economy and regard themselves as its guardians. They think that political control of business is necessary. They view "regulated industries" as minor exceptions in a market economy that is supposedly fundamentally free and look at antitrust as the alternative to regulation. Antitrust, they believe, is needed to keep the free market free. Antitrust as umpire sees to it that the game is played fairly and by the rules. Enforcement of the antitrust laws is supposed to protect a competitive system from those who might try to monopolize something the way Standard Oil is believed to have monopolized oil a century ago. Business practices, such as price discrimination (sales at different prices to different purchasers), exclusive dealing (sales on condition that the purchaser not buy from a competitor of the seller) and mergers, must be prevented where they might lessen competition or tend to create a monopoly such as Standard Oil, according to the antitrust community.

The antitrust believer's view of the economy arrogantly overstates the role of antitrust. The antitrust believer's assumed free market and concepts from microeconomic theory of "markets" and "market power" do not take account of much that has happened in the past 100 years or of much that now occurs in the real world. The U.S. economy is not free. Government creates barriers and helps favorites. Labor unions fix the price of labor. Government grants monopolies (patents). Government takes large shares of profits that would otherwise be available for investment.

The antitrust community sees antitrust as the main event. Regulated industries are viewed as a sideshow even though the American Bar Association's *Antitrust Law Developments* (5th ed.) lists under "regulated industries" the following: agriculture, communications (including broadcasting, common carriers, and cable television), energy (including natural gas, electric power, and federal lands programs), financial institutions and markets, government contracts, health care, insurance, organized labor, sports, and transportation (including motor, rail and air, and ocean shipping). Despite those acknowledged exceptions, a policy in favor of competition is supposed to be fundamental. Harvard professors tell students, "Antitrust . . . looks to perfect competition for guidance, but the analysis inevitably emphasizes the myriad and complex imperfections of actual markets."[1]

The Sherman Act of 1890, the basic antitrust statute, does not contain the word "competition." The statute refers to "trade or commerce." The other antitrust statute, the Clayton Act, adopted in 1914, contains the phrases "substantially to lessen competition" and "injure, destroy, or prevent competition," but provides no definition of the word "competition." Congress favors competition but only if it is fair. In the Federal Trade Commission Act,[2] adopted in the same year as the Clayton Act, Congress declared unlawful "unfair methods of competition" and created a federal commission to prevent them. Congress left it to the commission to define which methods of competition are unfair. (The Federal Trade Commission Act is not among the acts defined as an "antitrust law" in the Clayton Act.)

In 1922 the Supreme Court ruled that staging baseball games is not interstate commerce and therefore does not involve competition subject to the federal antitrust statutes.[3] The antitrust community refers to this as "the baseball exemption."[4] Neither football[5] nor basketball[6] has a similar exemption. The Curt Flood Act of 1998[7] added a provision to the Clayton Act revoking baseball's antitrust exemption insofar as it relates to the employment of major league players. The statute leaves unchanged the exemption from the antitrust laws of the minor leagues (including the player draft) and of matters not involving player-management relations.

In 1933 the Supreme Court concluded that use of a common selling agency by 137 coal producers in four states to fix the price of coal should not be condemned simply because it eliminates "competition" between the sellers.[8] The court, with one dissent, did not see the elimination of this sort of competition as forbidden by the antitrust laws. Students at New York University Law School are told in a casebook, "In *Appalachian Coals*, the Court treated the arrangement as a legitimate joint sales agency (although it might well have seen the joint sales arrangement as a cover for a cartel)."[9] One pair of professors writes that the joint selling agency "was upheld on the rationale that it lacked market power."[10] Some today regard that decision as "an aberration of the 1930's."[11] Students at Georgetown Law School are told in a casebook that "a sophisticated characterization process is necessary" before something can automatically be labeled an illegal cartel.[12]

Academics acknowledge the existence of the *Appalachian Coals* decision, but the practicing antitrust community no longer finds it useful and seldom refers to it. Some decisions of the Warren Court are also disregarded. During the days of aggressive government merger prevention, that Court declared illegal every sort of merger, including those that might eliminate "potential" competition.[13] Today it can correctly be said, "Antitrust concern with conglomerate mergers seems to have disappeared without a trace."[14] The community is no longer interested in such mergers. Current merger guidelines relate only to "horizontal mergers" (those between parties said to be "competing firms"). On one hand, the guidelines are more permissive than the Court decisions. On the other hand, with regard to price-stabilization combinations, the antitrust community prefers the more restrictive of two court declarations. In the *Appalachian Coals* case the Court declined to condemn a combination to fix the price of coal. In the *Socony-Vacuum* case[15] the Court upheld a criminal conviction of a combination to fix the price of oil. The antitrust community has adopted the latter and ignores the former. Those are illustrations of the "dynamic" nature of antitrust free of "what exactly are the words of the statute."[16]

Two professors have described an episode illustrating the shallowness of the U.S. commitment to competition as follows:

> The New Deal's initial response to the Depression was to abandon enforcement of the antitrust laws. In the pursuit of a national remedy to revive the economy, the antitrust laws were expressly abrogated by the National Industrial Recovery Act of 1933. Contrary to the conventional economic wisdom of the day, which advocated balancing the budget and cutting wages and other costs, the NRA was an attempt to "reflate" the economy by forming cartels in the major sectors of the economy. The NRA administrator ordered former competitors to meet together, to include labor organizations and consumer groups, and jointly to prepare codes governing

each industry that restricted or eliminated competition in
that industry. The Codes specified every commercial aspect
including prices, conditions of work, and the terms of trade
for each product and service in the economy.[17]

During this period the United States had a clear policy as to
business competition. The policy was to eliminate as much competition as possible, whether fair or unfair. The Supreme Court held the
National Industrial Recovery Act unconstitutional as an improper
delegation of power to the president and beyond congressional
power to regulate interstate commerce.[18] No consistent policy has
been developed since.

It is not clear whether corporate acquisitions should be seen as
destructive of competition or as a method of competition. It is not
clear what methods of competition should be seen as fair or unfair.
It is not clear when contracts will be regarded as lawful because
they promote competition or unlawful because they suppress competition. It is not clear when activities will be regarded as lawful
efforts to compete or unlawful efforts to obtain or abuse a monopoly.
Lacking a definition of competition, we, as the public, do not know
how to measure it or how to tell whether or not it is being lessened.
We have no consistent policy as to when we favor it or oppose it.
When court decisions about competition seem to contradict each
other, antitrust professors tell students, "Perhaps each case is a
product of convictions dominant at the time it was decided."[19] "Convictions" could be translated as "hunches" or "whims," and one
might ask, "Whose convictions about what?"

There is no consensus on what meaning to give to the word
"competition." Most people in business say they favor competition,
and yet they use government to protect themselves from it any way
they can. At least five different meanings of the word "competition"
have been suggested: (1) rivalry, (2) the absence of restraint over
one person's economic activities by another, (3) that state of the
market in which the individual buyer or seller does not influence
the price by his purchases or sales, (4) the existence of fragmented
industries and markets preserved through the protection of viable,
small, locally owned businesses, and (5) "any state of affairs in which
consumer welfare cannot be increased by moving to an alternative
state of affairs through judicial decree."[20] In the real world, politics

controls business rivalry through patents, licenses, selective exemptions, quotas, subsidies, price supports, fuel economy standards, environmental controls, minimum wages, and taxes and tax credits, and through random, selective enforcement of ambiguous antitrust statutes. The assertion that antitrust "looks to competition for guidance" is meaningless. It depends on who is doing the looking and where that person looks.

Pre-1980 Enforcement—Mutually Exclusive Goals

One pair of scholars describes the erratic enforcement history of the antitrust statutes as follows:

> From the origins of the Sherman Act and throughout its history, a list of terms of ambiguous content seem (sic) to have influenced both enforcement initiatives as well as the caselaw. In the beginning there were such terms as "trusts," "monopolies," and "cut-throat competition." During the Depression and beyond, "bigness," "concentration," "collusion," "conscious parallelism," "leverage," "coercion," "foreclosure," "market power," "monopoly power," and "merger movement" became the basis of enforcement action.[21]

The period from the late 1950s, following the creation of the section of antitrust law by the American Bar Association, to the late 1970s was one of directionless activism in antitrust. During the closing days of the Eisenhower administration a "revitalized"[22] FTC vigorously enforced section 2 of the Clayton Act, seeking to rid the garment industry of advertising and promotional payments by manufacturers not made available on proportionally equal terms to all competing customers—a widespread practice in clear violation of the statute. One enforcement action went all the way to the Supreme Court.[23] At that time the antitrust community was debating how to protect competition without protecting competitors. Some were saying that when competitors are eliminated competition is lost, so competitors (frequently labeled "small business") must be protected. Others were saying that, as long as competition remained healthy, the loss of individual competitors should not be of great concern. Adoption of the single goal of consumer welfare was later suggested as a solution to this puzzle.

Preserving competition, rather than protecting individual competitors, gained ascendancy as antitrust's purpose. Steady efforts to have all corporate mergers declared unlawful continued. Attacking big business became more appealing than protecting small business. The Justice Department began an investigation of IBM in 1967 and filed a complaint in 1969, alleging that IBM had monopolized general-purpose digital computers.[24] In the same year President Richard Nixon asked the ABA for a professional appraisal of the FTC. In due course the chairman of an ABA study committee was appointed chairman of the FTC. Another revitalization of the institution followed. This time, rather than attacking garment manufacturers, the FTC pursued bigger targets. In 1972 the commission alleged that four makers of ready-to-eat cereal shared a monopoly and that the industry should be restructured.[25] In 1976 the commission alleged that General Motors had unlawfully monopolized a portion of its own auto parts inventory. The commission sought to force GM to change its parts distribution system.[26]

Frederick Rowe's book on price discrimination,[27] published in 1962, intellectually destroyed section 2 of the Clayton Act. That section of one of the two basic antitrust statutes lost favor among the antitrust community. Section 2 of the Clayton Act is in such low repute that the antitrust community prefers not to think of it as an antitrust law and refers to it as "the Robinson-Patman Act." A task force consisting of senior members of the section of antitrust law of the ABA prepared a report titled "The State of Federal Antitrust Enforcement—2004" in which it recommended "repeal of Sections 2 (c) and 3" of the Robinson-Patman Act. There is no section 2 (c) of the Robinson-Patman Act. The task force meant to refer to section 2 (c) of the *Clayton* Act, as amended by section 1 of the Robinson-Patman Act, and to section 3 of the Robinson-Patman Act.

That careless error is indicative of the casual attitude of the antitrust community toward statutes. The error is not immaterial. Section 2 of the Clayton Act prohibited price discrimination but was interpreted in such a way as to provide insufficient protection to small grocery retailers competing with chain stores. Section 1 of the Robinson-Patman Act of 1936 amended section 2 of the Clayton Act to remedy the perceived problem. Section 2 of the Clayton Act, as amended by the Robinson-Patman Act, remains one of the antitrust laws defined by Congress as the basis for possible treble damage actions.

In addition to section 1, which extended by amendment the Clayton Act's civil prohibition of price discrimination, the Robinson-Patman Act contains other provisions that are not "antitrust laws." For example, section 3 of that act makes it a criminal offense to sell "at unreasonably low prices for the purpose of destroying competition or eliminating a competitor."[28]

Following the 1950 amendment of section 7 of the Clayton Act extending that statute's coverage, most notably to asset as well as to stock acquisitions, both the FTC and the Justice Department pursued active merger prevention programs. Robert Bork, while a Yale professor of antitrust law, described the atmosphere as follows:

> The imminent concentration of all ownership in a few giant corporations, with the concomitant demise of small business, is the standard, Mark I, all-weather antitrust hobgoblin. This congealing of the economy has been prophesied freely at least since the debates on the Sherman Act of 1890, always on the basis of overwhelming current trends, and it never comes to pass. It also never ceases to frighten people. The evil of this predicted economy-wide concentration appears to be so enormous and self-evident that critical faculties are overwhelmed.[29]

Studies were published about market structure. An oligopoly model was developed. It linked market structure with higher profits and anticompetitive behavior. The idea gained acceptance that, if increased concentration is a good reason for stopping mergers, "deconcentration" may be called for. After all, merger prevention only preserves the dominant position of the already-dominant. Why not break 'em up and do some real good? A 1968 White House Task Force on Antitrust Policy recommended enactment of a Concentrated Industries Act to reduce concentration in any industry in which "any four or fewer firms had an aggregate share of 70% or more during at least seven of the ten and four of the most recent five base years." Sen. Phillip Hart proposed an Industrial Reorganization Act directed at the largest companies in seven industries.

The "concentration" fever did not last. In 1971 John McGee published *In Defense of Industrial Concentration*.[30] He produced graphs and algebraic equations in defense of concentration to refute those that had been used to condemn it. Other economists such as Harold Demsetz[31] and Yale Brozen[32] undermined both the theoretical and the empirical bases for concerns about concentration. Legislative proposals to break up industry were abandoned. In 1982 the FTC gave up on its cereal case. That same year, after five years of litigation with General Motors over auto parts distribution, the commission concluded that "the parties have pretty much battled to a stand off." Realizing there was nothing it could do about the situation anyway (because it could not force GM to sell to specific buyers), the FTC abandoned the case. Also in 1982 the Justice Department quit its fruitless 15-year pursuit of IBM's alleged monopoly of computers. By 1984 it could be said that the oligopoly model "embodies the stale vision of a bygone age."[33] This does not mean that it has been eliminated from the antitrust psyche. In fact it has a prominent role in the current merger guidelines. Fear of corporate consolidation remains a central element of antitrust.

Attempt at a Rational Basis in Economic Theory

By 1980 protecting small business through vigorous enforcement of section 2 of the Clayton Act and preventing concentration through blanket enforcement of section 7 of the Clayton Act had lost their appeal. The Justice Department's use of section 2 of the Sherman Act to attack IBM's alleged monopolization of computers and the FTC's attack on the shared monopoly of cereal makers both turned out to be fiascoes. Antitrust needed a new rationale. What has been called "the Chicago school" supplied one.

As Daniel Gifford and Leo Raskind noted, "By the late 1970's, it had become clear that allocative efficiency had emerged as the dominant criterion in the judicial interpretation of the antitrust laws."[34] The thinking went as follows: Monopolies are bad because they allow the monopolist to raise price above marginal cost and obtain monopoly profits at lower volume. As a result, resources are misallocated and consumer welfare is lessened. Antitrust should be directed toward the single goal of preventing monopolistic practices that harm consumer welfare. Everything else is useless or mischievous. Economics is the key.

In 1976 Richard Posner, a University of Chicago Law School professor, suggested repeal of all antitrust laws other than section 1 of the Sherman Act because "redundant antitrust statutes . . . have stimulated an uncritical and unwise expansion of the prohibitory scope of antitrust."[35] Two years later, Bork, a University of Chicago

Law School alumnus, urged antitrust reform "to strike at three classes of behavior": (1) horizontal agreements to fix prices and divide markets; (2) horizontal mergers "creating very large market shares" leaving "fewer than three significant rivals in any market"; and (3) "deliberate predation," with "care ... taken not to confuse hard competition with predation." Some condemned conduct should be permitted—"agreements on prices, territories, refusals to deal, and other suppressions of rivalry that are ancillary ... to an integration of productive activity ..., small horizontal mergers, all vertical and conglomerate mergers, vertical price maintenance and market division, tying arrangements, exclusive dealing and requirements contracts, 'predatory' price cutting, [and] price 'discrimination.' "[36]

Bork concluded that "the only legitimate goal of American antitrust law is the maximization of consumer welfare" and that "the legislative histories of the antitrust statutes ... do not support any claim that Congress intended the courts to sacrifice consumer welfare to any other goal."[37]

Posner and Bork believed in antitrust and sought reform, not abolition. They changed antitrust rhetoric. Without any amendment of the statutes, the prohibitory scope of antitrust had been narrowed. As to price discrimination prohibited by section 2 of the Clayton Act, a task force of the ABA section of antitrust law noted in a 2001 report "the essential elimination of federal enforcement activity over the last quarter century" and "nearly complete bipartisan neglect of the statute."[38] Amendment of section 7 in 1976, requiring notice to the government of proposed mergers, has made section 7 impossible to ignore in the way section 2 has been ignored, but indiscriminate merger prevention has ceased. Bork's recommendation that vertical and conglomerate mergers should be permitted has been followed. More than 95 percent of reported mergers are left unmolested.

Consumer Welfare Economics Takes Over as Rhetoric— Protectionist or Fairness Strain Lives On

Some members of the antitrust community saw Chicago-school thinking as a threat to their existence, and for a time it was. Ronald Reagan's election as president resulted in the appointment of James C. Miller, an economist rather than a lawyer, to chair the FTC, and a Stanford law professor, William Baxter, to head the antitrust division at the Justice Department. Baxter had been a member of the 1968 White House task force that recommended breaking up concentrated industries, but by 1981 he had changed his mind about concentration. Antitrust activity, along with other regulatory activities, slowed down. It was rumored that one prominent Washington law firm had to borrow money to meet the monthly payroll. The firm that former Justice Department antitrust chief Herbert Bergson had started in the early 1950s began downsizing and eventually disappeared. Ralph Nader and Fred Furth, an experienced antitrust plaintiff's lawyer, held a revival meeting at their personal expense at Airlie Center in northern Virginia not far from Washington. Most of the leaders of the antitrust community were invited and attended. Academic traditionalists made efforts to prevent "the pendulum" from swinging "too far."[39] In 1987 the Georgetown University Law Center dean said "failures to act and loose rhetoric have contributed to a foolish and wasteful surge of giant consolidations" and urged that "a more vigorous, pragmatic antitrust enforcement policy should be restored."[40] Another prominent member of the antitrust community lamented that the antitrust "religion" was "dying" and that this was "the loss of a precious cultural resource."[41]

The antitrust religion was not dying. It remains alive and well. Attendance at the 2006 spring meeting of the ABA's section of antitrust law was at an all-time high. Antitrust has simply changed clothes from protection of small business and prevention of concentration to advancing consumer welfare. One creator of the new rhetoric for antitrust has looked upon his work with favor in the following words:

> Beginning around 1970, increased consensus and sophistication in the economic analysis of antitrust encouraged a more sophisticated approach to antitrust law and, beginning in the 1980's, coincided with a more positive public attitude toward capitalism. The "big business" chimera was largely forgotten. Efficiency became the only generally accepted goal of antitrust. More judges and lawyers learned the rudiments of antitrust economics, and antitrust economists became more effective as consultants and expert witnesses. It is fair to say that at the beginning of its second century antitrust law has become a branch of applied economics, has achieved a high degree of rationality and predictability, and is a success story of which all branches of the law and allied disciplines can be proud.[42]

Note this antitrust believer's use of the term "antitrust" and the absence of any reference to the antitrust statutes. It is the "analysis of antitrust" and the "goal of antitrust" that is in question. What is being discussed is religious doctrine, not the meaning of statutory language. The argument is over how to clothe antitrust. Belief in the Standard Oil legend and fear of corporate consolidation are still basic elements of the faith. But what remains is for the antitrust community to adjust to the new rhetoric and adapt it to the goals of the faith. This is possible because economic theory cannot supply normative rules of behavior. Economics, even if accepted as science, can tell us what was, what is, and sometimes what will be. It cannot tell us what ought to be. Antitrust can.

Even the Chicago school's rhetorical victory has been overstated. Acceptance of efficiency as the only goal of antitrust is less than complete. As antitrust scholar Herbert Hovenkamp told students:

> The Chicago School's approach to antitrust is defective for two important reasons. First of all, the notion that public policymaking should be guided exclusively by a notion of efficiency based on the neoclassical market efficiency model is naïve. That notion both overstates the ability of the policymaker to apply such a model to real world affairs and understates the complexity of the process by which the policymaker must select among competing policy values. Second, the neoclassical market efficiency model is itself too simple to account for or to predict business firm behavior in the real world.[43]

Hovenkamp is yet another antitrust community member who accepts the existence of "antitrust" as something independent of legal rules. There is no pretense of the enforcement of statutes by judges. Antitrust must be approached in a more sophisticated way. Antitrust decisions are policy decisions. Through a complex process, the decider selects among competing policy values.

The Chicago school tried to give antitrust enforcement a single goal to provide rationality and predictability in place of what was seen as the Warren Court's tendency to select among competing policy values and enforce "its own social preferences."[44] There is now broad acceptance that allocative efficiency has become *one* of the goals of antitrust, but substantial sentiment remains among the antitrust community that antitrust has more than one goal from which those making antitrust decisions can choose, leaving the decisionmakers free to enforce their own policy preferences. One pair of experts sees the choice of goals as follows:

> These goals generally fall into four categories: (1) consumer welfare goals, including the efficient allocation of existing resources and avoiding wealth transfers to participants with market power; (2) fostering innovation and technological progress; (3) protecting individual firms through fairness and equity goals; and (4) maintaining decentralized power.[45]

The claim that antitrust law has achieved rationality and predictability can be supported by citations to Supreme Court decisions that moved in that direction. The Court has recognized the implausibility of predatory price cutting[46] and declined to hold that blanket licenses of copyrighted music are automatically illegal.[47] Nor, said the Court, are agreements between buyer and seller necessarily illegal simply because they restrict the buyer's freedom to resell.[48] Still, it is difficult to maintain that applied economics has given any precision to the problem of identifying illegal monopolization or that today's merger regulation has any predictability at all. Ambiguous phrases in the antitrust statutes empower government officials to interfere in business activity but do not supply much guidance as to when or where or why to do so. A century of court decisions has provided little clarification. There is little reason to believe that microeconomic theory will bring much change. Even if allocative efficiency were to be accepted as the sole rationale for decisions enforcing the antitrust statutes, fairness and equity goals, still widely and firmly cherished, could be pursued through imaginative application of the imaginary concept of market power. Indeed, market power has replaced concentration as the all-purpose antitrust hobgoblin and the primary evil at which the ceremonial process of antitrust is now directed.

4. The Magic of "Market Power"

The antitrust community uses market power, an imaginary concept from economic theory, as though the term describes something that actually exists. Antitrust is *pro* competition. To what is antitrust anti? The antitrust statutes don't contain an answer to that question. The antitrust community has supplied one. Antitrust is *anti* market power. The basic evil at which antitrust activities are said to be directed is market power. The thinking goes something like this: The bad thing about monopolization is that the monopolist acquires market power. The bad thing about some mergers is that they may result in market power. One of the central elements of antitrust is a belief that firms can and do exercise market power and that it is up to government to prevent their doing so. Official doctrine declares, "At its core, antitrust policy is aimed at preventing firms from obtaining, retaining, or abusing market power."[1]

Two elements of antitrust—belief in the legend of Standard Oil and fear of corporate consolidation—are shared by many literate Americans. The third element—belief in the existence of market power, as well as the responsibility of government to do something about it—belongs to professional antitrust experts. Most Americans have never heard of it. What is market power?

> Economists define 'market power' as the ability of a firm or group of firms within a market to profitably charge prices above the competitive level for a sustained period of time. Although any firm can raise its price, not every firm can profitably do so. As a result, a distinguishing characteristic of a firm or group of firms with market power is that their prices can be raised without the firm or group of firms losing so many sales that the price increase is unprofitable. If there are close substitutes or others could easily begin producing close substitutes, a firm will not profit from a price increase and thus, by definition, does not have market power.[2]

In other words, you have market power if you have market power. This market power is not real. It is an analytical concept of economic theory. It comes from textbook models of perfect competition and monopoly. The concept carries no assumption that market power has ever been possessed by any firm or group of firms or that it ever could be. It is an imagined power, like witchcraft. It is the power that a firm or group of firms would have in an imagined situation—a situation in which the firm or group of firms has no competitors for a sustained period of time and that no close substitutes or potential close substitutes exist. This imagined capacity of an imagined firm or group of firms in an imagined situation has been imported into the interpretation and enforcement of rules of law that contain the words "restraint of trade," "monopolize," and "lessen competition" as though market power is real—as though it describes a situation that actually exists—as though possession of such hypothetical power can be a matter of factual proof.

The Sherman Act forbids contracts "in restraint of trade or commerce among the several States or with foreign nations" and monopolizing or attempting to monopolize "any part of the trade or commerce among the several States, or with foreign nations." The Clayton Act forbids mergers "where in any line of commerce . . . in any section of the country, the effect . . . may be substantially to lessen competition, or to tend to create a monopoly." The judicial inquiry as to whether conduct violates those vague and ambiguous normative standards in the antitrust statutes turns into what the antitrust community calls "market analysis." Decisions are given a gloss of rationality by discussion of "the relevant market." The process is described as follows:

> Market analysis begins with the definition of the relevant market. Without defining the relevant market, there is no meaningful context within which to assess the restraint's competitive effects. A relevant market has both product and geographic dimensions. After defining the relevant market, the Court considers whether the defendant has "market power"—typically defined as "the ability to raise prices above those that would be charged in a competitive market." Courts generally have held that proof of defendant's market power is an absolute prerequisite for a plaintiff seeking to use market analysis to satisfy its burden of proving likely anticompetitive effect.[3]

The antitrust community takes this process seriously because court opinions written in these terms are used as rules by which to judge conduct. Market power in this formulation is not just a theoretical concept. It is an ability that the defendant can achieve and exercise. Possession of market power can be a matter of "proof"—something that judges and juries can find as a fact. In that sense Justice John Paul Stevens has called market power a "special ability . . . to force a purchaser to do something."[4] In the same sense, the Commentary on the Horizontal Merger Guidelines (2006) published by the Federal Trade Commission and the Justice Department states on page 1 that "the core concern of the antitrust laws, including as they pertain to mergers between rivals, is the creation or enhancement of market power" and that "mergers should not be permitted to create or enhance market power or to facilitate its exercise."

The authors of the Commentary write as though the antitrust laws are people. People have concerns. Statutes do not. Someone has concerns about the creation, enhancement, and exercise of market power. Government must respond to such concerns.

Antitrust experts point out: "Market power often is not easily assessed; 'the' analysis certainly requires a fact-specific and detailed inquiry into the underlying competitive conditions, which may be complex."[5] Market power "is possessed to some degree by every firm that is not constrained by perfect competition."[6] In other words, every kid with a lemonade stand has *some* market power. "In markets with differentiated products, the absence of localized competition may enable a firm to exercise market power."[7] How do we know when the defendant possesses sufficient market power intentionally achieved to be a criminal in violation of the Sherman Act? How do we know when a merger may result in the creation of such an unacceptable amount of market power that it should be prevented? "Economic theory alone . . . does not provide a bright line that indicates when such power raises concerns that violate the antitrust laws."[8] "The quantum of power required for judicial intervention varies with the nature of the antitrust challenge."[9] According to "the" analysis, "the courts must make a judgment of degree. . . . Performance tests obviously cannot detect power that has not yet been attained and thus cannot aid antitrust efforts to control conduct leading to market power. . . . Market power and its determinants are all matters of degree. . . . But decisions must be made even when available data are inconclusive."[10]

Why must such decisions be made? Why should we condemn conduct when all we have are inconclusive data? In his book *The*

Antitrust Paradox, Robert Bork described how some members of the antitrust community answer this question:

> Several hundred lawyers at a meeting of the Antitrust Section of the American Bar Association listened to a nationally prominent attorney, who subsequently became an Associate Justice of the Supreme Court, contend it was fruitless to worry about antitrust's intellectual problems. Antitrust, the attorney said, is in the good old American tradition of the sheriff of a frontier town: he did not sift evidence, distinguish between suspects, and solve crimes, but merely walked the main street and every so often pistol-whipped a few people.[11]

Antitrust believers feel a need to do something even if they can't be sure that it will accomplish anything. As Thurman Arnold said, "The crusade is not a practical one."[12] Even if attempts to deal with market power accomplish no more than did Theodore Roosevelt's trust-busting, the attempt has moral and ceremonial value.

How would someone prove the existence of market power? No one can prove it, but the antitrust community infers its existence from market share. "While market shares and concentration statistics are not perfect proxies for market power, they have become a proxy in the courts and before the agencies for the assessment of market power and the likely performance of a market."[13] The Chicago school's efforts to make antitrust law a branch of applied economics have resulted in the retention of concentration as a central element of antitrust.

"Market" Is Metaphor; It Can Only Be Assumed and Cannot Be Proven

To prove the existence of market power, a market must first be defined. The antitrust bible published by the ABA tells us:

> The definition of a relevant market is important in most antitrust cases and is often the central battleground issue. Although the courts have identified basic methodologies and factors to be considered in defining a market, applying these principles in particular cases often proves difficult and complex.[14]

The government's Horizontal Merger Guidelines define a market "as a product or group of products and a geographic area in which it is produced or sold such that a hypothetical profit-maximizing firm, not subject to price regulation, that was the only present and future producer or seller of those products in that area likely would impose at least a 'small but significant and nontransitory' increase in price, assuming the terms of sale of all other products are held constant."[15] The Guidelines also contain the statement: "In attempting to determine objectively the effect of a 'small but significant and nontransitory' increase in price, the Agency, in most contexts, will use a price increase of five percent lasting for the foreseeable future."[16]

Determinations of the market and market power are made through a self-hypnotic process of circular reasoning. The market is only a metaphor, not a description of reality. There is no actual market. This was explained by Frederick Rowe:

> Fundamentally, the market is metaphor, not actuality, a mental "picture in our heads." While many definitions, all circular, state attributes of what the market *is*, a market is a market is a market—there is no *there*, there. Like the law's concept of contract, economics' concept of market yields no answers for any but the blackletter textbook case. But unlike contract, which has been objectified by precedent, historical gloss, and case-by-case interpretation, the market has no objective content outside itself. Without empirical referents, identification of *the* market is perforce arbitrary, a façade for decisions elsewhere derived. Inevitably, *the* market entails a mix of intuition, judgment, and choice, relative for each case and every question at hand. (Derivative norms of "market power" then wax delusive or piffling, for such power exists everywhere or nowhere, and becomes meaningful only as a variable of time and degree for any given case.). . . The market itself cannot be the predictive premise, the analytic constant for inferring positive or negative prospects of particular enterprise events in any actual case. . . . The rub is not with economic models as models, but their misuse as legal norms.[17]

The Guidelines' market definition requires the assumption that, while the hypothetical price increase on which the market definition is to be based continues (a 5 percent increase for the foreseeable future), "the terms of sale of all other products are held constant." The attempt is to make a static analysis of a dynamic world by making an assumption about an unknown future, and the assumption is most probably wrong. The one thing we know about the future is that things do not stand still. Definition of the market is based on an assumption that could be true only in a dream world, not the real world.

To deal with this problem, the antitrust community has employed the concept of "barriers to entry," another metaphor needed to give a surface plausibility to the market metaphor. Supposedly, because of barriers to entry, hypothesized higher prices do not attract additional sellers:

> The existence or absence of barriers to entry is a critical market characteristic that is inevitably considered in one form or another in every market and market power analysis. Both the courts and the economic literature recognize that a monopolist or collusive group will not be able to increase prices above the competitive level for sustained periods of time where entry into a relevant market is easily accomplished.[18]

This neatens up the doctrine but merely leads to further difficulty in imposing the concepts onto facts in the real world. According to the *Market Power Handbook*, "there remains significant disagreement over both the definition of entry barriers, and the best method of evaluating the ease or difficulty with which a new competitor will be able to enter a market."[19]

If it is possible to exercise market power because there are barriers to entry, when were the barriers erected and by whom? Were they in place before the market power was obtained? One pair of economists concludes: "There is no general consensus about what precisely constitutes a barrier to entry."[20] It may be that the only effective barriers to entry are those maintained by government through special legislation or patents.[21]

Market Power—Imagined and Unverifiable

Market "power" is the imagined power that a seller might have if an assumed future, in which all other things remain unchanged and which cannot be verified, were to occur. Government forces citizens to pay taxes. That is real power. Business firms cannot force citizens to pay for anything. Power cannot be achieved by high sales volume. There is no right to sell. No one can be forced to buy.

Antitrust believers derive—out of circular assumptions—a miraculous power of some sellers to force sales on buyers. Market definition depends on an assumed power and that power, in turn, depends on definition of the market. Both depend on assumptions about a future that no one can know. Application of the term "market power" to a consensual relationship of buyer and seller confuses thought on the subject. The only real power a seller has is derived from satisfying buyers. Absent government coercion, it is only the buyer, not the seller, who has any power.

The antitrust community must use available terms to get results, given existing antitrust doctrines. Every seller has a monopoly at a particular time and place, but everything competes with everything else for the buyer's dollar. The antitrust community attempts to reconcile these two truisms with the necessity of giving some meaning to the terms "monopolization" and "competition." At the present time, "market analysis" is the only tool available. The antitrust community is stuck with that tool, given existing antitrust doctrines. Lawyers merely apply those doctrines and cannot be expected to provide assistance at developing intelligent public policy.

Belief in market power is critical for the antitrust community. If there is no such thing as market power, there is no point to antitrust. Where would the Apostle's Creed be without the virgin birth? Belief in the effect of a placebo, like belief in the power of prayer, may do some good and does no harm to nonbelievers. By comparison, belief in market power carries a potential for mischief and provides no rational basis for normative rules.

When a judge or jury finds that a defendant possesses market power, it can lead to a conclusion of illegal monopolization, with possible treble damages and breakup of the defendant to follow. When a government official concludes that a merger might lead to creation of substantial market power, the merger must be prevented. In the dream world of antitrust, as sales volume rises to the point that a particular market share is reached, like magic the sellers have obtained market power. Now they can raise prices above the "competitive" level, cut production, and make monopoly profits. But success is risky. If market share is a proxy for market power, the rule for the boldly creative and productive entrepreneur becomes at some point: hold down sales volume and avoid improvements in price, quality, and service or face antitrust prosecution. The enforcement of the antitrust laws is based on that theory. It takes an expert to believe in it.

"Market Power" Label—A Disguise for Subjective Decisions

The "market power" label is used to provide a façade for subjective decisions as to what the decisionmaker feels is fair. Whether a given defendant has an unacceptable amount of market power—whether that defendant has violated the law—is a matter of judgment. On what basis is the judgment made? Economic theory provides no "bright line" to guide the decision. Nor do the facts. Identification of the market is arbitrary, "a façade for decisions elsewhere derived."[22] As Rowe has written, market definition "entails a mix of intuition, judgment, and choice, relative for each case and every question at hand."[23] The judgment or choice is made to find that the defendant has, or did have or might have, substantial market power. Did the judge or jury find that the defendant had substantial market power because the defendant actually did have such power, or did the power exist only because the judge or jury found that it did?

Antitrust doctrines of market analysis bestow on antitrust decisionmakers the power to make arbitrary decisions based on hunch or whim disguised as reason. Those who understand what they are doing can further their own personal or political objectives, including the desire for fairness and social justice. Those who do not understand what they are doing are simply acting at random, or in whatever direction they can be led by effective advocates. As one chairman of the ABA section of antitrust law has written:

> Every antitrust case now involves a battle of economic experts, and it is very difficult for judges and juries untutored in antitrust economics to evaluate the presentation of economic experts effectively and, thus, the experts often simply cancel each other out of the case.[24]

Some decisionmakers may understand what they are doing. Some may not. In either case, they are not doing what they are supposed to do in our system—apply announced written rules to proven facts to decide whether a law has been violated.

5. Monopolization

The primary goal of antitrust is protection of the public from monopolization by the "trust." The antitrust community has been unable to develop a specific description of the primary villain of antitrust—the trust. The Sherman Act, the original *anti*-trust law, declared it a federal crime, punishable by fine and imprisonment, to "restrain trade" and to "monopolize" any part of the trade or commerce among the several states or with foreign nations. Those activities were what the Standard Oil trust and other trusts were supposed to have done. Trusts were believed to have monopolized parts of trade. Clayton Act prohibitions—such as those against price discrimination, tying, and mergers—are not criminal. They were adopted later to prevent practices that purportedly might lead to monopolization.

As several authors have observed, the antitrust community favors competition but lacks a consensus on how to define it. Law professors Daniel Gifford and Leo Raskind wrote as follows:

> The Sherman Act was enacted as a response to the dominant political phrases of the day—"trusts," and "monopolies." As the legislative history of the Sherman Act attests, the congressional debates that led to its enactment did not provide a clear direction for interpreting the statute as enacted.[1]

According to law professors Eleanor Fox and Lawrence Sullivan, when the Sherman Act was passed the public saw trusts as an "intolerable evil."[2] Congress acted to combat that evil "despite doubts about precisely what the statute meant or would accomplish."[3] The action was similar to the way today's politicians respond to public dissatisfaction with gasoline prices by proposals to do something about "price gouging" without being able to define it. In 1890 public dissatisfaction with trusts seemed to require doing something about monopolization although the term wasn't defined—and even though oil industry prices were declining at the time. Doubts about what the statute meant or would accomplish were no obstacle to congressional action.

The antitrust community has struggled ever since to give meaning to the statutory prohibition of monopolization. It is impossible to construct a factual foundation for the term. Like market power (and unlike, say, robbery) there remains only a prohibited concept of evil without factual reference. No one has developed a formulation that can distinguish legitimate from illegitimate competitive efforts by a single firm acting alone. Is the firm successfully competing, which is thought to be desirable, or is it monopolizing, which the statute condemns? There is no way to tell the difference on the basis of ascertainable facts.

In 2006 the Justice Department and the Federal Trade Commission held a series of joint public hearings to examine "whether and when specific types of single-firm conduct" may violate the Sherman Act "by harming competition and consumer welfare, and when they are procompetitive or benign."[4] At the initial hearing the FTC chairman indicated that the problem of how to define illegal monopolization "still vexes" and announced a new goal of antitrust—"undistorted competition."[5] The concept of "distorting" competition may help capture the elusive concept of monopolization.

Belief in antitrust begins with the Standard Oil legend. Antitrust believers are opposed to what the Standard Oil trust is believed to have done. Antitrust is *anti* the Standard Oil trust. Why? In the late 19th century, American businessmen attempted to consolidate corporations under a legal device known as the "trust." They transferred securities to trustees who then possessed authority to run the new entity as one unified corporation. Standard Oil formed the first trust in 1882 and, within a decade, other industries did the same.[6] In 1911 the Supreme Court held that Standard Oil Company of New Jersey was an illegal monopoly prohibited by the Sherman Act because Standard had unified "power and control over petroleum and its products."[7] The Court dissolved the evil trust into dozens of geographically dispersed companies. The legend of Standard Oil was established.

Professors of antitrust law preserve the legend. Phillip Areeda and Louis Kaplow accept as "clear facts" that Standard "had achieved undoubted dominance of domestic oil production and distribution through numerous mergers, some of which were *coerced*, and oppressive tactics against competitors, including the *coercion* of competitors' suppliers and customers."[8] Fox and Sullivan tell their students how this "dominance" was exercised:

> The enormous buying power of that trust was used to *force* the railroads to give the trust low rates while charging its competitors high rates. As a seller, the Oil Trust charged high prices to customers in monopoly areas, while engaging in local price cutting designed to *force* recalcitrant competitors to sell out to the trust or be destroyed.[9]

Fox and Sullivan suggest that "the railroads, needing Standard Oil's business, were afraid to offend it."[10]

The Standard Oil legend is a starting point for belief in antitrust in somewhat the same way that belief in the virgin birth supports the Apostle's Creed. Without an acceptance of the Standard Oil legend, the collection of fears, assumptions, and predictions that constitute the antitrust religion would have nothing to build on. If the legend were shown to be without factual foundation, the Sherman Act may have been aimed at something that never existed. Legal action to enforce the statute might be chasing a ghost. That could be the reason it is so difficult to define monopolization—it never happened. Antitrust might be, as professor D. T. Armentano has asserted, a "hoax."[11]

Not everyone agrees with Areeda and Kaplow that the "clear facts" show Standard Oil achieved "dominance" of domestic oil production through "coerced" mergers and "oppressive tactics" against competitors. It may be that many firms were eager to be bought out by Standard.[12] Furthermore, at the peak of Standard's supposed dominance of the industry, "the costs and prices for refined oil reached their lowest levels in the history of the petroleum industry."[13] According to professor Thomas DiLorenzo, "there never was any evidence that the trusts and 'combinations' of the late nineteenth century actually harmed consumers in the way that monopolies are supposed to harm consumers—by colluding to restrict production to drive up prices."[14] Robert Crandall and Clifford Winston of the Brookings Institution concluded that the decree dissolving Standard Oil had "little effect" and note that real crude oil prices were falling before Standard Oil was brought to trial and rose after the breakup. They point out that Standard Oil's market share of refinery capacity in the United States had fallen before the decree from 82 percent in 1899 to 64 percent in 1911.[15] Professor

Simon Whitney concluded, "decline in the share of refining done by Standard Oil even before 1911, and a continued decline of successor companies as a group, indicate that the decree merely supported current trends."[16]

Armentano wrote that Standard Oil was more efficient:

> [The legend] has almost nothing in common with the actual facts. . . . Standard Oil's efficiency made the company extremely successful: it kept its costs low and was able to sell more and more of its refined product, usually at a lower and lower price, in the open marketplace. . . . In 1911 at least 147 refining companies were competing with Standard, including such large firms as Gulf, Texaco, Union, Pure, Associated Oil and Gas, and Shell. . . . Standard Oil . . . secured its market position in petroleum primarily through internal efficiency and merger, not systematic predatory practices.[17]

Professor John McGee examined the thousands of pages of the trial record in the Standard Oil case and concluded that the record shows "Standard Oil did not use predatory price discrimination to drive out competing refiners, nor did its pricing practice have that effect."[18]

Whatever the truth in the historical record, one might ask how the trust could "coerce" buyers to buy and sellers to sell without the assistance of government. What was the basis of Standard's so-called "dominance" of domestic oil production and distribution? What was the source of Standard's "power and control" over petroleum? How does a shipper of goods make railroads "afraid to offend it?" Was Standard's "power" to "force" others to enter into commercial transactions of buying and selling wielded at gunpoint or with baseball bats? If so, the trust could have been prosecuted for robbery. There would have been no need for adoption of an antitrust law.

The antitrust community acknowledges that it is difficult to put into words the concept of monopolization and that it is difficult to state a normative rule of just what is prohibited by declaring monopolization a crime. Antitrust believers see the difficulty as one of identification and description of the wicked monopolist, a matter of distinguishing between a good trust and an evil trust. Hearings are held to discuss the problem, but the community cannot accept the conclusion that the difficulty of defining monopolization may derive from the possibility that, without support from government, no one can monopolize any part of trade or commerce for long enough that we need a law against it. Without a belief in monopolization there would be no need for a law to prevent it and no need for a law to prevent business practices that might lead to it.

To gain a better understanding, let us compare the crime of monopolization with the crime of robbery. The crime of robbery has a clear definition based on provable facts. It is defined as "the taking, with intent to steal, of the personal property of another, from his person or in his presence, without his consent or against his will, by violence or intimidation."[19] Each of the elements of the crime of robbery has an anchor in the real world. Such concepts as "taking" and "by violence" have real meaning.

The offense of monopolization cannot be defined the way robbery can. The supposed elements of monopolization have no anchor in the real world. They can only be imagined. The American Bar Association's antitrust law section refers for a definition of monopolization to the *Grinnell* case[20] in which the Supreme Court identified what it referred to as "the elements of the offense" as follows:

> The offense of monopoly under section 2 of the Sherman Act has two elements: (1) the possession of monopoly power in the relevant market and (2) the willful acquisition or maintenance of that power as distinguished from growth or development as a consequence of a superior product, business acumen, or historic accident.[21]

Unlike a statement of the elements of the offense of robbery, that statement by the Supreme Court is useless as an operative, normative rule by which to guide and judge conduct. The statement is simply a doctrinal verbalization. Taking by force can be observed by witnesses who can be questioned under oath. Possession of monopoly power cannot be observed by anyone. One either believes in it or one doesn't. Proof of the existence of monopoly power depends on assumptions and predictions that cannot be verified. There are no witnesses who can be questioned, only expert theorists who can offer opinions that "often simply cancel each other out."[22]

Even doctrinally the Supreme Court's statement relied upon by the antitrust community for a definition of monopolization leaves unresolved the tension between competing values. As Fox has written:

> The meaning of "monopolize" has been one of the puzzles of U.S. antitrust law for the entire century of its existence. The challenge is to formulate a liability rule or standard that takes wise account of the tension between providing incentives to be the best and preventing unjustified creation and abuses of monopoly power. The balance has shifted over time.[23]

Without the assumptions inherent in the concepts of "the market" and "market power," there is no tension that needs balancing. Without the assumptions of static analysis applied to a dynamic world, there is no defining of "the" market and no "market power." The problem of defining monopolization is in the concept, that is, in the impossibility of encouraging winners and protecting losers at the same time. Belief in antitrust allows belief in a kind of competition in which some win but none lose. Antitrust believers like Fox are attempting to reconcile competition with social justice. They have a dream.

The Supreme Court's definition of monopolization uses the term "monopoly power." Is there any difference between market power and monopoly power? The ABA *Market Power Handbook* answers as follows:

> Some scholars have distinguished between the two terms. Those scholars point out that firms may have trivial amounts of market power, perhaps because the firm has transitory advantages that will be competed away as other firms innovate. That market power should not raise antitrust concerns. In contrast, firms with a substantial amount of market power may be said to have monopoly power or "antitrust monopoly power," which does raise antitrust concerns. . . . Many economists would distinguish antitrust monopoly power as a circumstance where a firm (or group of firms) has substantial market power. The presence of substantial market power is reflected in the firm's (or group of firms') ability to raise a price significantly above competitive levels for a sustained period of time; the firm (or group of firms) is insulated from competition over the long run by significant barriers to entry as opposed to minor differences in product attributes.[24]

In other words, without barriers to entry market power does not equal monopoly power. Firms may have "trivial" amounts of market power that will be competed away, but such market power does not raise "antitrust concerns." Only substantial market power made possible by significant barriers to entry raises such concerns. What are significant barriers to entry? Once again, the student of antitrust confronts an economic concept, like market and market power, defined by result and based on assumption, not ascertainable facts.

The ABA *Market Power Handbook* concludes its chapter on barriers to entry with the following:

> The likelihood of entry is a fact-specific inquiry that, like market power and relevant market analysis, requires a comprehensive assessment of the structural and behavioral characteristics of the market and firms at issue. No single test exists for whether entry will be likely, timely or successful. Rather, the analysis must consider a wide range of evidence.[25]

Once antitrust concerns have been raised, it does not necessarily follow that illegal conduct has occurred; only that a fact-intensive process of antitrust analysis should begin. Comprehensive assessment is called for. No single test is available. Everything is relevant and nothing is determinative. "The analysis" includes not only facts but also assumptions and predictions that cannot be verified. If the decisionmaker is so inclined, the label "anticompetitive" is applied, and the conduct pronounced illegal. There is no normative rule by which to guide or judge conduct. Results depend not so much on what the facts are but on how they are characterized by skillful advocates and theorists. A decision is reached as to whether something has happened that should be disapproved of—whether the defendant is a doer of evil, and whether a victim has been treated unfairly. If so, the defendant is accused of acting not competitively but *anti*-competitively. Then the conclusory label is applied and the conduct ruled illegal. There is no rule that can be stated in advance to guide and evaluate conduct. The conduct is evaluated first, and then a ruling is made. The conduct is not disapproved because it violates a rule. The rule can't be stated until the conduct has been exhaustively examined and disapproved on the basis of assumptions and predictions.

The antitrust process of deciding who is illegally monopolizing rather than just competing has been discussed as a matter of choosing standards. Steven Salop, professor of law and economics at Georgetown University, acknowledging that there is "great intellectual ferment over the proper antitrust liability standard governing allegedly

53

exclusionary conduct," finds "two main competing liability standards."[26] He prefers one over the other and says that making it "the" standard would "unify antitrust law and make the doctrine more coherent."[27] Prominent antitrust lawyer Mark Popofsky, apparently unconcerned about unity or coherence, identifies five different proposed definitions of exclusionary conduct. He says that the search for a unitary test should be abandoned, that courts must apply "different" legal tests and "select between rules" depending on the case.[28] Law professor Andrew Gavil says the following of the antitrust community's attempts to define monopolization:

> As an antitrust community we have long been of two minds about monopoly. On the one hand, the evils of monopoly are widely recognized: restricted output, higher prices, perhaps diminished incentives to pursue cost-cutting measures and innovation, and increased incentives to pursue rent-seeking strategies, as with predation. . . . Yet we also are aware of the potential dangers of too readily condemning the actions of monopolists for fear that legal standards will erode the very incentive that drove them to compete hard and succeed in the first place. . . . Identifying operative legal rules that resolve the obvious tension between these two competing values has proven to be an elusive goal.[29]

Gavil concludes that the goal of stating an operative legal rule should be abandoned because "a unitary and inflexible standard will necessarily under- or over-deter."[30] Rather than adopt Popofsky's recommendation that it be left to judges to select a rule to fit the case, Gavil suggests "dominant firms" should be asked to "adhere to a higher code of responsibility."[31] He does not say where this code can be found. Perhaps in the Golden Rule. It can't be found in the written provisions of the Sherman Act.

Counseling to avoid prosecution for monopolization is impossible. There is no way to know or predict what rule or standard, if any, will be selected to decide the case. How does the successful competitor avoid raising antitrust concerns? Cutting sales, so that inefficient competitors may more easily survive, may help to avoid government scrutiny. But the evil may already have been done. An unsuccessful competitor may sue for treble damages. For a fee, an imaginative and articulate economist may label some past competitive action of the defendant with a sinister term such as "exclusionary" or "predatory." Facts may be presented with sufficient skill such that the label sounds plausible to a jury sympathetic to the plaintiff. An enterprising lawyer may invent a class of injured parties and demand payment for damages so high that the successful competitor must either settle or face bankruptcy. That's not the rule of law but of roulette.

Unsuccessful Attempts to Give Meaning to the Statutory Prohibition of Monopolization

The history of government action against monopolization provides no cause for optimism that an operative definition of monopolization will ever be found. Antitrust believers struggling to make sense of the ambiguity in antitrust statutes reach for an analogy with common law development as though federal courts can develop a law of monopolization the way that old English courts developed tort and contract law. Professors E. Thomas Sullivan and Herbert Hovenkamp write that the Sherman Act "was designed to set forth only general principles so that the courts would be able to determine the legality of challenged practices on a case-by-case basis within the context of common law principles."[32] Areeda and Kaplow assert that the Sherman Act "may be little more than a legislative command that the judiciary develop a common law of antitrust."[33]

The common law analogy is misleading and confuses thought. The Sherman Act is a statute enacted by a legislature of limited powers delegated in a written constitution. Federal courts are not courts of general jurisdiction like those that developed English common law inherited by our state courts. Under our constitution, all federal law is statutory. There is no federal common law. Neither Congress nor the federal courts can create one. If the Sherman Act were, as Areeda and Kaplow suggest, only a command to develop a common law of antitrust, the act would be an unconstitutional delegation of legislative powers to the judiciary, without any intelligible principle to guide the judiciary in fleshing out the provisions of the statute.

A law subjecting the citizen to possible fine or imprisonment should be explicit as to what one may or may not safely do and should not leave too much to the discretion of prosecutors, judges, and juries. The Supreme Court, however, has rejected the argument that the Sherman Act is deficient in this respect.[34] The court said that "the law is full of instances where a man's fate depends on his estimating rightly, that is, as the jury subsequently estimates it, some matter of degree," and gave the example of "murder, manslaughter, or misadventure" resulting from an automobile accident.[35] But that analogy does not fit well with determinations of market power and barriers to entry. Perhaps that's why prosecutors have been reluctant to invoke the criminal sanctions of the Sherman Act. The ABA explains as follows:

> Sections 1 and 2 of the Sherman Act give the government the authority to proceed against violations by criminal indictment or by civil contempt. Although the language of the statutes offers no criteria for determining whether a particular violation should most appropriately be addressed criminally or civilly, the Antitrust Division has a long-standing policy of seeking criminal indictment only where it believes it can prove a clear, purposeful violation of the law.[36]

From Standard Oil to IBM to Microsoft—the Successful Competitor Turned upon When He Wins

Government attacks on alleged monopolization are rare, but there is always a danger to successful competitors, especially innovators, that competitive losers will pressure activist government officials to do something. Assisted by creative lawyers and economists, losers can place on the winner heavy financial burdens to defend business success against private treble damage actions with unpredictable results.

Prosecution of Standard Oil ended in victory for the government. The defendant was dissolved, a symbolic but useless victory for the Justice Department. In 1915 former president Theodore Roosevelt said of the prosecution of Standard Oil that "not one particle of good resulted to anybody and a number of worthy citizens of small means were appreciably injured."[37]

Similarly, the prosecution of IBM was a complete fiasco. The government began an investigation in 1967 and filed a complaint in January 1969.[38] Trial began in May 1975. The United States sought dismissal in January 1982.[39] Law professor John Lopatka describes the case as follows:

> The numbers astound: 700 trial days over the course of nearly seven years, preceded by six years of discovery; 87 live witnesses; 860 deposition witnesses (whose testimony was read

aloud to an empty bench, a process that consumed 70 trial days); 104,400 trial transcript pages; 17,000 exhibits. . . . The government estimated that it spent $16.8 million, not including expert witness fees, litigating the case; the defendant estimated that the total annual cost—*annual*—to all parties was between $50 million and $100 million, an estimate that presumably does not include the incalculable indirect costs of the litigation. And after fifteen years after its investigation began, the United States simply dropped its case against IBM, Assistant Attorney General William Baxter concluding that the government would lose and fearing that it might win.[40]

The government alleged that IBM had monopolized a market of general-purpose digital computers, having reached sales of about 74 percent of that market. The government did not charge that IBM had acquired its market share unlawfully but that it had maintained its position through anticompetitive acts. According to author and former federal appellate judge Robert Bork, "There was no sensible explanation for IBM's dominance in the computer industry at the time other than superior efficiency, and, as the firm's relative superiority declined, the market began to erode IBM's position."[41]

A private party, Telex, also attacked IBM for its business success.[42] In the *Telex* case, Telex first alleged that IBM had monopolized and attempted to monopolize data-processing equipment and then, in an amended complaint, charged IBM with monopolization of plug-compatible peripheral products attached to IBM central-processing units. Rather than just defend, IBM fought back. In a counterclaim, IBM charged Telex with unfair competition, theft of trade secrets, and copyright infringement. After an exhaustive trial, a U.S. district judge concluded that IBM should pay Telex $259.5 million, plus $1.2 million in costs and attorneys' fees. A court of appeals reversed that decision. The court concluded that the evidence established that IBM's actions constituted "valid competitive practice"[43] and ordered Telex to pay IBM on the counterclaim $17.5 million in compensatory damages and $1 million in punitive damages. Telex filed a petition for review in the Supreme Court but later withdrew the petition after a settlement in which each party released its claims against the other.[44] The case nicely illustrates the difficulty of distinguishing illegal monopolization from valid competitive practice. The parties, probably advised by the most expensive experts available, were unwilling to risk a decision in the Supreme Court as to which is which. The *Telex* case makes it difficult to maintain that there is any rule of law with regard to monopolization.

Chapter 1 describes the meandering procedural history of the *Microsoft* case.[45] Though the proceedings clarified nothing, they showed the subjective nature of decisions about monopolization and the absence of any discoverable rule by which to guide or judge conduct. Competitive losers complained to the Federal Trade Commission about Microsoft's conduct. Two commissioners would have done nothing about it. Two would have. Because the fifth commissioner declined to participate in the decision, the commission did nothing. The Justice Department pursued the case. After several years in the courts, involving two district judges and three circuit judges and an unsuccessful attempt by another circuit judge to mediate the case, a district judge found that Microsoft had illegally monopolized Intel-compatible PC operating systems and illegally attempted to monopolize Internet browsers. He concluded that the company should be broken up. A panel consisting of seven circuit judges, one of whom had been in charge of the antitrust division at the Justice Department before being appointed to the court of appeals, reversed most of the district judge's decision and turned the matter into a "tying" case that was settled out of court with the parties agreeing to regulatory provisions supposedly designed to protect complaining competitors. Chapter 7 will discuss tying.

On June 1, 1938, trial began on a complaint by the Justice Department that Aluminum Company of America had illegally monopolized aluminum. The government urged that the company be dissolved. The trial lasted two years and generated 40,000 pages of testimony. After another two years, a district judge dismissed the complaint. Two years after that, the Supreme Court announced that it couldn't assemble a quorum of six justices to review the case but referred the matter to the U.S. Court of Appeals for the Second Circuit. That court's opinion,[46] written by Chief Judge Learned Hand, has been called a "classic" that "did much to shape the modern law of monopolization."[47] The opinion is certainly a classic but might more accurately be described as having done more to perpetuate confusion than to shape law. The opinion contains statements that have lasted, such as: "A single producer may be the survivor out of a group of active competitors, merely by virtue of his superior skill, foresight and industry"[48] and "The successful competitor, having been urged to compete, must not be turned upon when he wins."[49] But the court then proceeded to do just that. The court concluded that Alcoa was an illegal monopoly and had illegally monopolized the ingot market. Alcoa argued that it had conducted its business with skill, energy, and initiative, and that it should be commended, not dismembered. The court replied:

> It was not inevitable that [Alcoa] should always anticipate increases in the demand for ingot and be prepared to supply them. Nothing compelled it to keep doubling and redoubling its capacity before others entered the field. It insists that it never excluded competitors; but *we can think of no more effective exclusion than progressively to embrace each new opportunity as it opened, and to face every newcomer with new capacity already geared to a great organization, having the advantage of experience, trade connections and the elite of personnel.* Only in case we interpret "exclusion" as limited to manoevres not honestly industrial, but actuated solely by a desire to prevent competition, can such a course, indefatigably pursued, be deemed not 'exclusionary.' So to limit it would in our judgment emasculate the Act; would permit just such consolidations as it was designed to prevent.[50]

The court condemned Alcoa for efficiency. The court had to do so. Otherwise, the Sherman Act would have been emasculated. The existence of Alcoa, like that of Standard Oil, was the very thing that antitrust is supposed to prevent. Thus was the modern law of monopolization shaped.

Antitrust proceedings pervert traditional legal procedure. Our system of law enforcement requires an ascertainable rule by which conduct can be measured. The system assumes that facts can be found establishing noncompliance with the rule. Findings of fact differ from statements of law. The judge states the law to the jury. The jury finds the facts and applies the law to the facts, and the result follows. In cases tried without a jury, the judge finds the facts.

Reaching a conclusion that the defendant has monopoly power, has used it anti-competitively, and is therefore an illegal monopoly cannot be done by traditional legal procedure without debasing the system. Whether the defendant has been shown to have taken something of value from another by force is a factual question. Whether the defendant has antitrust monopoly power is not. The gaseous theoretical concepts of antitrust mix questions of law and economics with questions of fact. When a judge hears a monopolization case without a jury, the judge can issue the decision and support it with an essay in which conglomerations of facts, assumptions, suppositions, predictions, guesses, theories, and conclusions are labeled as "findings of fact." In a jury trial, the judge can finesse much of the decision to the jury through supposed instructions as to the law, leaving it to the jury to make assumptions disguised as findings of fact and to resolve the case on any basis it chooses, including a personal sense of fairness. Such a decision is difficult for a court of appeals to review. Because there is no operative normative rule defining monopolization, instructing the jury in such cases is a challenging task.

The antitrust community maintains the pretense that monopolization law exists on which a jury can be instructed. At the same time, some community members urge that the search to define monopolization law should be abandoned. The community, attempting to assist the judge in the task of stating to a jury that which cannot be stated, has published model jury instructions supported by footnotes referring to court precedents.[51] They have been published in book form by the ABA Section of Antitrust Law. That volume's preface states that "the Section believes that the instructions accurately and fairly state the law" and that they "present a single, clear view of the law based on Supreme Court and Court of Appeals decisions."[52]

Many of the ABA's suggested instructions are open-ended and filled with abstractions. The successful competitor cannot be confident that success will be the only criterion for a conclusion of unlawful monopolization. A suggested instruction on proof of monopoly power includes the following:

> A market share above 50 percent may be sufficient to support an inference that defendant has monopoly power, but in considering whether defendant has monopoly power it is also important to consider other aspects of the relevant market, such as market share trends, the existence of barriers to entry, the entry and exit by other companies, and the number and size of competitors. Along with defendants' market share, these factors should inform you as to whether defendant has monopoly power. The likelihood that a company has monopoly power is stronger the higher that company's share is above 50 percent.[53]

With regard to "barriers to entry," the ABA suggests that juries be instructed as follows:

> Barriers to entry make it difficult for new competitors to enter the relevant market in a meaningful and timely way. Barriers to entry might include intellectual property rights (such as patents or trade secrets), specialized marketing practices, and the reputation of the companies already participating in the market (or the brand name recognition of their products).
>
> Evidence of low or no entry barriers may be evidence that defendant does not have monopoly power, regardless of defendant's market share, because new competitors could enter easily if defendant attempted to raise prices for a substantial period of time. By contrast, evidence of high barriers to entry along with high market share may support an inference that defendant has monopoly power.[54]

Concerning "anticompetitive conduct," the ABA suggests that juries be instructed as follows:

> The difference between anticompetitive conduct and conduct that has a legitimate business purpose can be difficult to determine. . . . In determining whether defendant's conduct was anticompetitive or whether it was legitimate business conduct, you should determine whether the conduct is consistent with competition on the merits, whether the conduct provides benefits to consumers, and whether the conduct would make business sense apart from any effect it has on excluding competition or harming competitors.[55]

Whether the successful business will be penalized for success may depend on the jury's hunch as to whether some executive's decision made "business sense" or not. The Golden Rule might have greater precision.

Economists have shown ingenuity at developing sinister-sounding concepts, such as "buyer-side market power,"[56] to characterize competitive activity as not making business sense and to put successful competitors to the expense of defending their success in court. The 2005 *Weyerhaeuser* case[57] illustrates the process. The case is a replay of the Standard Oil legend. An integrated producer profitably supplies finished product at continually declining prices. Less-efficient operators at a single level of the competitive chain go out of business. Standard Oil was broken up. Weyerhaeuser was allowed to continue in its existing form but was ordered to pay some of its assets to the less efficient because it supposedly engaged in "predatory" buying.

The Court of Appeals for the Ninth Circuit upheld a damage award of $26 million (trebled to $78 million). A unanimous panel of three judges used the concept of inelastic demand and speculation about what price level might or might not benefit consumers in the long run to distinguish the *Weyerhaeuser* case from a Supreme Court decision[58] that had rejected a claim of "predatory" selling. The Court of Appeals accepted the label of the case by the plaintiffs' economist as one of "predatory overbidding (i.e., paying a higher price for sawlogs than was necessary)." Testimony by a Weyerhaeuser former employee that the company could "influence prices in the alder sawlog market," evidence that prices had risen in that market, and the former employee's opinion that the company had paid more than necessary for sawlogs were seen as sufficient support for concluding that it "had engaged in anticompetitive conduct through predatory overbidding." The court sustained a claim of an unlawful attempt to monopolize sawlogs, as well as the jury's estimate of damages based on "the fundamental assumption that Weyerhaeuser maintained artificially high costs in the sawlog market during the damages period." Imaginative, articulate economic theorists were decisive. Lawyers argued over esoteric, doctrinal questions concerning standards for identifying "predatory" buying and selling.

The court of appeals did not state a rule by which to advise how to avoid this trap of business success into which Weyerhaeuser fell. There is no clue in the court's opinion as to what the defendant should have done that it did not do or what it should not have done that it did do. The case illustrates vividly the impossibility of distinguishing legitimate competition from unlawful attempts to monopolize and the symbolic political nature of the law of monopolization.

6. Mergers

"Vigorous" enforcement of section 7 of the Clayton Act has produced Supreme Court declarations that give government a legal basis to prevent any substantial corporate merger. Fundamental to antitrust is a concern that mergers unsupervised by government may lead to development of an evil trust. Antitrust believers fear corporate consolidation because they see it as a means to monopolize a good or service in the way they believe Standard Oil monopolized oil. The fear was expressed vividly by Supreme Court Justice William O. Douglas in a concurring opinion in a beer merger case in 1966.[1] The Court declared a merger unlawful in each of three ways: (1) the merged firm would have 23.95 percent of beer sales in Wisconsin, (2) the merged firm would have 11.32 percent of beer sales in the three-state area of Wisconsin, Illinois, and Michigan, and (3) the merged firm would have 4.49 percent of beer sales nationwide. Justice Douglas concurred with each of the Court's conclusions and asserted that any other decision would lead "to a form of concentration . . . described" in an appendix to his opinion. He attached a newspaper column of humorist Art Buchwald in which Buchwald observed that mergers were occurring and that "if the trend continues, the whole country will soon be merged into one large company." Buchwald went on to suggest that by 1978 all companies west of the Mississippi would have merged into one corporation and all companies east of the Mississippi into another corporation, those two companies would merge into one, and that company would then negotiate "with the President to buy the United States."

Justice Douglas believed in antitrust. He feared corporate consolidation. The clear implication of his opinion and its supporting appendix was that, if the government could not prevent a merger that would result in the merged company selling 4.49 percent of beer in the United States, all firms might be able to merge into one and might do so. The notion is so absurd that it is never explicitly articulated, but it is a persistent unstated assumption of antitrust. Irrational

63

fear of corporate consolidation remains one of the enduring elements of the antitrust religion. Much antitrust activity is directed at responding to that fear.

Supreme Court doctrine on monopolization contains no clear statement of what the law allows or prohibits. By comparison, Court doctrine as to mergers is clear. Section 7 of the Clayton Act prohibits mergers that may "lessen competition" or "tend to create a monopoly." The Supreme Court has interpreted the statute to cover all mergers. Under the Court's statutory interpretation there are no mergers that cannot be said to lessen competition or tend to create a monopoly. In effect, mergers are per se unlawful.

The campaign against mergers during the 1960s, described in chapter 1, was a complete success. The government prevented mergers of every type and won every case except one. In that case, the *General Dynamics* case,[2] decided in 1974, Warren Burger had replaced Earl Warren as chief justice. The Court rejected an attempt to prevent the merger of two coal companies. The Court saw no possibility of future competition between the companies, absent the merger, because one of the companies had limited reserves of coal. The Court concluded that the merger would have no competitive effect proscribed by the statute. *General Dynamics* was the last case in which the Supreme Court said anything substantive about mergers.

In 1962, in the *Brown Shoe* opinion, Chief Justice Warren had extolled "small business" as the "way of life" to be preserved by section 7 of the Clayton Act.[3] The following year, in the *Philadelphia National Bank* case, the Court condemned any "merger which produces a firm controlling an undue percentage share of the relevant market and results in a significant increase in the concentration of firms in that market."[4] Backed up by the Supreme Court, the Justice Department hit mergers threatening to raise concentration in markets for "frozen dessert pies," for "artificial Christmas trees," for "vandal-resistant plumbing fixtures" used in prisons, for local towel rental services, for "custom-compounded reinforced thermoplastics," for drapery hardware, or for commercial trash hauling in Dallas. The Federal Trade Commission moved against mergers threatening to raise concentration in markets for frozen pizza, for carburetor kits, for urological catheters, and for "knockdown casket parts."[5]

Some lower court decisions since 1975 have "not adhered closely to the letter or spirit of the Supreme Court's merger jurisprudence."[6]

Supreme Court antitrust decisions in nonmerger matters have been said to "provide grounds for inferring that the Court approves the evolution of lower court merger jurisprudence," but "the Court has never directly repudiated the teaching of its antitrust decisions."[7] Andrew Gavil, William Kovacic, and Jonathan Baker have suggested that "the foundations of U.S. merger policy rest upon the assumption, without the benefit of the Court's own direct guidance, that the Court no longer means what it once said."[8] Nevertheless, the merger doctrines of the Warren Court remain substantially intact. They are used to prevent mergers involving such products as ice cream, sardines, and mashed fruits and vegetables, although it is impossible to imagine the creation of a monopoly of any of those items or how a merger could tend to create one. Antitrust "market analysis" supplies a rationale for preventing such mergers. Markets are assumed in "superpremium" ice cream,[9] sardine "snacks,"[10] and "baby food."[11] In such markets the merger is said to lessen competition and is, therefore, illegal.

The campaign against mergers resulted in Supreme Court interpretations of section 7 of the Clayton Act that had the effect of declaring unlawful all mergers. The authorities had to face the fact that they did not intend to prevent all mergers. They were forced to be selective. They had to be more permissive than the law. Reluctant to contradict declarations of the Supreme Court or to renounce unlimited discretion to stop any merger should it become politically important to do so, the authorities have been unwilling to state unambiguously which mergers might be allowed.

All Mergers Are Illegal—Some May Be Allowed

Once it became apparent that the government could prevent any merger it chose to prevent, enforcement officials issued "guidelines" originally intended to give some guidance on which mergers might be allowed. From time to time, the Justice Department and the FTC have issued written documents misleadingly titled Merger Guidelines. These so-called guidelines were first published by the Justice Department in 1968.[12] It issued a complete revision in 1982,[13] and the FTC issued its own enforcement policy statement concerning horizontal mergers that same year.[14] The Justice Department's 1982 revision contained the following footnote:

> There is some economic evidence that, where one or two firms dominate a market, the creation of a strong third firm enhances competition. The Department has considered this evidence but is not presently prepared to balance this possible gain against the certainty of substantially increased concentration in the market.

Thus, in enforcing a statute prohibiting mergers that may "lessen competition," the Justice Department was stating a readiness to prevent mergers that increase concentration even though they *enhance competition.* Two years later, it revised its statement and omitted that footnote.[15] In 1992, the FTC joined with the Justice Department in a new statement.[16] In 1997, they added a section on "Efficiencies," resulting in a 36-page statement with 39 footnotes.[17] In March 2006, they published Commentary on the Horizontal Merger Guidelines.[18] It consists of 68 pages without footnotes.

In recent years, the treatment of "horizontal" mergers (between firms said to be competing with each other in some assumed market) has differed from the treatment of other types of mergers. Although Supreme Court doctrines are available to prevent vertical mergers (between suppliers and their customers) and conglomerate mergers (between firms that are not actual or potential competitors and do not have an actual or potential customer-supplier relationship), preventing such mergers has fallen out of fashion since the Reagan Revolution and the antitrust community's adoption of Chicago-school rhetoric. Some community members have deplored the failure to continue more complete merger prevention. They have urged that a "more vigorous" antitrust enforcement policy be "restored."[19] But restoration has not occurred. There has been no "counter-revolution."[20] Merger policy has remained "consistent across administrations."[21]

The reason may be that horizontal mergers offer enough professional activity to keep the antitrust community busy, and they are easy to attack. Horizontal mergers are by definition prohibited by the statute. Horizontal mergers are mergers of competitors. Because it can be assumed that the combined company will not compete with itself, any merger of competitors will eliminate the competition that existed between the parties before the merger and, thus, lessen competition to that extent.

Guidelines That Do Not Guide

The Guidelines give a doctrinal framework within which to rationalize decisions already made but don't give a basis for predicting which way a decision will be made. Originally intended as indications of which mergers might be allowed, the Guidelines have become restatements of concepts and doctrines used to rationalize merger prevention.

The latest Guidelines version discusses "market definition and concentration," "potential adverse competitive effects of mergers," "entry analysis," "efficiencies," and "failure and exiting assets." Although there is no demonstrable correlation between concentration and competition, under "Concentration and Market Shares" the document introduces a pseudo-scientific measurement of concentration:

> Market concentration is a function of the number of firms in a market and their respective market shares. As an aid to the interpretation of market data, the Agency will use the Herfindahl-Hirschman Index ("HHI") of market concentration. The HHI is calculated by summing the squares of the individual market shares of all the participants. Unlike the four firm concentration ratio, the HHI reflects both the distribution of the market shares of the top four firms and the composition of the market outside the top four firms. It also gives proportionately greater weight to the market share of the larger firms, in accord with their relative importance in competitive interactions.
>
> The Agency divides the spectrum of market concentration as measured by the HHI into three regions that can be broadly characterized as unconcentrated (HHI below 1000), moderately concentrated (HHI between 1000 and 1800), and highly concentrated (HHI above 1800).[22]

As if rules by which to evaluate conduct are being declared, the document's authors characterize discussions of concepts like market definition and market concentration as "standards." The first page of the document reads:

> It is not possible to remove the exercise of judgment from the evaluation of mergers under the antitrust laws. Because the specific *standards* set forth in the Guidelines must be applied to a broad range of possible factual circumstances,

mechanical application of those standards may provide misleading answers to the economic questions raised under the
antitrust laws. Moreover, information is often incomplete
and the picture of competitive conditions that develops from
historical evidence may provide an incomplete answer to
the forward-looking inquiry of the Guidelines. Therefore, the
Agency will apply the standards of the Guidelines reasonably
and flexibly to the particular facts and circumstances of each
proposed merger.[23]

The 2006 Commentary on the Horizontal Merger Guidelines
states: "Merger analysis depends heavily on the specific facts of each
case."[24] Thomas Leary, while a member of the FTC, told a Joint U.S./
E.U. Conference on Merger Remedies in Paris in January 2002:

Merger cases are highly fact-intensive. People with the same
basic philosophy can and do come to different conclusions
on individual transactions.[25]

In other words, as to any particular proposed merger, one person
may read the Guidelines to prohibit the transaction and another
person may read the Guidelines to permit it. The Guidelines do not
guide parties considering whether to merge, nor do they guide
government officials considering whether to prevent or permit a
merger.

Examples of Unpredictability

When presented with PepsiCo's proposed acquisition of Quaker
Oats Co., FTC members split 2-2 on whether to oppose it, and then
voted 4-0 to close the investigation. Two commissioners stated that
allowing "PepsiCo to further consolidate its soft drink position by
acquiring Quaker Oats and its popular Gatorade products raises
obvious and significant concerns that competition will be lost in the
highly concentrated soft drink industry." The other two commissioners raised the question "whether Quaker Oats, with its Gatorade
product, has the potential to be a significant third competitive force
in the marketplace." They added that "predictions of future effects
are difficult and that reasonable people can differ even when they
apply the same tools of analysis."[26]

When General Mills Inc. proposed to acquire Pillsbury Co. in 2001,
the FTC considered two proposals: (1) a settlement integrating terms

offered by the parties and (2) a preliminary injunction to stop the merger. Only two votes could be obtained for either proposal.[27]

In that same year the FTC closed its investigation of the merger of Phillips Petroleum Corp. and Tosco Corp. with a statement that the merger is not "likely to harm competition and consumers" because the firms operated in different parts of the country, their combined shares were low where their marketing overlapped, and no consolidation of Alaska North Slope reserves or production would result.[28]

In 2001, retiring after six years as FTC chairman during which an estimated 26,000 mergers were approved, Robert Pitofsky pointed with pride to having obtained a court of appeals reversal of a district court decision that would have permitted the Heinz and Beechnut baby food merger.[29] The district judge had found the following:

> The Commission made its prima facie case by showing increased market concentration. The defendants rebutted that case with proof that the proposed merger will in fact increase competition. The Commission responded to the rebuttal case essentially with only structural theory.[30]

Chairman Pitofsky told the *Wall Street Journal* that the decision overruling the district judge "holds the line" on antitrust enforcement. In an interview with *Legal Times* he said, "Our role is mostly to play defense and preserve the status quo."[31] On succeeding Pitofsky as FTC chairman, Timothy J. Muris said that he would have allowed the merger.[32]

Unpredictability is inherent in the merger regulation process. As the Guidelines point out, standards cannot be mechanically applied. Historical evidence may provide an incomplete answer. The inquiry is forward-looking. Regulators feel they must make assumptions about a future that cannot be known.

The 2006 Commentary on the Horizontal Merger Guidelines contains what are described as "short summaries of matters that the Agencies have investigated . . . [in order] to further understanding of the principles under discussion." Indications are given as to how the investigations ended, but the reader is told that "none of the summaries exhaustively addresses all the pertinent facts or issues that arose in the investigation." None of these examples provides any guide as to how another "fact-intensive" future investigation will end because (1) examples of past decisions do not contain all the "pertinent facts," and (2) no future case will present exactly the same facts.

The "standards" in these documents can be cited in support of a decision to stop any horizontal merger, but they are no obstacle to allowing a merger—even a merger that not just eliminates competition but actually creates a monopoly. When Boeing Co. bought McDonnell Douglas Corp. and thereby obtained a complete monopoly of U.S. commercial aircraft manufacture, the FTC allowed the merger to proceed without any conditions.[33] "The merger's industrial policy, foreign trade, and national defense implications generated political tension. . . . Some Executive Branch officials and members of Congress applauded moves to reinforce Boeing's lead in commercial aircraft production. . . . Department of Defense also welcomed the Boeing-MDC consolidation as a way to preserve the firms' defense capabilities and eliminate excess production capacity."[34] Under those circumstances, the FTC published a statement rationalizing its way to the conclusion that this merger of what it called "two direct competitors" would not substantially lessen competition or tend to create a monopoly.

Neither 36 pages of Guidelines nor 68 pages of Commentary provide any guide to predict which merger will be allowed or which merger will be prevented. The documents inform the antitrust community of language that should be used to discuss a proposed merger no matter what the real considerations are. They illustrate how antitrust doctrines will be used to describe a decision to prevent a merger once a prevention decision has been made. The Guidelines do not prohibit the presentation of facts and argument that may be truly pertinent to a decision to allow a merger, but they provide no guidance as to what those facts and argument may be.

The 2006 Commentary states on the first page: "The core concern of the antitrust laws, including as they pertain to mergers between rivals, is the creation or enhancement of market power" and "the Agencies challenge mergers that are likely to create or enhance the merged firm's ability . . . to exercise market power." Such statements provide no rule or guidance. To define a market (and the derivative market power) requires application of a static analysis to a dynamic world. Conclusions cannot be reached without assumptions. To define a market requires an assumption that, except for the merger, the world will stand still. In the course of that exercise those who share the same basic philosophy can and do come to different conclusions on individual transactions. Those individual judgments are impossible to predict.

Government harassment of mergers is arbitrary and unpredictable and is done in secret and randomly driven by complaints of competitors. At the time of the Warren Court pronouncements on corporate mergers and the Justice Department retreat from them in the original Guidelines, it was possible to merge first and then await a government attempt to obtain the facts and undo the merger. Congress changed that in 1976 by the addition to the Clayton Act of section 7A,[35] which requires premerger notification of all mergers above a minimum size and a waiting period before the merger can be completed.

There were premerger notification filings of 1,695 proposed mergers in fiscal year 2005. Federal regulators challenged 18 of them.[36] More than 98 percent were allowed to proceed without government interference. There is no way to tell why a proposed merger fell into the 98-plus percent that were ignored.

High-profile proposed mergers sometimes arouse public interest, which may prompt an announcement in antitrust language, such as "this merger is not likely to give the merged entity market power,"[37] if the government decides not to object to the merger. There is no systematic disclosure of decisions to allow mergers. The public record of challenged mergers provides few clues as to which mergers will be allowed. In 2004 a federal district court refused to stop a merger to duopoly (two sellers) in "high function software,"[38] and the Justice Department accepted the result without appeal. At the same time it opposed a merger to near monopoly in sardine snack products.[39] The FTC allowed a merger to monopoly in commercial aircraft manufacture[40] but an increase in concentration of jarred baby food was vigorously opposed,[41] and a merger in the retail market for "superpremium" ice cream was prevented.[42]

Since the early 1980s objections to some mergers have been disposed of by partial divestitures. Mergers are permitted on condition that some assets are sold off. These have included agreements to get rid of

> two bakeries, one brewery, four grocery stores, one cement
> plant, one casket plant, a suntan oil line, and eight nursing

homes. Shrewd merger planners came to like a little overlap as antitrust insurance, for it bought peace by providing a token offering for a cosmetic decree.[43]

The antitrust community refers to merger review as "merger enforcement." Annual Reports to Congress by the Justice Department and the FTC contain sections headed "Merger Enforcement Activity." At the 2005 spring meeting of the Section of Antitrust Law of the American Bar Association, the assistant attorney general in charge of the Justice Department's antitrust division spoke of "calling balls and strikes in merger enforcement" and stated his belief that "merger enforcement is a necessary part of antitrust."[44]

Most mergers are allowed. A few mergers are prevented. Some mergers are modified. *No* mergers are enforced. The antitrust community uses the term "merger enforcement" even though no mergers are being enforced because it likes to think of what it is doing as law enforcement. Merger regulation is not law enforcement. No ascertainable rule is being enforced. It is an element of the antitrust belief that antitrust is a desirable alternative to regulation. Antitrust believers do not wish to acknowledge that the existing process of merger review is not law enforcement but whimsical government regulation of mergers. Merger review, merger prevention, merger control, and merger regulation are called "merger enforcement" by the antitrust community to preserve the fiction that government interference with mergers is law enforcement. The antitrust believer likes to think of unpredictable selective prevention of mergers as "calling balls and strikes," acting as an umpire to keep the economy fair and free of regulation.

No Rule of Law as to Corporate Mergers

The statute and its interpretation by the Supreme Court state a law against mergers, but there is no rule by which to predict when the law will be enforced. Like highway speed limits, section 7 of the Clayton Act gives the merger police arbitrary power to select those against whom the law will be enforced. A merger may be substantial enough that a filing fee and waiting period are imposed, and thereby presumptively prohibited by law, but the merger may be allowed by a secret decision of unidentified, unelected, unaccountable government officials. Will the merger be put with the 95-plus percent to be ignored or the few percent to be looked at more closely? Does the merger arouse "antitrust concerns"? In whom? Will the merger be reviewed by the Justice Department or the FTC? Mergers are destabilizing. They threaten the status quo. Is the merger likely to cause any unhappiness? Might the merger cause unhappiness to anyone of political significance? Someone may lose a job, a sales account, or a satisfactory relationship of some kind. Those threatened may complain to a politician or directly to the antitrust authorities.

The ceremonial ritual of merger review consumes much of the antitrust budget. (An FTC press release in October 2000 said that "merger enforcement accounted for more than 70 percent of the FTC [antitrust] resources."[45]) Formal proceedings that might weaken Warren Court doctrines are seldom necessary. The ritual begins when two prominent companies propose to merge. They file notification forms. "Antitrust concerns" are expressed. Government officials demand further information. Being forced to wait, the parties may call off the merger. Executive branch officials, legislators, state government officials, consumer groups, customers, suppliers, and competitors are heard from privately, some in support and some opposed. The Guidelines provide a language in which to state objections. Phrases like "market power," "lessen competition," and "increase concentration" are intoned. Sometimes government attorneys broker a political solution. Sacrificial offerings may be made, such as promises to sell off a bakery, a brewery, or a casket plant. Whether the merger goes through or is called off, antitrust concerns are taken care of. The statutes and Warren Court interpretations remain in place. Fear of corporate consolidation is allayed. Antitrust is celebrated. Belief in antitrust is preserved.

7. "Tying" and "Exclusive" Dealing

Combination offers are labeled "tying," and selection of customers is called "exclusive dealing"—both of which sound sinister and suggest possession and exercise of power by the seller. Monopolization law is tidy but meaningless. The doctrine has no factual reference to the real world. There is no way to distinguish illegal monopolization from legitimate competition. The antitrust statute on mergers has been interpreted in such a way as to prohibit all mergers, but, like highway speed limits, there is no predictability as to when the law will be enforced. A former FTC chairman has said that merger regulation is based on "quicksand." It "lacks a firm foundation" because of "the uncertain empirical basis of existing theories for attacking mergers."[1]

The law on what the antitrust community calls "tying" is no better. Professors Daniel Gifford and Leo Raskind call tying "a troublesome antitrust issue."[2] Tying doctrine is acknowledged to be "in a somewhat uncertain state."[3] There is no consensus as to what tying is, when tying is illegal, or why it should be. Professors Eleanor Fox and Lawrence Sullivan have suggested that "The Supreme Court's evolving treatment of tying provides a microcosm of today's evolving and conflicting antitrust attitudes."[4]

It is said that "a tying arrangement exists when a producer of a desired product sells it only to those who also buy a second product."[5] If buyers agree to take all their requirements of one product from the seller without regard to any other product, this is called an "exclusive dealing" contract.[6]

Prejudice against tying and exclusive dealing is best understood as rejection of perceived evil. Professors Phillip Areeda and Louis Kaplow imagine an element of coercion in tying. The seller coerces buyers, forcing them to buy. As Areeda and Kaplow see it:

> Although a tying agreement is a particular kind of exclusive dealing, the latter term usually refers only to nontying exclusive dealing arrangements. In all events, both invoke Clayton Act sec. 3 and its concern with *coercing* buyers and *foreclosing* a rival's opportunities.[7]

Note the personification of the inanimate. Written words are said to have a "concern." The Clayton Act is just words on paper. How can words have concerns? Do the professors have this concern? Should we? Why? The Clayton Act doesn't say anything about "coercing" or "foreclosing."

Antitrust believers have many concerns and one of them is with tying. Antitrust believers are concerned about coercion of buyers and foreclosure of sellers. They believe that, as Justice John Paul Stevens has written, a seller with "control" over one product can "force" a buyer to buy a second product and prevent another seller from selling it.[8]

The case law on tying has been summarized as follows:

> Judicial analysis of tying arrangements has undergone important adjustments in the past twenty years. . . . Although the Supreme Court continues to classify some tying arrangements as per se violations, the test courts now use to determine whether the per se rule should be applied to a particular arrangement increasingly resembles a rule of reason inquiry because in deciding which test to apply the courts have shown a willingness to consider business justifications for tie-ins and sometimes have analyzed the economic effect of the arrangement. . . . Tying cases display inconsistent approaches to defining and applying the elements of a per se violation, but it is possible to identify several commonly accepted elements of the offense.[9]

"Per se" in antitrust language means "in and of itself"—without a "rule of reason" inquiry in which everything is relevant and nothing is determinative.

The elements of tying are said to be: (1) two separate products, (2) sale of one product conditioned on purchase of another, (3) "the seller has sufficient economic power in the market for the tying product to enable it to restrain trade in the market for the tied product," and (4) "a not insubstantial amount of interstate commerce in the tied product is affected."[10] According to professors E. Thomas Sullivan and Herbert Hovenkamp, "No general definition of a 'product' for purposes of the law of tying arrangements has yet been produced."[11] Bork explained tying as follows:

> Every person who sells anything imposes a tying arrangement. This is true because every product or service could be broken down into smaller components capable of being sold

separately, and every seller either refuses at some point to break the product down any further or, what comes to the same thing, charges a proportionally higher price for the smaller unit. The automobile dealer who refuses to sell only the chassis or the grocer who declines to subdivide a can of pears are engaged in tying. . . . There is no way to state the "inherent" scope of a product. The judge who attempts it either decides according to product dimensions that seem to him natural because he is accustomed to them, or explicitly decides on grounds of efficiency. . . . Economies of scale determine the definition of the product.[12]

"Tying" and "Exclusive Dealing"—Terms Used to Regulate Contracts to Prevent Evil

Neither of the terms "tying" or "exclusive dealing" can be found in the antitrust statutes. Antitrust believers have invented those supposed evils.

Tying has been condemned as a violation of section 1 of the Sherman Act (as a contract between buyer and seller that unreasonably restrains trade), as well as of section 3 of the Clayton Act. Andrew Gavil, William Kovacic, and Jonathan Baker state, "Section 3 . . . includes a *specific* prohibition of tying."[13] That assertion is frequently made but not quite correct. Section 3 prohibits sales "on the condition . . . that the . . . purchaser . . . not use or deal in the goods . . . of a competitor . . . of the . . . seller, where the effect . . . may be to substantially lessen competition or tend to create a monopoly." Clayton Act prohibitions are more specific than those of the Sherman Act, but there is no specific prohibition of tying in the Clayton Act. The word does not appear in either statute.

Fox and Sullivan describe the origin of section 3 of the Clayton Act as follows:

> In the early 1900s, large and powerful sellers often required their customers to deal exclusively with them, blocking opportunities of sales by their rivals and limiting the freedom of their customers to choose alternative sources of supply. Such requirements were widely perceived as oppressive.[14]

According to that biblical account of the early days of antitrust, some sellers were not only large but also "powerful." They had the power of "coercion" with which Areeda and Kaplow say the Clayton

Act is "concerned." Powerful sellers didn't just choose their customers in those days. They coerced and oppressed them. Sellers forced customers to buy only from them and not from others. It is not obvious how large sellers stayed large by behaving this way, in that buyers cannot be forced to buy but are free to refrain from buying or to buy from whomever they choose, including sellers who might not attempt to impose any such requirements. Nevertheless, oppression by powerful sellers is said by Fox and Sullivan to have occurred "often" in the early 1900s.

Antitrust believers thought the practice was doubly evil. It deprived customers of freedom to buy from someone else, and it prevented rivals of the seller from making sales. Political action was thought to be called for. Rep. Henry D. Clayton proposed a bill to declare illegal *all* sales that prohibited the buyers from using the goods of a competitor of the seller. That proposal was not adopted. The law enacted applies not to all sales that are on that condition but only to those where the "effect . . . may be to substantially lessen competition or tend to create a monopoly in any line of commerce."

The antitrust community has had difficulty stating how tying can lessen competition or tend to create a monopoly. Early cases involved patents. In 1917, the Supreme Court held illegal a license of a patented motion picture machine. The license limited use of the machine to the licensor's films. When films other than those of the licensor were used in the machines, the licensor sued for patent infringement. The defendant argued that the restrictive condition in the patent license was void, and the Court agreed. The Court said, "A restriction which would give to the plaintiff such a potential *power for evil . . .* would be gravely injurious to that public interest, which we have seen is more of a favorite of the law than is the promotion of private fortunes."[15]

In 1947, the Court held illegal a lease of patented machines that injected salt into canned products on condition that the lessees buy salt for use in the machines from the lessor. The Court said, "The tendency of the arrangement to accomplishment of monopoly seems obvious."[16]

Those cases inspired explanations such as the following by Earl Kintner, a former FTC chairman.

> All manufacturers naturally desire to maximize the sales of
> their goods, and any aid to this end is willingly embraced.

Early in the twentieth century several devices were developed to achieve this purpose. One of these devices, the tie-in sale, utilized the market power of one product to increase the market power of another product. For example, a manufacturer of salt might develop a machine for the processing of salt which is more desirable than any comparable machine. If the machine is sold or leased only on the condition that the user purchase all his salt from the manufacturer, a tie-in sale has taken place. The market strength of the manufacturer's salt, the tied product, is thereby raised to the market strength of the processing machine, the tying product. . . . The manufacturer's competitors would be denied customers not on the basis of the competitive merit of their product but simply because of their inability to offer their customer the particular inducement available from the offending manufacturer. In the situation involving the salt-processing machine this inability might lead to a virtual monopoly by the tying manufacturer.[17]

Bork has questioned that rationale for prohibiting tying in the following manner:

The tie-in tended to the accomplishment of *what* monopoly? In the machines? Requiring a purchaser to take salt does not build a monopoly in the machines; it would tend to have the opposite effect. In salt? It is inconceivable that anybody could hope to get a monopoly, or anything remotely resembling a monopoly, in a product like salt by foreclosing the utterly insignificant fraction of the market represented by the salt passing though these leased machines.[18]

The classic doctrinal statement of the evil nature of tying was restated in 1958 by the Supreme Court in the *Northern Pacific* case. In that case the Court found illegal land contracts with the condition that the buyer ship all goods produced on the land on the seller's railroad, with the following comments:

Indeed, tying arrangements serve hardly any purpose beyond the suppression of competition. . . . They are unreasonable in and of themselves whenever a party has sufficient economic power with respect to the tying product to appreciably restrain free competition in the market for the tied product and a not insubstantial amount of interstate commerce is affected.[19]

79

This statement may be translated as follows: "It is sufficient if the tying product has sufficient power to command the arrangement, which is to say that a tie-in is illegal if it exists."[20]

Tie-ins have sometimes been explicitly allowed. A tie-in of cable access television equipment and service was permitted during the development period of a new industry.[21] A tie-in of a patented silo and a patented unloading device was upheld where there had been substantial customer dissatisfaction with unloaders purchased alone.[22] These cases might have been more easily resolved doctrinally by concluding that only a single product was being sold and that no tying of separate products occurred.

Bork argued that "the entire theory of tying arrangements as menaces to competition is completely irrational"[23] and that "there is no validity to the law's explanation of tying arrangements."[24] More recently, Robert Levy made it clear that, "Tying arrangements are neither predatory nor exclusionary . . . they are bargains between sellers and buyers, not collusion between competitors."[25] Levy has explained how selling two products together may be a method of competition, not a means of preventing it:

> First, if the tying and tied products are functionally related, there may be cost savings through economies of joint production or distribution. Second, if the tied product is integral to the operational efficiency of the tying product, or if the tying product is sensitive to the quality of the tied product, there are obvious performance advantages in avoiding inferior substitutes—especially when it is difficult for the consumer to determine whether operating problems are due to low-quality inputs.[26]

Levy has also pointed out additional legitimate uses of tying, including protection against unauthorized copying of software, and providing a means by which to engage in lawful price discrimination through metering, risk sharing, and optimal product bundling.[27]

Courts remain unpersuaded by such thinking. In 1984, in the *Jefferson Parish* case, a divided Supreme Court reversed a lower court decision that had held illegal a contract between a hospital and a group of anesthesiologists. Although the Court ruled in favor of the defendant, included in the Court's opinion was the statement: "It is far too late in the history of our antitrust jurisprudence to question the proposition that certain tying arrangements pose an unacceptable risk of stifling competition and therefore are unreasonable 'per se'."[28] Justice Sandra Day O'Connor concurred in the judgment but muddled the doctrine further with a complex treatise of her own as to when a tie-in should be found illegal.

Neither empirical facts, logical economic theory, nor common sense can overcome the intuition of antitrust believers that there is something evil about tying, that, as the Supreme Court has said, there is a "power for evil" in tying. Antitrust adherents believe that, as Justice Felix Frankfurter declared in the *Standard Stations* case, without any empirical or theoretical support, "tying arrangements serve hardly any purpose beyond the suppression of competition."[29] (In that case, the Court held illegal exclusive dealing contracts of oil companies with retail gasoline stations. Justice William O. Douglas deplored the decision as one that "promises to wipe out large segments of independent filling-station operators.")

Concerned that market power can exist and be misused, antitrust believers cannot rid themselves of a belief in leverage. Like Justices Frankfurter and Stevens, they retain a belief that a monopolist can extract monopoly profits in one market, extend his market power to another market, and extract additional monopoly profits in the second market as well. They believe that a seller with a monopoly, or market power, over one product can force buyers to buy that product in combination with another product and, by doing so, exclude competitors from the market for the second product.

"The best known and most influential exclusionary conduct case . . . was an opinion by a gifted district court judge, Charles Wyzanski," Fox and Sullivan wrote.[30] In that case, the *United Shoe Machinery* case, Judge Wyzanski expounded a theory of exclusion. He found that United Shoe had illegally monopolized shoe machinery by a method of leasing machines to shoe manufacturers.[31] The theory of automatic exclusion had also been used by Justice Douglas in the *Griffith* case. In that case the Court found illegal monopolization in a motion picture chain's practice of negotiating with each distributor a master agreement for all its theaters.[32] The theory of exclusion in these cases has two defects: "reliance on a nonexistent motivation for economic behavior and reliance upon the fallacy of double counting."[33]

Antitrust believers cling to theories that exclusion can result from linking two markets by lease, contract, or merger or by combined sales of separate products. The community resists the theory of "one monopoly profit," a theory of microeconomics that a monopolist has the power to extract monopoly profits only once and cannot extend this power to other products or locations or by placing restrictions on customers.

According to generally accepted microeconomic theory, the presence of more than one seller means that price is determined by supply and demand. Sellers compete on price down to marginal cost of production. Resources are allocated efficiently, and the consumer benefits. Where there is only one seller, or monopolist, however, it can control output and price. He cannot be forced to sell. The monopolist can produce less, set price above marginal cost, and extract monopoly profits. He benefits but the consumer does not, and resources are allocated less efficiently.

Without support from government, monopolies can exist only temporarily, but during their existence they can extract monopoly profits. If the monopolist sells the product, the price obtains the monopoly profit. The monopolist can do this only once. He cannot sell a second time something that has already been sold. If he leases out the product, he can extract the monopoly profit in rent or in some other lease provision, but he cannot set the rent at a level that extracts the monopoly profit and then obtain some additional profit by means of an exclusionary lease term. It makes no difference if the monopolist sells at retail or to a retailer. There is still only one monopoly profit to be had. Likewise, if the monopolist sells the product over which he has a monopoly in combination with another product as to which there is a price set by the market, the monopolist can still take the monopoly profit in the tying product only once. The monopoly profit has to be captured in the price of the combination. The seller cannot obtain monopoly profits on the tying product and a second time on the tied product.

Consider this illustration in Levy's book:[34] Mr. P has a monopoly product that he prices at $1,000. In an attempt to extend his market power, P requires his customer, Mr. C, to purchase a worthless tied product for an additional $100. Assume further that the tied product is pure profit to P (i.e., his costs are zero), and pure loss to C (i.e., the product has zero value for use or resale). At first blush, it would seem that P has transformed a single monopoly into two. Note, however, that the package price for the two products would be the same whether P priced the tying product at the full $1,100 or priced the two products separately. In either case, C has two choices. He can accept the offer, which indicates that he values the tying product at $1,100 or more; or he can reject the offer, which indicates that he values the tying product at less than $1,100. Those two options are identical—with or without the tie-in. P's monopoly is in the tying product only.

The theory of one monopoly profit has gained some acceptance since the publication of Bork's book, but not yet by the Supreme Court or the broader antitrust community. Acceptance of the theory would threaten much of antitrust, not only tying and exclusive dealing but also attempts to monopolize and so-called vertical restraints (restrictions placed on buyers by their suppliers such as where, to whom, and at what price to resell). Belief in the evil of tying is an important element of the antitrust religion.

Persistence of belief in exclusionary theory finds some support in the creative assertion of professors Thomas Krattenmaker and Steven Salop that "in carefully defined circumstances, certain firms can attain monopoly power by making arrangements with their suppliers that place their competitors at a cost disadvantage."[35] Tying supposedly can harm competition because "in carefully defined circumstances" the exclusion that results from tying can raise rivals' costs, making it difficult for them to compete, or something like that. Explained with the help of charts and not easily summarized or understood, the theory of "raising rivals' costs" is by its own terms of only limited application. Like the theory of market power, it is a theory of academic economics, a hypothetical condition that might exist somewhere sometime given an assumed set of circumstances, not necessarily a description of anything in the real world. Nevertheless, the theory is said to have been "highly influential at the federal antitrust enforcement agencies, particularly during the Clinton administration."[36]

Does Prohibition of Tying Make All Sales on Credit Illegal?

Enforcement of an asserted statutory prohibition against tying has resulted in a Supreme Court declaration in the *Fortner* case that sales on credit may be illegal. Attacking evil through the "ceremonial channels" of enforcement referred to by former assistant attorney general Arnold can have curious results.

In the *Schwinn* case, the Supreme Court declared unlawful a distribution practice widely used for years by most franchisors. Contracts between buyers and sellers contained provisions that the buyers would resell only within a specified territory or only to designated customers.[37] Prompted by the Justice Department, the Court declared that *any* agreement between seller and buyer that restricts the buyer's freedom where and to whom resales may be made is a per se violation of the Sherman Act. This novel interpretation in 1967 of a statute enacted in 1890 made widely employed contracts of long-standing use subject to criminal prosecution as a felony.

No criminal prosecutions were brought, but 10 years later the Supreme Court reversed the ruling, the only explicit reversal of a prior doctrine in antitrust history.[38] After the reversal, one prominent member of the antitrust community, concerned for the vigor of antitrust enforcement, urged careful distinction between price and non-price vertical restrictions so that the reversal not be allowed to permit "the pendulum" to swing "much too far."[39] Swinging of a pendulum is an unfortunate analogy for what are supposed to be rules of law but an apt one for antitrust.

A case that hasn't been reversed illustrates the mischief that can be done by attempts to combat the supposed evil of tying. In the *Fortner* case, the tying pendulum swung in a bizarre direction when the Supreme Court came close to declaring sales on credit illegal. Fortner, a real estate developer, financed the purchase of land and the construction of prefabricated homes by borrowing money from U.S. Steel Credit Corp., a subsidiary of U.S. Steel Corp. As a condition of the loan, Fortner agreed to erect homes manufactured by U.S. Steel on the land purchased with the proceeds of the loan. U.S. Steel Credit Corp. provided 100 percent financing, which was unavailable elsewhere. After acceptance of the loan agreement, a dispute arose over price and quality of the manufactured homes. Fortner sued U.S. Steel and the credit corporation, alleging violations of sections 1 and 2 of the Sherman Act, seeking treble damages for lost profits and a decree enjoining the enforcement of the supposed tie-in provision. A district court decided summarily for defendants, holding that Fortner had failed to establish that the defendants had sufficient economic power over the tying product, credit, and foreclosure of a substantial amount of commerce with respect to the tied product—prefabricated houses.[40] A court of appeals affirmed.[41]

The Supreme Court reversed.[42] The Court found the "sale" of credit by U.S. Steel Credit Corp. separable from the sale of houses by U.S. Steel. One dissenting justice saw the case as simply "a sale of a single product with the incidental provision of financing." Another wrote, "The logic of the majority opinion . . . casts great doubt on credit financing by sellers."

The Court sent the case back to the district court. Ten years of further litigation followed. The district court found the tie-in illegal because the credit offered was unique in that it covered all of the buyer's costs and at a low interest rate. A court of appeals agreed. When the case reached the Supreme Court a second time, the Court found insufficient the evidence of the uniqueness of the credit offered by U.S. Steel Credit Corp. and, therefore, that there was no illegal tie.[43] A lengthy, expensive, fruitless search for a villain had been made possible by antitrust tying doctrines. The defendants were finally let go, but the doctrines remain in place.

Unsuccessful Government Effort to Break Up Microsoft— Further Obfuscation of Tying Law

The government broke up Standard Oil. Theodore Roosevelt concluded "not one particle of good resulted."[44] Arnold agreed, stating that Roosevelt's trust-busting "never accomplished anything."[45] But a legend of evil was created. The latest high-profile attempt to break up a successful competitor, Microsoft, also failed, ending with consent to a regulatory regime of licensing requirements and product policing to protect competitors from practices of Microsoft thought to be unfair.

Tying "is sometimes cast in the form of a charge of monopolization."[46] In the course of the attempt to break up Microsoft, the Court of Appeals for the District of Columbia Circuit rejected a government effort to have Microsoft's inclusion of its Internet browser with its operating system declared a per se illegal tie-in but sent the case back to the district court for further proof. The appeals court included in a *per curiam* opinion—an opinion endorsed by all the circuit judges but not authored by any individual judge—a 22-page essay on tying.[47] The government thereafter abandoned its complaint as to tying.[48]

The antitrust community is embarrassed about the impossibility of distinguishing competitive business behavior from unlawful attempts to monopolize. The Antitrust Modernization Commission has the problem under consideration. The antitrust community sees no need, however, for modernizing existing doctrines as to tying. Like the suggestion to study whether any empirical foundation exists for the belief that antitrust activity produces a net benefit to consumers, tying is not on the Antitrust Modernization Commission's agenda.

Why do antitrust tying doctrines persist when they are so demonstrably without validity? Courts, law professors, and practicing lawyers must assume that statutes enacted by Congress have some meaningful content that can be discovered, even if they do not. Decisions and declarations of the Supreme Court must be taken as given and treated seriously by lower court judges and practicing lawyers. And, of course, tying doctrine is no threat to the welfare of the antitrust community. The prohibition against tying can be a useful tool for government and private plaintiffs to protect losers against unacceptably successful competitors thought to be making too much money and acting unfairly. Tying and exclusive-dealing doctrines fit in nicely with the other elements of belief in antitrust.

8. Price Fixing

Courts have interpreted laws prohibiting contracts in restraint of trade as allowing criminal conviction for price fixing without proof that any price was fixed or that anyone was adversely affected. Antitrust is not what it once was. Enforcement of section 2 of the Clayton Act, which prohibits some forms of price discrimination, has been abandoned. Most mergers substantially lessen competition and therefore violate section 7 of the Clayton Act, but only a few are challenged. The IBM antitrust case was a fiasco and gave the anti-monopolization provision in section 2 of the Sherman Act a black eye that the Microsoft case has not erased. Pressed to defend irrelevance, incoherence, and irrationality, the antitrust believer responds, "What about price fixing?" Defenders of the faith cling to the concept of the price fixer as a villain who should be vigorously prosecuted.

The antitrust community calls agreements affecting price "price-fixing conspiracies." Grand juries frequently investigate such agreements in preparation for criminal proceedings aimed at fines and imprisonment. "Criminal cartel enforcement" is the "top priority" of federal prosecutors.[1] Yet price-fixing agreements can be seen as partial, temporary mergers. Independence of the parties and some competition between them is preserved. In his book *Regulating Big Business: Antitrust in Great Britain and America 1880–1990*, Tony Freyer concluded that "in the United States the use of antitrust to outlaw cartels channeled investment decisions toward mergers engendering greater managerial centralization."[2] In other words, resolute prosecution of price fixing has tended to increase concentration.

The per se ban on price fixing is the product of "evolution."[3] The crime, like that of tying, has been defined by ideology, not by an act of Congress. Section 1 of the Sherman Act declared every contract in restraint of trade a felony. Since every contract restrains some trade, taking that prohibition seriously could have brought commerce to a standstill. Professors Eleanor Fox and Lawrence Sullivan have pointed out that Congress passed the Sherman Act "[d]espite doubts about precisely what the statute meant or would accomplish."[4] In an attempt to make some sense of it, the Supreme Court rewrote the statute to read, in effect, "every contract in *unreasonable* restraint of trade," reserving to the courts the determination of which contracts are unreasonable.[5] The Court later declared that any contract that affects price is inherently unreasonable no matter what price is agreed on[6] and even if the agreement is to keep prices down.[7]

Agreement is the crime. Agreement need not be proven by direct evidence. It may be inferred from circumstances that suggest agreement even when there is no agreement. One of the few undisputed rules of antitrust law is this simple admonition: Do not discuss prices with competitors. Any communication between competitors about prices is perilous. If survival without price cooperation is in doubt, it may be better to consider a merger.

The full law of price fixing is not so simply stated. Originally enacted to protect the public from evil trusts, the Sherman Act has become a club to use on local sign painters[8] and cement producers.[9] In 1927 the Supreme Court upheld a criminal conviction of plumbing fixture manufacturers for combining "to fix prices."[10] But during the ensuing depression, the Court refused to enjoin a common selling agency even though the underlying agreement gave "the selling agency power substantially to affect and control the price of bituminous coal."[11]

In 1940 the Court upheld a criminal conviction of oil companies and declared as follows:

> Under the Sherman Act a combination formed for the purpose and with the effect of raising, depressing, fixing, pegging, or stabilizing the price of a commodity in interstate or foreign commerce is illegal per se.[12]

But in 1979 the Court allowed an agreement among copyright holders fixing a fee for a blanket license.[13] "Notwithstanding the literal agreement on price, the Court concluded that per se analysis was inappropriate because such an agreement was necessary for a new product—the blanket license—to be available at all."[14]

Antitrust Law Developments (5th ed.) states that "naked price-fixing" is treated as "illegal per se with virtually no factual inquiry."[15] The editors of that publication say that the Supreme Court "explained" that "the aim and result of every price-fixing agreement, if effective, is the elimination of competition."[16] They finesse the question of effectiveness with further "explanation" that such agreements

> may well be held to be in themselves unreasonable or unlawful restraints, without the necessity of minute inquiry whether a particular price is reasonable or unreasonable as fixed and without placing on the government . . . the burden of ascertaining from day to day whether it has become unreasonable through the mere variation of economic conditions.[17]

That a merger might result in efficiency used to be regarded as a reason to condemn the merger. In the Procter & Gamble case, Justice William O. Douglas declared that "possible economies cannot be used as a defense to illegality" in merger cases.[18] The antitrust community has overruled Justice Douglas and now recognizes an efficiency defense. A revision of the Horizontal Merger Guidelines published in 1997 added a section on efficiencies. Section 4 states that "efficiencies generated through merger can enhance the merged firm's ability and incentive to compete, which may result in lower prices, improved quality, enhanced service, or new products."[19] In announcing acceptance of the consolidation of Bell South into AT&T in 2006, the assistant attorney general for antitrust stated that one of the reasons for allowing the merger was that it "would likely result in cost savings and other efficiencies."[20]

Antitrust is flexible, allowing reversal of doctrine without any amendment of the statute and without even acknowledgment of a reversal. One prominent member of the antitrust community described the period during which efficiency went from a minus to a plus as one of "essential stability of merger policy" and its "core principles."[21]

If efficiency can justify a merger that supposedly eliminates competition, why can't it justify price cooperation that is only a partial merger? "Tensions" are "emerging" in the law of price fixing.[22] An efficiency defense could evolve out of this tension. To do so, it would have to overcome the antitrust community's strong emotional attachment to seeing price fixing as theft. According to the assistant attorney general for antitrust, "This type of conduct deprives consumers of their right to competitive pricing."[23] Like belief in the Standard Oil legend and fear of corporate consolidation, antipathy to agreements affecting price is deep and wide.

Justice Hugo Black once gave an entertaining explanation for disapproval of price fixing. He declared that agreements to fix prices "cripple the freedom of traders and thereby restrain their ability to sell in accordance with their own judgment."[24] Of course, any trader who voluntarily signed such an agreement would have been exercising his freedom and his ability to sell in accordance with his own judgment. That paradox must not have occurred to Justice Black.

The Supreme Court under Chief Justice Earl Warren had a protective attitude toward small business—an attitude that often gave rise to bizarre statements. For example, in the *Schwinn* case, Justice Abe Fortas, out of concern for what he called "smaller enterprises," condemned agreements between buyers and sellers that define territories for resale. He said that to allow such agreements "would violate the ancient rule against restraints on alienation."[25] Apparently, Justice Fortas believed he could enforce the rule against restraints on alienation by imposing his own restraint on alienation.

Some Agreements as to Price May Produce Efficiencies—Some May Not

Price fixing is a crime even if no price is fixed. Courts can infer agreement and impose a fine or imprisonment without any consideration of two questions: (1) Was the agreement effective? and (2) Was any harm done?

Scholars have found little evidence that price-fixing prosecutions affect consumer welfare. In 1988 Howard Marvel, Jeffrey Netter, and Anthony Robinson found an "absence of effective collusion in many of the criminal cases."[26] In 1993 Michael Sproul saw "little doubt that in the great majority of cases antitrust prosecution does not lead to lower prices. In general, an indictment for price fixing results in slightly higher prices."[27] In 2003 Robert Crandall and Clifford Winston concluded, "To be sure, there are well known examples where firms have clearly colluded to raise prices, including recent cases involving lysine, citric acid and vitamins. However, researchers have not shown that government prosecution of alleged collusion has systematically led to significant nontransitory declines in consumer prices."[28]

A contract to fix prices cannot be enforced and is not likely to endure. According to Robert Levy, "Experience teaches that cartels do not hold: once prices exceed market levels, the temptation to break the agreement becomes all but irresistible."[29]

Professor Richard Epstein wrote, "In comparison with the risks of government action, the dangers from private cartels look small, if only because of the inherent tendency to yield to individual members' cheating against the cartel for their short-term advantage."[30] If a price is fixed below the market price, the market clears and the public benefits. If a price is fixed at the market price, the agreement has no effect. If a price is fixed above the market price, each seller has an incentive to undercut the fixed price, surreptitiously, in an attempt to achieve higher profits. Ultimately, the cartel is likely to collapse.

No evidence has been found that agreements as to price are necessarily sufficiently damaging to consumer welfare to outweigh the cost of government action against them. Perhaps some are and some are not. There is no way to tell in advance which are which. Antitrust believers assume that unobjectionable instances of price fixing are "rare."[31] The only available empirical data[32] suggest otherwise.

The effect of an action cannot be known without looking at results. As professor D. T. Armentano has explained:

> Support for a per se illegality approach to price-fixing schemes presumes that it is possible to know beforehand which business combinations will generate net social efficiency and which will not. This presumes that the very information provided by the working out of the market process can be known before that market process is allowed to operate.[33]

Without knowledge of the effects of an agreement there is no way to tell whether or not the agreement results in efficiency. Guesses can be made, but they are only guesses. And who should do the guessing? Guesses are a poor basis on which to impose fines and prison sentences. Prosecutors have no incentive to explore the question of whether or not an agreement is socially beneficial. As long as the per se rule persists, convictions can be obtained either way.

"Deterrence" is offered as justification for the per se rule against price fixing.[34] But what conduct is being deterred? How much of that conduct was truly anti-competitive? The maxim "Better to free a guilty person than to punish an innocent one" is reversed. The per se rule on price fixing says, "Better to punish the innocent than to let the guilty go free."

The antitrust community is at its most united and self-righteous when pursuing price fixing. With government approval, unions negotiate agreements that fix the price of labor on a broad scale. Yet a few producers in Indianapolis discuss local cement prices and are prosecuted as criminals.[35] Antitrust believers learn to live with that pervasive contradiction. The value of enforcement of the per se rule against agreements affecting price has not been demonstrated by empirical data, but the rule clearly has benefits for the antitrust community. The rule obviates any need to discuss markets or market power, making convictions easier to obtain. By criminalizing price fixing, the rule strengthens the antitrust community's sense of self-righteousness and satisfaction that its activities are in the public interest.

Antitrust rhetoric is consistently anti-price fixing. Enforcement has been erratic. Price fixing by plumbing fixture manufacturers and producers of petroleum products was stopped.[36] Price fixing by coal mine operators and copyright owners was not.[37] Price-fixing cartels are tolerated or even sponsored when they have political support. Just as antitrust found a way to approve a politically desirable merger-to-monopoly in commercial aircraft manufacture,[38] antitrust authorities have found ways to allow politically desirable cartels.

In his 2002 book *Globalization and Its Discontents*, Joseph Stiglitz provided an eyewitness account of the impotence and irrelevance of antitrust when substantial political interests are at stake. In 1994 the international price of aluminum had dropped. There was a general global slowdown, and, because of new designs for soft drink containers, demand declined. With a cutback in production of military planes, Russia had more aluminum to sell. Stiglitz was then chairman of the Council of Economic Advisers. Paul O'Neill, later Secretary of the Treasury, was the chief executive officer of Alcoa, the same Alcoa that had been prosecuted for illegal monopolization and condemned in 1945 for excluding competitors by "embracing new opportunities" and having "a great organization" with "the advantage of experience, trade connections and the elite of personnel."[39]

According to Stiglitz, O'Neill "engineered the global aluminum cartel."[40] In a subcabinet meeting, a decision was made to support

O'Neill's proposal. The State Department supported it, as did Robert Rubin, who was head of the National Economic Council and played a decisive role. Stiglitz wrote, "The US government was at the center of creating a global cartel in aluminum."[41]

In January 1994 representatives of 17 nations (including three lawyers from the antitrust division of the Justice Department) met in Brussels.[42] Agreement to cut aluminum production was reached. In the third quarter of 1995 prices for ingot rose 20 percent from a year earlier.[43] Stiglitz said "people" at the Justice Department were "livid" at the subcabinet decision to support the creation of the cartel.[44] They were not so livid as to do anything about it, except to shield its existence.

In February 1996 a seller of painted aluminum signs for gasoline stations was fined and placed under six months' house arrest and 42 months' probation. The FBI had searched his office and that of a competitor and found evidence of an agreement on prices. As a buyer of aluminum, the defendant was probably a direct victim of the government-created cartel. On filing the criminal action against him in April 1996, the assistant attorney general for antitrust stated: "Those who conspire to drive up the price of products should expect to face criminal charges."[45]

In May 1997 the general counsel of the Aluminum Association received a letter from the Justice Department, stating that an investigation of the activities of major aluminum producers had been closed and that no violations of the antitrust laws had been found.[46] The assistant attorney general for antitrust had previously been quoted as saying that production cuts under the global agreement were "individual decisions by producers."[47]

The report of the International Competition Policy Advisory Committee in February 2000 contained a section on the "Surge in US International Cartel Prosecutions." The report stated that the antitrust division "since 1995 has given top priority to aggressive enforcement against international cartels."[48] The report contains no mention of the aluminum cartel. Disguising sponsorship of that conspiracy allowed continuation of a high moral tone in announcements of criminal prosecutions. The antitrust faith was kept.

The Ivy League Cartel was handled differently. In 1958 the eight Ivy League colleges and MIT organized a system to prevent price competition by extracting and sharing financial information from applicants for admission to match tuition discounts called "financial aid." Fearing that Stanford was luring students by larger tuition discounts and merit scholarships, which were prohibited by written agreement of the Ivy League members, the group attempted to recruit Stanford to join the conspiracy. Stanford refused on advice of counsel that the cartel was violating the Sherman Act.

In 1991 the Justice Department brought a civil suit but abstained from criminal action. The eight Ivy colleges consented to a prohibitory decree. MIT chose to litigate. After a nonjury trial, a district court issued detailed findings, most of which could not be disputed, and ordered an end to the joint determination of the price to be paid by a prospective student "whether identified as tuition, family contribution, financial aid awards, or some other component of the cost of providing the student's education."[49]

MIT appealed. During the course of further litigation, the White House changed hands. The new administration dropped the case after accepting a promissory letter from MIT in December 1993.[50] Having absolved colleges of a blatant cartel violation that had gone on for decades, the authorities then winked at creation of a cartel of aluminum producers. Stability of policy was maintained by prosecution of aluminum buyers and pursuit of other international cartels. Politics trumped law, but the antitrust community's belief in the villainy of price fixing was preserved.

That Standard Oil monopolized the oil industry and its breakup was publicly beneficial is a primary element of the antitrust faith. A second element is the belief that, without government interference, many more corporations would merge and become Standard Oil look-alikes, controlling everything. Antitrust believers are convinced that, when a seller reaches some high market percentage, he can then control prices and force people to buy. With such beliefs, it is easy to be frightened by the prospect that some group of competitors might cooperate on a price at which they will sell.

Fringe issues over the meaning of the per se rule are discussed within the antitrust community. Is it a rule of law, a rule of evidence, a rule as to who has the burden of proof, or only a rule that a defense will not be allowed?[51] Answers cannot be found in the laws. As the assistant attorney general for antitrust has said, it is not so much "what exactly are the words of the statute. . . . In antitrust it really is much more dynamic."[52] Although it acknowledges that some agreements as to price may be beneficial, the antitrust community is satisfied with the assumption that most price cooperation is pernicious. There is no debate within the community about that.

Erosion of the per se rule could revive the question of constitutionality of criminal prosecution for violation of section 1 of the Sherman Act. Our legal system does not allow fines or imprisonment for violation of rules that are vague. Does a law prohibiting "every contract that unreasonably restrains trade" provide sufficient notice of what conduct is criminal or does it leave too much discretion to prosecutors, judges, and juries?

In 1913 the Supreme Court considered a challenge to a criminal conviction under the Sherman Act. The Court rejected an argument that "the crime ... contains ... an element of degree as to which estimates may differ, with the result that a man might find himself in prison because his honest judgment did not anticipate that of a jury of less competent men." The Court said that "the law is full of instances where a man's fate depends on his estimating rightly, that is, as the jury subsequently estimates it, some matter of degree." The Court gave examples of "murder, manslaughter, or misadventure" resulting from an automobile accident.[53] Prosecutorial restraint and the per se rule have foreclosed opportunity to question that reasoning.

The policy of the Justice Department's antitrust division on antitrust criminal prosecution has been stated as follows:

> The Supreme Court has held that the Sherman Act is not unconstitutionally vague. But an indictment in a particular case might unfairly attack conduct not known to the defendants to be unlawful. The solution of the Antitrust Division to this problem of potential unfairness has been to lay down the firm rule that criminal prosecution will be recommended to the Attorney General only against willful violations of the law, and that one of two conditions must appear to be shown to establish willfulness. First, if the rules of law alleged to have been violated are clear and established—describing per se offenses—willfulness will be presumed.... The Supreme Court held more than 30 years ago that price fixing was a per se violation of the law—one for which no justification or defense could be offered.... Second, if the acts of the defendant show intentional violations ... willfulness will be presumed.[54]

If the rule of law as to price fixing becomes less clear and established, if some price-fixing agreements become defensible on grounds of efficiency, some cases now being prosecuted criminally might be challenged because the indicted conduct was not known by the defendants to be unlawful.

Any weakening of confidence in the rightness of criminal enforcement would tend to undermine the self-righteous tone of prosecution. The antitrust community derives much psychic and other income from this process. Grand jury investigations provide an ongoing source of employment for government and private personnel. Fear of such investigations justifies meticulous antitrust audits and compliance programs that require many billable hours. The per se rule provides a foundation for this activity. Weakening the rule could weaken that foundation. The antitrust community may sense that placing overriding value on efficiency could bring down the whole antitrust house of cards.

Treble Damage Actions—No Obvious Benefit to the Public

Criminal prosecution is not the only weapon against the evil of price fixing. There is another method to punish the trust: the threat of treble damages. Even if the Justice Department shows discretion in prosecution of Sherman Act violations, state attorneys general and enterprising private lawyers can make allegations of price fixing that cannot easily be brushed off.

To punish trusts thought to be evil, antitrust law provides increased rewards for private suits against them. The Clayton Act says that any person "injured in his business or property by reason of anything forbidden in the antitrust laws" may sue for *three times* his damages plus "the cost of suit, *including a reasonable attorney's fee.*"[55] Assisted by the per se rule, enterprising lawyers combine that provision and the modern class action procedure to produce dramatic results.

In a competitive economy, matching of prices is common. A price-fixing agreement can be imagined. A class of victims can be supposed. A client can be recruited. The client has nothing to lose. A complaint, skillfully drafted, is filed. A court certifies that the victim class can sue. Big costs can be incurred. Large damages are possible. Evidence gathering begins. Defendants' files and e-mails are

scoured. Ambiguous words of mid-level executives may be uncovered. Evidence gathering continues. A trial date is scheduled. The
threat of bankruptcy looms. Settlement becomes realistic and is
reached. Money changes hands.

In December 2003 allegations of tying and an attempt to monopolize were settled in a class action in a U.S. District Court in New
York. The complaint accused Visa and MasterCard of illegally tying
their debit products to their credit cards. No adjudication of the
merits of the claims occurred. Defendants agreed to create a settlement fund of $3.05 billion to be shared by five million merchants,
giving them $610 each. Lawyers for the class sought reimbursement
for costs of $18 million and a fee of $609 million. The Court ordered
defendants to pay the costs and $220 million in attorneys' fees.[56]
Some would say the attorneys earned it. They punished an evil trust.

9. In Conclusion

The antitrust laws provide a vehicle for the antitrust community to carry on a useless, mischievous activity portrayed as law enforcement. Antitrust has been called "a subcategory of ideology,"[1] "a religion without a cause,"[2] and "a hoax."[3] Whatever antitrust may be, it is not law enforcement. Justice Abe Fortas wrote: "Antitrust in the United States is not . . . a set of laws by which men may guide their conduct. It is rather a general sometimes *conflicting* statement of articles of faith and economic philosophy."[4]

Antitrust resulted from Congress's desire to do something even though nothing could be done. The antitrust statutes are pious declarations against evil. Antitrust was founded on the desire to solve a basic problem of capitalism: What to do about the losers? The statutes reflect a hope of preserving a nation of farmers, craftsmen, and traders in small towns before industrialization and corporate organizations transformed America into factories, offices, and cities. Antitrust is celebrated by a ritual of legal proceedings supposed to keep trade both free and fair.

Supreme Court antitrust decisions attempt to give meaning to what Justice Fortas called "conflicting" statements of "articles of faith." Decisions do not follow from principles on a case-by-case basis as they do in the development of English common law. Decisions do not clarify marginal ambiguities in statutory prohibitions or make rules precise. Instead, Supreme Court decisions are compromises over differing personal predilections of individual members of the Court as to what is evil. Lawyers and law professors search in the opinions for rules. Most court opinions simply muddy the water.

Reformers

Although "the will of Congress contains internal contradictions,"[5] judges, professors, and advocates assume that the legislature had something definite in mind when it adopted the antitrust statutes. Reformers don't accept Thurman Arnold's suggestion that antitrust is ceremonial moralizing.[6] Reformers are attempting reform, not abolition. Reformers, as professors of law, cannot acknowledge that a statute that incorporates "internal contradictions" makes no sense and cannot be reformed. That is not something professors of antitrust law can say. They have to believe that, if federal judges are taught enough microeconomic theory, antitrust law will achieve "a high degree of rationality and predictability" and "become a branch of applied economics."[7]

Economics will not turn antitrust into law enforcement. Theoretical discussion of markets and market power is based on static analysis, not on facts in the real world. The definitions in the analysis assume a world standing still. Belief in market power requires ignoring the long run. In the antitrust world there is no long run. It's all about an imaginary now.

Not all antitrust practitioners are true believers. A few see antitrust as a meaningless word game without merit but rewarding to those who play it well. Others are skeptical about some basic antitrust beliefs but see antitrust as needed protection against short-run market distortions. They recognize that what they see as market imperfections can't survive the long run. They see antitrust as justified by the need for action now. Fixing the point at which the short run turns into the long run is unresolved. The Court of Appeals in the *Microsoft* case spoke of "the relatively near future."[8] The proceedings in that case had an air about them of the need to act quickly before it's too late, before the problem has taken care of itself, before it becomes obvious that antitrust is irrelevant.

Development of a global economy through the Internet is shortening the long run. Long-run results arrive more quickly than they used to. It is becoming more difficult to ignore the long run. And, it is becoming more difficult to sustain belief in a static analysis based on assumptions that the world will stand still.

Antitrust Belief Embedded in American Psyche—Repeal of Antitrust Statutes Politically Impossible

The antitrust community cannot look critically at antitrust. There is "little empirical evidence that past interventions have provided much direct benefit to consumers or significantly deterred anticompetitive behavior,"[9] but the prevailing attitude of most of the antitrust community was expressed in 1982 by professor Milton Handler:

"We now have an excellent body of antitrust doctrines that, over all, have worked extremely well."[10]

Gary Hull of Duke University has written:

> Most Americans believe that the antitrust laws preserve our free market system, protect consumers from rapacious corporations, and ensure fair competition in the marketplace. However, the reverse is true. Antitrust is based on bad economics and on a false interpretation of the history of American business. It violates the sanctity of contract. . . . The laws do not need to be clarified, scaled back or applied more judiciously. Those laws must be abolished."[11]

Economics professor D. T. Armentano has called for repeal.[12] He argues as follows: (1) the antitrust laws misconstrue the nature of competition and monopoly, (2) the laws have often served to shelter inefficient firms from lower prices and innovations, (3) section 2 of the Clayton Act is intended to restrict price rivalry, (4) section 7 of the Clayton Act is destructive of a competitive process, (5) the laws are a form of regulation that makes the economy less efficient, (6) enforcement requires assumption of knowledge that is not available, and (7) the laws have been enforced arbitrarily and interfere with the rights of property owners to make voluntary agreements.

Those arguments, however valid, will not shake the nation's emotional commitment to antitrust because they do not undermine the foundational elements of antitrust belief. Antitrust fills emotional needs. As long as the Standard Oil legend is alive, concentration is feared. As long as "market power" can be believed to exist and be used, antitrust will survive, despite Armentano's case for repeal and despite the lack of evidence that antitrust does much good.

Armentano has described antitrust's primary source of support:

> Antitrust attorneys, private plaintiffs, consultants, and the antitrust bureaucracy have much to gain from a continuation of antitrust regulations and much to lose from any repeal of or reduction of antitrust enforcement. Consequently, the beneficiary groups have every incentive to strenuously resist reform and repeal and to denounce all antitrust critics in the most strident tones. Ordinary citizens and consumers, on the other hand, have little incentive to rally against the antitrust juggernaut, little incentive even to educate themselves as to the antitrust facts of life.[13]

Active members of the antitrust community must constantly articulate and advocate antitrust doctrines. Personal recitation of doctrine
instills belief. The doctrines give their advocate a sincere feeling of
self-righteousness. He is standing up for fairness and protecting the
weak against the greedy and powerful.

The believer personifies antitrust. Antitrust does things. It makes
assumptions and seeks results.[14] It makes "mistakes"[15] and suffers
"defeats."[16] Antitrust becomes like an old friend who helps the
believer feel that his activity is not just profitable for himself, but
worthwhile for others. The antitrust community profits handsomely
from antitrust, but that is only a reinforcing factor, not proof of
insincerity of the community's belief in antitrust.

There is strong support for antitrust outside the antitrust community. Opinion makers in journalism and many intellectuals feel antipathy toward commercial activity. They feel good expressing concern
for "the consumer," whom they regard as a potential victim of
corporate greed. The anointed see antitrust as important for social
justice. They are a formidable obstacle to change.

Repeal of the antitrust statutes might lead to something worse in
their place. Antitrust believers assert that antitrust law "preserves
and protects markets as an alternative to a more intrusive regulation
or control of the economy."[17] They believe that overall public control
of business in one form or another is absolutely necessary. Thomas
DiLorenzo has pointed out, "There was never any evidence that the
trusts and 'combinations' of the late nineteenth century actually
harmed consumers in the way that monopolies are supposed to harm
consumers—by colluding to restrict production to drive up prices."[18]

Nevertheless, "the myth persists that monopoly is an intrinsic
feature of capitalism that must be controlled and regulated by
enlightened antitrust regulation."[19]

Something worse than antitrust is already in place—the Federal
Trade Commission—a group of five political appointees empowered
by the Federal Trade Commission Act of 1914 to define and prevent
"unfair" methods of competition. That open-ended authority to regulate trade has been left mostly undeveloped. The commission has
relied on antitrust doctrines instead. Were the antitrust statutes to
be repealed, aggressive use of broad FTC authority could take
their place.

Education of judges, government officials, law professors, and
journalists could dissolve antitrust. Understanding the nature of

antitrust and its lack of factual foundation undermines its appeal. Education about antitrust history not generally known but not difficult to understand might make a difference. History shows that the breakup of Standard Oil accomplished nothing. It was "part of a moral conflict."[20] It was like preaching against sin without defining it. Corporate consolidation need not be feared. No amount of magic "market power" can force buyers to buy. For anyone interested in developing intelligent public policy, those ideas are not difficult to absorb.

Should Microsoft be allowed to add a media player? Should GE be allowed to acquire Honeywell? Should IBM be broken up? Antitrust supplies a vocabulary to discuss those questions but does not provide answers, no matter how much help is obtained from economic theory. Antitrust judgments are subjective choices of the judge about public policy. Law students should be taught that antitrust is not law enforcement. Journalists and opinion makers should be encouraged to ask themselves, "Do we really need to fear that some greedy capitalist will monopolize sardine snacks or mashed fruits and vegetables?" The public should be told what is going on, that antitrust decisions are political decisions misleadingly portrayed as law and economics. Those in a position to do so should force more discussion of such questions as, "Can salaried government officials in Washington make better decisions about how many distributors of office supplies there should be in, say, Wheeling, West Virginia, than people whose capital is at stake?"

Although today's antitrust community is alive and well, antitrust is atrophying. It is becoming a relic, an anachronism, the irrelevant debris of past political demagoguery. Education in the antitrust facts of life could accelerate the process.

Notes

Introduction

1. Thurman Arnold, *The Folklore of Capitalism* (Yale University Press, 1937), pp. 211–12.

Chapter 1

1. Phillip Areeda and Louis Kaplow, *Antitrust Analysis*, 5th ed. (New York: Aspen Law and Business, 1997), pp. 11–12.

2. Ibid., p. 12.

3. Eleanor M. Fox and Lawrence A. Sullivan, *Cases and Materials on Antitrust* (St. Paul, MN: West Publishing Co., 1989), pp. 9, 11.

4. Ibid., p. 738.

5. *Antitrust and Trade Regulation Report* 84 (January 17, 2003): 35.

6. *Chicago Board of Trade v. United States*, 246 U.S. 231, 238 (1918).

7. *United States v. Grinnell Corp.*, 384 U.S. 563, 570–71 (1966).

8. *Brown Shoe Co. v. United States*, 370 U.S. 294 (1962).

9. *United States v. Von's Grocery Co.*, 384 U.S. 270 (1966).

10. *Brown Shoe Co.*, 370 U.S. 294.

11. *Hart-Scott-Rodino Antitrust Improvements Act of 1976*, 15 U.S.C. 15, § 18a (2000).

12. FTC and U.S. Department of Justice, Commentary on the Horizontal Merger Guidelines 2006, p. 1.

13. FTC and U.S. Department of Justice, Annual Report to Congress: Fiscal Year 2005 Pursuant to Subsection (j) of Section 7A of the Clayton Act (2006) Hart-Scott-Rodino Antitrust Improvement Act of 1976 (Twenty-eighth Report).

14. *United States v. Microsoft Corp.*, 159 F.R.D. 318 (D.D.C. 1995).

15. *United States v. Microsoft Corp.*, 56 F.3d 1448, 1462 (D.C. Cir. 1995).

16. *Microsoft Corp.*, 56 F.3d 1448, 1465.

17. *United States v. Microsoft Corp.*, 980 F. Supp. 537 (D.D.C. 1997).

18. *United States v. Microsoft Corp.*, 147 F.3d 935 (D.C. Cir. 1998).

19. *United States v. Microsoft Corp.*, 84 F. Supp. 2d 9, 12–112 (D.D.C. 1999).

20. *United States v. Microsoft Corp.*, 97 F. Supp. 2d 59, 62 (D.D.C. 2000).

21. *Microsoft Corp.*, 97 F. Supp. 2d 59, 62.

22. *Microsoft Corp.*, 97 F. Supp. 2d 59, 63.

23. *United States v. Microsoft Corp.*, 253 F.3d 34 (D.C. Cir. 2001).

24. *Microsoft Corp.*, 253 F.3d 34, 51–59.

25. *Microsoft Corp.*, 253 F.3d 34, 72, 74.

26. Justice Department Press Release, September 6, 2001.

27. "Roundtable Conference with Enforcement Officials," *Antitrust Law Journal* 68 (2000): 581, 614.

28. Paul Rand Dixon, "Merger Policy and the Preservation of the Competitive System," *Antitrust Law Journal* 30 (1966): 86, 90.

29. "An Interview with the Honorable Donald F. Turner," *Antitrust Law Journal* 34 (1967): 122.

30. Robert H. Bork, *The Antitrust Paradox* (New York: Basic Books, 1978).

31. Richard A. Posner, *Antitrust Law* (Chicago: University of Chicago Press, 1976), p. 212.

32. D. T. Armentano, *Antitrust Policy* (Washington: Cato Institute, 1986) p. 74.

33. Robert W. Crandall and Clifford Winston, "Does Antitrust Policy Improve Consumer Welfare? Assessing the Evidence," *Journal of Economic Perspectives* 17 (2003): 3.

Chapter 2

1. *United States v. Bergson*, 119 F. Supp. 459 (D.D.C. 1954).

2. Spencer Weber Waller, "Prosecution by Regulation: The Changing Nature of Antitrust Enforcement," *Oregon Law Review* 77 (1998): 1383, 1444.

3. Waller, "Prosecution by Regulation," 1383, 1445–46.

4. *Antitrust* 16 (Summer 2002): 4.

5. See the 50th anniversary luncheon program published as an insert to *Antitrust* 16 (Summer 2002): 4.

6. Simon N. Whitney, *Antitrust Policies: American Experience in Twenty Industries*, Vol. II (New York: Twentieth Century Fund, 1958), p. 442.

7. "House Judiciary Committee Chairman Proposes Panel to Revamp Antitrust Law," *Antitrust and Trade Regulation Report* 80 (June 29, 2001): 614. Special Report, *Antitrust and Trade Regulation Report* 88 (January 21, 2005).

8. Robert H. Bork, *The Antitrust Paradox* (New York: Basic Books, 1978), p. 415.

9. For example, see Milton Handler, "Reforming the Antitrust Laws," *Columbia Law Review* 82 (1982): 1287–1364. The author, a pioneer at combining teaching with law practice, concluded: "We now have an excellent body of antitrust doctrines that, over all, have worked extremely well for almost a century." They have worked especially well for members of the antitrust community, but there is "little empirical evidence that past interventions have provided much direct benefit to consumers or significantly deterred anticompetitive behavior." Also see Robert W. Crandall and Clifford Winston, "Does Antitrust Policy Improve Consumer Welfare? Assessing the Evidence," *Journal of Economic Perspectives* 17 (2003): 3, 4.

10. Thomas B. Leary, "Lessons from Real Life: True Stories that Illustrate the Art and Science of Cost-Effective Counseling," The Antitrust Source, March 2003, www.antitrustsource.com.

11. Waller, "Prosecution by Regulation," 1383, 1444.

12. For example, Eleanor M. Fox and Lawrence A. Sullivan, *Cases and Materials on Antitrust* (St. Paul, MN: West Publishing Co., 1989).

13. E. Thomas Sullivan and Herbert Hovenkamp, *Antitrust Law, Policy and Procedure*, 4th ed. (Charlottesville, VA: Lexis Law Publishing, 1999), p. xiii.

14. Andrew I. Gavil, William E. Kovacic, and Jonathan B. Baker, *Antitrust Law in Perspective: Cases, Concepts and Problems in Competition Policy* (St. Paul, MN: Thomson/ West Publishing Co., 2002).

15. "A Casebook for Our Time," book review, The Antitrust Source, March 2003, www.antitrustsource.com.

16. Phillip Areeda and Louis Kaplow, *Antitrust Analysis,* 5th ed. (New York: Aspen Law and Business, 1997), p. 12.

17. Ibid.

18. Eleanor M. Fox and Lawrence A. Sullivan, *Cases and Materials on Antitrust* (St. Paul, MN: West Publishing Co., 1989), p. v.

19. Herbert Hovenkamp, "Antitrust Policy after Chicago," *Michigan Law Review* 84 (1985): 213, 284, quoted in Robert Pitofsky, Harvey J. Goldschmid, and Diane P. Wood, *Trade Regulation* (New York: Foundation Press, 2003) at pp. 9–11.

20. "From the Section Chair," *Antitrust* 16 (Summer 2002): 3.

21. "From the Section Chair," *Antitrust* 20 (Fall 2005): 3.

22. Final Report of the International Competition Policy Advisory Committee to the Attorney General and to the Assistant Attorney General for Antitrust (2000), www.usdoj.gov/atr/icpac/finalreport.htm.

23. "International Competition Network Adopts Initiatives to Improve Antitrust Enforcement," *Antitrust and Trade Regulation Report* 90 (May 12, 2006): 549.

24. "ICN Conference Addresses Merger Vetting Improvements, Savors Anticartel Advances," *Antitrust and Trade Regulation Report* 88 (June 10, 2005): 621.

25. "FTC Chairman Offers Support for Agency's FY 2007 Appropriation," *Antitrust and Trade Regulation Report* 90 (April 7, 2006): 380.

26. "From the Section Chair," *Antitrust* 20 (Fall 2005): 3.

Chapter 3

1. Phillip Areeda and Louis Kaplow, *Antitrust Analysis,* 5th ed. (New York: Aspen Law and Business, 1997), p. 12.

2. Federal Trade Commission Act, 15 U.S.C. (1914) §§ 41–58.

3. *Federal Baseball Club v. National League of Professional Baseball Clubs,* 259 U.S. 200 (1922).

4. American Bar Association Section of Antitrust Law, *Antitrust Law Developments,* 5th ed. (Chicago: ABA Publishing, 2002), p. 1385.

5. *Radovich v. NFL,* 352 U.S. 445 (1957).

6. *Haywood v. NBA,* 401 U.S. 1204 (1971).

7. *Curt Flood Act,* 112 Stat. 2824 (1998); 15 U.S.C. § 27a.

8. *Appalachian Coals, Inc. v. United States,* 288 U.S. 344 (1933).

9. Eleanor M. Fox and Lawrence A. Sullivan, *Cases and Materials on Antitrust* (St. Paul, MN: West Publishing Co., 1989), p. 426.

10. Daniel J. Gifford and Leo J. Raskind, *Federal Antitrust Law Cases and Materials,* 2d ed. (Cincinnati, OH: Anderson Publishing Co., 2002), p. 99.

11. Areeda and Kaplow, *Antitrust Analysis,* p. 190. The authors continue, "Although it has long been assumed that the holding of *Appalachian Coals* may have little contemporary relevance, more recent claims relating to fair competition and fair prices in the international trade and agricultural contexts invoke notions similar to those articulated in *Appalachian Coals*" (pp. 190–91).

12. Robert Pitofsky, Harvey J. Goldschmid, and Diane P. Wood, *Trade Regulation,* 5th ed. (Westbury, NY: Foundation Press, 2003), p. 325.

13. *FTC v. Procter & Gamble Co.,* 386 U.S. 568, 581 (1967).

14. Robert H. Bork, Epilogue of *The Antitrust Paradox,* Rev. ed. (New York: The Free Press, 1993), p. 434.

15. *United States v. Socony-Vacuum Oil Co.,* 310 U.S. 150 (1940).

16. Joel Klein, Assistant Attorney General, Antitrust Division, speaking at a spring meeting of the ABA Section of Antitrust Law, *Antitrust Law Journal* 68 (2000): 614.

17. Gifford and Raskind, *Federal Antitrust Law Cases and Materials*, pp. 18–19.

18. *Schechter Poultry Corp. v. United States*, 295 U.S. 495 (1935).

19. Fox and Sullivan, *Cases and Materials on Antitrust*, p. 307.

20. Robert H. Bork, *The Antitrust Paradox* (New York: Basic Books, 1978), p. 61.

21. Gifford and Raskind, *Federal Antitrust Law Cases and Materials*, p. 28.

22. Earl W. Kintner, "The Revitalized Federal Trade Commission," *New York University Law Review* 30 (1955): 11, 43.

23. *FTC v. Jantzen, Inc.*, 386 U.S. 228 (1967).

24. *In re IBM Corp.*, 687 F.2d 591 (2d Cir. 1982).

25. Kellogg Co., 99 F.T.C. 8 (1982).

26. General Motors Corp., 99 F.T.C. 464 (1982).

27. Frederick M. Rowe, *Price Discrimination under the Robinson-Patman Act* (Boston: Little Brown, 1962).

28. Robinson-Patman Act of 1936, 15 U.S.C. § 13a.

29. Bork, *The Antitrust Paradox* (New York: Basic Books, 1978), p. 202.

30. John S. McGee, *In Defense of Industrial Concentration* (New York: Praeger Publishers, 1971).

31. Harold Demsetz, *Economic, Legal, and Political Dimensions of Competition* (Amsterdam: North Holland, 1982).

32. Yale Brozen, *Concentration, Mergers, and Public Policy* (New York: Macmillan, Burns, Malcolm, 1982).

33. Frederick M. Rowe, "The Decline of Antitrust and the Delusions of Models," *Georgetown Law Journal* 72 (1984): 1511. This article contains a thoroughly documented history of the rise and decline of the economic concentration hobgoblin.

34. Gifford and Raskind, *Federal Antitrust Law Cases and Materials*, p. 28.

35. Richard A. Posner, *Antitrust Law* (Chicago: University of Chicago Press, 1976), p. 212.

36. Bork, *The Antitrust Paradox* (New York: Basic Books, 1978), pp. 405, 406.

37. Ibid., pp. 51, 66.

38. ABA Section of Antitrust Law, Report of the Task Force on the Federal Antitrust Agencies—2001 (2001), pp. 41, 42, www.abanet.org/antitrust/pdf_docs/antitrustenforcement.pdf.

39. Robert Pitofsky, "The Sylvania Case; Antitrust Analysis of Non-Price Vertical Restrictions," *Columbia Law Review* 78 (1978): 1, 3; Eleanor Fox, "The Modernization of Antitrust: A New Equilibrium," *Cornell Law Review* 66 (1981): 1140; Victor H. Kramer, "Antitrust Today: The Baxterization of the Sherman and Clayton Acts," *Wisconsin Law Review* 1981 (1981): 1287, 1302.

40. Robert Pitofsky, "Does Antitrust Have a Future?" *Georgetown Law Journal* 76 (1987): 321, 326.

41. Frederick M. Rowe, "The Decline of Antitrust and the Delusions of Models," *Georgetown Law Journal* 72 (1984): 1511, 1570.

42. Richard A. Posner, *The Problematics of Moral and Legal Theory* (Cambridge, MA: Harvard University Press, 1999), p. 229.

43. Herbert Hovenkamp, "Antitrust Policy after Chicago," *Michigan Law Review* 84 (1985): 213, quoted in Pitofsky, Goldschmid, and Wood, *Trade Regulation*, p. 11.

44. Bork, *The Antitrust Paradox* (New York: Basic Books, 1978), p. 65.

45. Lawrence A. Sullivan and Warren S. Grimes, *The Law of Antitrust: An Integrated Handbook* (St. Paul, MN: West Group 2000), sec. 1.5b, quoted in Gifford and Raskind, *Federal Antitrust Law Cases and Materials*, p. 55. Note that this is a handbook of the law of antitrust, not a handbook of antitrust law, much less a handbook of the antitrust statutes.

46. *Matsushita Electric Co. v. Zenith Radio Corp.*, 475 U.S. 574 (1986).

47. *Broadcast Music, Inc. v. Columbia Broadcasting System, Inc.*, 441 U.S. 1 (1979).

48. *Continental T.V., Inc. v. GTE Sylvania, Inc.*, 433 U.S. 36 (1977).

Chapter 4

1. ABA Section of Antitrust Law, *Market Power Handbook* (Chicago: ABA Publishing, 2005), p. vii.

2. Ibid., pp. 1–2.

3. ABA Section of Antitrust Law, *Antitrust Law Developments*, 5th ed. (Chicago: ABA Publishing, 2002) pp. 67–68.

4. *Jefferson Parish Hospital District No. 2 v. Hyde*, 466 U.S. 2 (1984).

5. ABA, *Market Power Handbook*, p. 117.

6. Phillip Areeda and Louis Kaplow, *Antitrust Analysis*, 5th ed. (New York: Aspen Law and Business, 1997), p. 554.

7. ABA, *Market Power Handbook*, p. 87.

8. Alan J. Daskin and Lawrence Wu, "Observations on the Multiple Dimensions of Market Power," *Antitrust* 19, no. 3 (Summer 2005): 57.

9. Phillip Areeda and Herbert Hovenkamp, *Antitrust Law*, para. 802c (1996), quoted in ABA Section of Antitrust Law, *Market Power Handbook* (Chicago: ABA Publishing, 2005), p. 7.

10. Areeda and Kaplow, *Antitrust Analysis*, pp. 553, 559, 561, 572.

11. Robert H. Bork, *The Antitrust Paradox* (New York: Basic Books, 1978), p. 6.

12. Thurman Arnold, *The Folklore of Capitalism* (New Haven, CT: Yale University Press, 1937), p. 211.

13. ABA, *Market Power Handbook*, p. 100.

14. ABA, *Antitrust Law Developments*, p. 525.

15. Ibid., pp. 1483–84.

16. Ibid., p. 1486.

17. Frederick M. Rowe, "The Decline of Antitrust and the Delusions of Models," *Georgetown Law Journal* 72 (1984): 1511, 1563, 1564, 1565.

18. ABA, *Market Power Handbook*, pp. 119–21.

19. Ibid., p. 121.

20. Daskin and Wu, "Observations on Multiple Dimensions," 53, 57 n. 7.

21. Robert A. Levy, *Shakedown* (Washington: Cato Institute, 2004), pp. 200–01.

22. Rowe, "The Decline of Antitrust," 1511, 1564.

23. Ibid.

24. Donald C. Klawiter, "From the Section Chair," *Antitrust* 20 (Fall 2005): 4.

Chapter 5

1. Daniel J. Gifford and Leo J. Raskind, *Federal Antitrust Law Cases and Materials*, 2d ed. (Cincinnati, OH: Anderson Publishing Co., 2002), p. 5.

2. Eleanor M. Fox and Lawrence A. Sullivan, *Cases and Materials on Antitrust* (St. Paul, MN: West Publishing Co., 1989), p. 33, citing William H. Taft, *The Anti-Trust Act and the Supreme Court* 2 (1914).

3. Fox and Sullivan, *Cases and Materials on Antitrust*, p. 36.

4. "FTC, DOJ Announce Upcoming Forum on Implications of Single-Firm Conduct," *Antitrust and Trade Regulation Report* 90 (June 9, 2006): 653.

5. Deborah Platt Majoras quoted in "FTC and DOJ Open Hearings on Implications of Single-Firm Conduct," *Antitrust and Trade Regulation Report* 90 (June 23, 2006): 712–13.

6. Tony Freyer, *Regulating Big Business* (Cambridge: Cambridge University Press, 1992), p. 37.

7. *Standard Oil Company v. United States*, 221 U.S. 1 (1911).

8. Phillip Areeda and Louis Kaplow, *Antitrust Analysis*, 5th ed. (New York: Aspen Law & Business, 1997), p. 449 (emphasis added).

9. Fox and Sullivan, *Cases and Materials on Antitrust*, p. 208 (emphasis added).

10. Ibid., p. 84.

11. D. T. Armentano, *The Myths of Antitrust* (New York: Arlington House, 1972), p. 279.

12. John S. McGee, "Predatory Price Cutting: The Standard Oil (N.J.) Case," *Journal of Law and Economics* 1 (October, 1958): 144–48, cited in Armentano, *Myths of Antitrust*, p. 69.

13. Armentano, *Myths of Antitrust*, p. 77.

14. Thomas J. DiLorenzo, *How Capitalism Saved America* (New York: Crown Forum, 2004), p. 135.

15. Robert W. Crandall and Clifford Winston, "Does Antitrust Policy Improve Consumer Welfare? Assessing the Evidence," *Journal of Economic Perspectives* 17 (2003): 3, 7, 8.

16. Simon N. Whitney, *Antitrust Policies* (New York: Twentieth Century Fund, 1958), p. 182.

17. D. T. Armentano, *Antitrust Policy* (Washington: Cato Institute, 1986), pp. 24, 25, 43.

18. McGee, "Predatory Price Cutting: The Standard Oil (N.J.) Case," 137, 168, quoted in Robert H. Bork, *The Antitrust Paradox* (New York: Basic Books, 1978), p. 39.

19. Justin Miller, *Handbook on Criminal Law* (St. Paul, MN: West Publishing Co., 1934), p. 391.

20. *United States v. Grinnell Corp.*, 384 U.S. 563 (1966).

21. *Grinnell Corp.*, 384 U.S. 563, 570–71.

22. Donald C. Klawiter, "From the Section Chair," *Antitrust* 20 (Fall 2005): 4.

23. Eleanor M. Fox, "Is There Life in *Aspen* after *Trinko*?" *Antitrust Law Journal* 73 (2005): 153.

24. ABA Section of Antitrust Law, *Market Power Handbook* (Chicago: ABA Publishing, 2005), pp. 3, 5.

25. Ibid., p. 139.

26. Steven C. Salop, "Exclusionary Conduct, Effect on Consumers, and the Flawed Profit-Sacrifice Standard," *Antitrust Law Journal* 73 (2006): 311–12.

27. Ibid., 311, 374.

28. Mark S. Popofsky, "Defining Exclusionary Conduct," *Antitrust Law Journal* 73 (2006): 435, 481.

29. Andrew I. Gavil, "Exclusionary Distribution Strategies by Dominant Firms: Striking a Better Balance," *Antitrust Law Journal* 72 (2004): 3.

30. Ibid., 3, 74.

31. Ibid., 3, 81.

32. E. Thomas Sullivan and Herbert Hovenkamp, *Antitrust Law, Policy and Procedure*, 4th ed. (Charlottesville, VA: Lexis Law Publishing, 1999), p. 31.

33. Areeda and Kaplow, *Antitrust Analysis*, p. 4.

34. *Nash v. United States*, 229 U.S. 373 (1913).

35. *Nash*, 229 U.S. 373, 376.

36. ABA Section of Antitrust Law, *Antitrust Law Developments*, 5th ed. (Chicago: ABA Publishing, 2002), p. 729.

37. Whitney, *Antitrust Policies*, p. 104, citing Paul H. Giddens, *Standard Oil Company* (Indiana) (New York: Appleton-Century-Crofts, 1955), p. 131.

38. *United States v. IBM Corp.*, Dkt. No. 69-Civ.-200 (S.D.N.Y. complaint filed Jan. 17, 1969).

39. *In re IBM Corp.*, 687 F.2d 591, 593 (2d Cir. 1982).

40. John E. Lopatka, *"United States v. IBM*: A Monument to Arrogance," *Antitrust Law Journal* 68 (2000): 145–46.

41. Robert H. Bork, *The Antitrust Paradox*, Rev. ed. (New York: The Free Press, 1993), p. 431.

42. *Telex Corp. v. IBM Corp.*, 510 F.2d 894 (10th Cir. 1975).

43. *Telex Corp.* 510 F.2d 894, 897.

44. *Brobeck, Phleger, & Harrison v. Telex Corp.*, 602 F.2d 866, 867 (9th Cir. 1979).

45. *United States v. Microsoft Corp.*, 253 F.3d 34 (D.C. Cir. 2001).

46. *United States v. Aluminum Co. of America*, 148 F.2d 416 (2d Cir. 1945).

47. Fox and Sullivan, *Cases and Materials on Antitrust*, p. 114.

48. *United States v. Aluminum Co. of America*, 148 F.2d 416 (2d Cir.1945).

49. *Aluminum Co. of America*, 148 F.2d 416.

50. *Aluminum Co. of America*, 148 F.2d 416 (emphasis added).

51. ABA Section of Antitrust Law, *Model Jury Instructions in Civil Antitrust Case* (Chicago: ABA Publishing, 2005).

52. Ibid., pp. xv, xvi.

53. Ibid., p. C-17.

54. Ibid., p. C-18.

55. Ibid., p. C-27.

56. Steven C. Salop, "Anticompetitive Overbuying by Power Buyers," *Antitrust Law Journal* 72 (2005): 669.

57. *Confederated Tribes of Siletz Indians of Oregon v. Weyerhaeuser Co.*, Antitrust and Trade Regulation Report 88 (9th Cir. 2005). On February 20, 2007, the Supreme Court vacated and remanded the 9th Circuit's decision. *Weyerhaeuser Co. v. Ross-Simmons Hardwood Lumber Co., Inc.*, 549 U.S.___, slip. op. (2007).

58. *Brooke Group Ltd. v. Brown & Williamson Tobacco Corp.*, 509 U.S. 209 (1993).

Chapter 6

1. *United States v. Pabst Brewing Company*, 384 U.S. 546, 553 (1966).

2. *United States v. General Dynamics Corp.*, 415 U.S. 486 (1974).

3. *Brown Shoe, Inc. v. United States*, 370 U.S. 294, 333 (1962).

4. *United States v. Philadelphia National Bank*, 374 U.S. 321, 362–63 (1963).

5. Frederick M. Rowe, "The Decline of Antitrust and the Delusions of Models," *Georgetown Law Journal* 72 (1984): 1511, 1528, footnotes omitted.

6. Andrew I. Gavil, William E. Kovacic, and Jonathan B. Baker, *Antitrust Law in Perspective: Cases, Concepts and Problems in Competition Policy* (St. Paul, MN: Thomson-West, 2002), p. 440.

7. Ibid., p. 441.

8. Ibid.

9. Nestle S. A., FTC File No. 012-0174, *Antitrust and Trade Regulation Report* 84 (June 27, 2003): 653.

10. *United States v. Connors Bros. Income Fund*, Final Judgment April 18, 2005 (D.D.C.), www.justice.gov/atr/cases/f208700/208712.htm, *Antitrust and Trade Regulation Report* 87 (Sept. 3, 2004): 249.

11. *FTC v. H. J. Heinz Co.*, 246 F. 3d 708 (D.C. Cir. 2001).

12. U.S. Department of Justice, Merger Guidelines, 33 Fed. Reg. 23,442 (1968).

13. Ibid., 47 Fed. Reg. 28, 493 (1982).

14. FTC, Statement Concerning Horizontal Mergers (1982), reprinted in 2 Trade Reg. Rep. (CCH) para. 4516.

15. U.S. Department of Justice, Merger Guidelines, 49 Fed. Reg. 26,823 (1984).

16. U.S. Department of Justice and FTC, Horizontal Merger Guidelines (1992), reprinted in 4 Trade Reg. Rep. (CCH) para. 13,104.

17. U.S. Department of Justice and FTC, Revision to section 4 of Horizontal Merger Guidelines, reprinted in *Antitrust and Trade Regulation Report* 72 (April 10, 1997): 359.

18. Commentary on the Horizontal Merger Guidelines, *Antitrust and Trade Regulation Report* 90 (March 31, 2006): 357.

19. Robert Pitofsky, "Does Antitrust Have a Future?" *Georgetown Law Journal* 76 (1987): 321, 326.

20. Thomas B. Leary, "The Essential Stability of Merger Policy in the United States," *Antitrust Law Journal* 70 (2002): 105, 113.

21. William E. Kovacic, "Prepared Statement of the Federal Trade Commission: Petroleum Industry Consolidation," Testimony before the Committee on the Judiciary, U.S. Senate, February 1, 2006, p. 2.

22. U.S. Department of Justice and FTC, Horizontal Merger Guidelines, issued April 2, 1992, revised April 8, 1997, section 1.5.

23. Ibid., Section 0. Purpose, Underlying Policy Assumptions, and Overview (emphasis added).

24. U.S. Department of Justice and FTC, Commentary on the Horizontal Merger Guidelines (March 2006), p. 3.

25. Leary, "Essential Stability of Merger Policy," 105, 112.

26. "FTC Closes Pepsi/Quaker Merger Probe; Divided Commission Results in Clearance," *Antitrust and Trade Regulation Report* 81 (August 3, 2001): 99.

27. "Tie Vote Results in FTC Deadlock on General Mills/Pillsbury Merger," *Antitrust and Trade Regulation Report* 81 (October 26, 2001): 364.

28. "Phillips Petroleum, Tosco Receive Notice of FTC Investigation Closure; Merger to Proceed," *Antitrust and Trade Regulation Report* 81 (September 21, 2001): 239.

29. *H. J. Heinz Co.*, 246 F. 3d 708.

30. *FTC v. H. J. Heinz Co.*, Civil Action No. 00-1688 (D.D.C 2000), Slip Opinion, p. 22.

31. "The FTC's Enforcer," *Legal Times* (May 28, 2001).

32. Caroline E. Meyer, "A Steady Course for the FTC," *Washington Post*, Section E, June 8, 2001.

33. Acquisitions-Boeing Co., 5 Trade Reg. Rep. (CCH) para. 24, 295 (FTC, July 1, 1997).

34. Gavil, Kovacic, and Baker, *Antitrust Law in Perspective*, p. 73.

35. Hart-Scott-Rodino Antitrust Improvements Act, 15 U.S.C. § 18a.

36. FTC and Justice Department, Annual Report to Congress: Fiscal Year 2005, pp. 2, 3.

37. "DOJ Won't Attack Consolidation of Major Appliance Manufacturers," *Antitrust and Trade Regulation Report* 90 (March 31, 2006): 349, 350.

38. *United States v. Oracle Corp.*, 331 F. Supp. 2d 1098 (N.D. Cal. 2004).

39. *Connors Bros. Income Fund* (D.D.C.), *Antitrust and Trade Regulation Report* 87: 249.

40. Acquisitions-Boeing Co., 5 Trade Reg. Rep. (CCH), para. 24, 295.

41. *H. J. Heinz Co.*, 246 F. 3d 708.

42. Nestle S. A., FTC File No. 012-0174, *Antitrust and Trade Regulation Report* 84 (June 27, 2003): 653.

43. Frederick M. Rowe, "The Decline of Antitrust and the Delusions of Models," *Georgetown Law Journal* 72 (1984): 1511, 1529, footnotes omitted.

44. D. Jeffrey Brown, Paul Collins, and Kevin Rushton, "Symposium—Aspen Skiing 20 Years Later: The Aspen Skiing Case from a Canadian Competition Law Perspective," *Antitrust Law Journal* 73 (2005): 278.

45. "FTC Wraps Up Record Year in Antitrust Enforcement with New Mix of Litigation and Guidance," FTC Press Release, October 13, 2000.

Chapter 7

1. Timothy J. Muris, "The Government and Merger Efficiencies: Still Hostile After All These Years," *George Mason Law Review* 7 (1999): 729, 736, 752.

2. Daniel J. Gifford and Leo J. Raskind, *Federal Antitrust Law Cases and Materials*, 2d ed. (Cincinnati, OH: Anderson Publishing Co., 2002), p. 235.

3. Andrew I. Gavil, William E. Kovacic, and Jonathan B. Baker, *Antitrust Law in Perspective: Cases, Concepts and Problems in Competition Policy* (St. Paul, MN: Thomson-West, 2002), p. 634.

4. Eleanor M. Fox and Lawrence A. Sullivan, *Cases and Materials on Antitrust* (St. Paul, MN: West Publishing Co., 1989), p. 644.

5. Phillip Areeda and Louis Kaplow, *Antitrust Analysis*, 5th ed. (New York: Aspen Law & Business, 1997), p. 686.

6. Ibid., p. 769.

7. Ibid., (emphasis added).

8. *Jefferson Parish Hospital District No. 2 v. Hyde*, 466 U.S. 2 (1984).

9. ABA Section of Antitrust Law, *Antitrust Law Developments*, 5th ed. (Chicago: ABA Publishing, 2002), pp. 177, 178, 179.

10. Ibid., p. 179.

11. E. Thomas Sullivan and Herbert Hovenkamp, *Antitrust Law, Policy and Procedure*, 4th ed. (Charlottesville, VA: Lexis Law Publishing, 1999), p. 518.

12. Robert H. Bork, *The Antitrust Paradox* (New York: Basic Books, 1978), pp. 378–79.

13. Gavil, Kovacic, and Baker, *Antitrust Law in Perspective*, p. 691 (emphasis added).

14. Fox and Sullivan, *Cases and Materials on Antitrust*, p. 627

15. *Motion Picture Patents Co. v. Universal Film Manufacturing Co.*, 243 U.S. 502 (1917) (emphasis added).

16. *International Salt Co. v. United States*, 332 U.S. 392 (1947).

17. Earl W. Kintner, *An Antitrust Primer*, 2d ed. (New York: Macmillan, 1973), p. 47.

18. Bork, *The Antitrust Paradox*, p. 367 (emphasis added).

19. *Northern Pacific Ry. Co. v. United States*, 356 U.S. 1, 5–6 (1958).

20. Bork, *The Antitrust Paradox*, pp. 367–68.

21. *United States v. Jerrold Elect. Corp.*, 187 F. Supp. 545 (E.D. Pa. 1960), *aff'd per curiam*, 365 U.S. 567 (1961).

22. *Dehydrating Process Co. v. A.O. Smith Corp.*, 292 F.2d 653 (1st Cir.), *cert. denied*, 368 U.S. 931 (1961).

23. Bork, *The Antitrust Paradox*, p. 368.

24. Ibid., p. 380.

25. Robert A. Levy, *Shakedown* (Washington: Cato Institute, 2004), p. 191.

26. Ibid., p. 202.

27. Ibid., pp. 202–03.

28. *Jefferson Parish Hospital District No. 2*, 466 U.S. 2.

29. *Standard Oil Co. of California v. United States*, 337 U.S. 293 (1949).

30. Fox and Sullivan, *Cases and Materials on Antitrust*, p. 146.

31. *United States v. United Shoe Machinery Corp.*, 110 F. Supp. 295 (D. Mass. 1953), *aff'd per curiam*, 347 U.S. 521 (1954).

32. *United States v. Griffith*, 334 U.S. 100 (1948).

33. Bork, *The Antitrust Paradox*, p. 142.

34. Levy, *Shakedown*, p. 197.

35. Thomas G. Krattenmaker and Steven C. Salop, "Anticompetitive Exclusion: Raising Rivals' Costs to Achieve Power over Price," *Yale Law Journal* 96 (1986): 209, 213–14.

36. Gavil, Kovacic, and Baker, *Antitrust Law in Perspective*, p. 635.

37. *United States v. Arnold Schwinn & Co.*, 388 U.S. 365 (1967).

38. *GTE Sylvania Inc. v. Continental T.V.*, 433 U.S. 36 (1977).

39. Robert Pitofsky, "The Sylvania Case: Antitrust Analysis of Non-Price Restrictions," *Columbia Law Review* 78 (1978): 1, 3.

40. *Fortner Enters., Inc. v. United States Steel Corp.*, 293 F. Supp. 762 (W.D. Ky. 1966).

41. *Fortner Enters., Inc. v. United States Steel Corp.*, 404 F. 2d 936 (6th Cir. 1968).

42. *Fortner Enters., Inc. v. United States Steel Corp.*, 394 U.S. 495 (1969).

43. *Fortner Enters., Inc. v. United States Steel Corp.*, 429 U.S. 610 (1977).

44. Simon N. Whitney, *Antitrust Policies* (New York: Twentieth Century Fund, 1958), p. 104, citing Paul H. Giddens, *Standard Oil Company* (Indiana) (New York: Appleton-Century-Crofts, 1955), p.131.

45. Thurman Arnold, *The Folklore of Capitalism* (New Haven, CT: Yale University Press, 1937), p. 211.

46. Gifford and Raskind, *Federal Antitrust Law Cases and Materials*, p. 235.

47. *United States v. Microsoft Corp.*, 253 F.3d 34 (D.C. Cir. 2001).

48. Justice Department Press Release, September 6, 2001.

Chapter 8

1. "Three More Executives Are Indicted in Global DRAM Cartelization Conspiracy," *Antitrust and Trade Regulation Report* 91 (Oct. 20, 2006): 413, 414.

2. Tony Freyer, *Regulating Big Business* (Cambridge: Cambridge University Press, 1992), p. 6.

3. Andrew I. Gavil, William E. Kovacic, and Jonathan B. Baker, *Antitrust Law in Perspective: Cases, Concepts and Problems in Competition Policy* (St. Paul, MN: Thomson-West, 2002), p. 85.

4. Eleanor M. Fox and Lawrence A. Sullivan, *Cases and Materials on Antitrust* (St. Paul, MN: West Publishing Co., 1989), p. 36.

5. *Standard Oil Co. v. United States*, 221 U.S. 1 (1911).

6. *United States v. Trenton Potteries Co.*, 273 U.S. 392 (1927).

7. *Kiefer-Stewart Co. v. Joseph E. Seagram & Sons*, 340 U.S. 211 (1951).

8. "Company, President Face Charges of Rigging Bids on Aluminum Products," *Antitrust and Trade Regulation Report* 70 (April 25, 1996): 458.

9. "Indiana Concrete Producer, Officer Plead Guilty to Fixing Ready-Mix Concrete Prices," *Antitrust and Trade Regulation Report* 90 (April 26, 2006): 490.

10. *Trenton Potteries Co.*, 273 U.S. 392.

11. *Appalachian Coals, Inc. v. United States*, 288 U.S. 344 (1933).

12. *United States v. Socony-Vacuum Oil Co.*, 310 U.S. 150 (1940).

13. *Broadcast Music, Inc. v. CBS*, 441 U.S. 1 (1979).

14. ABA Section of Antitrust Law, *Antitrust Law Developments*, 5th ed. (Chicago: ABA Publishing, 2002), p. 92.

15. Ibid., p. 58.

16. Ibid., p. 82.

17. *Trenton Potteries Co.*, 273 U.S. 392, 397–98.

18. *FTC v. Procter & Gamble Co.*, 386 U.S. 568 (1967).

19. Revised Section 4 Horizontal Merger Guidelines Issued by the U.S. Department of Justice and the FTC, April 8, 1997.

20. "DOJ Closes AT&T/Bell South Probe; Merger Isn't Likely to Reduce Competition," *Antitrust and Trade Regulation Report* 91 (Oct. 13, 2006): 381.

21. Thomas B. Leary, "The Essential Stability of Merger Policy in the United States," *Antitrust Law Journal* 70 (2002): 105, 107, 118.

22. Gavil, Kovacic, and Baker, *Antitrust Law in Perspective*, p. 98.

23. *Antitrust and Trade Regulation Report* 90 (April 28, 2006): 490.

24. *Joseph E. Seagram & Sons, Inc.*, 340 U.S. 211, 213.

25. *United States v. Arnold Schwinn & Co.*, 388 U.S. 365, 380 (1967).

26. Howard P. Marvel, Jeffrey M. Netter, and Anthony M. Robinson, "Price Fixing and Civil Damages: An Economic Analysis," *Stanford Law Review* 40 (February 1988): 561, 575, quoted in Fred S. McChesney and William F. Shughart II, *The Causes and Consequences of Antitrust* (Chicago: University of Chicago Press, 1995), p. 31.

27. Michael F. Sproul, "Antitrust and Prices," *Journal of Political Economy* 101 (1993): 741, 753, quoted in McChesney and Shughart, *The Causes and Consequences of Antitrust*, p. 32.

28. Robert W. Crandall and Clifford Winston, "Does Antitrust Policy Improve Consumer Welfare? Assessing the Evidence," *Journal of Economic Perspectives* 17 (2003): 3, 15.

29. Robert A. Levy, *Shakedown* (Washington: Cato Institute, 2004), p. 311.

30. Richard A. Epstein, *Principles for a Free Society* (Cambridge, MA: Perseus Publishing, 1998), p. 91.

31. Gavil, Kovacic, and Baker, *Antitrust Law in Perspective*, p. 97.

32. Sproul, "Antitrust and Prices," quoted in McChesney and Shughart, *The Causes and Consequences of Antitrust*, p. 32; Crandall and Winston, "Does Antitrust Policy Improve Consumer Welfare?" 3, 15.

33. D. T. Armentano, *Antitrust Policy* (Washington: Cato Institute, 1986), p. 62.
34. Gavil, Kovacic, and Baker, *Antitrust Law in Perspective*, p. 97.
35. "Indiana Concrete Producer, Officer Plead Guilty," 90 *Antitrust and Trade Regulation Report* 490.
36. *Trenton Potteries Co.*, 273 U.S. 392; *Socony-Vacuum Oil Co.*, 310 U.S. 150.
37. *Appalachian Coals, Inc.*, 288 U.S. 344; *Broadcast Music, Inc. v. CBS*, 441 U.S. 1 (1979).
38. Acquisitions-Boeing Co., 5 Trade Reg. Rep. (CCH), para. 24,295 (FTC July 1, 1997).
39. *United States v. Aluminum Co. of America*, 148 F.2d 416 (2d Cir. 1945).
40. Joseph E. Stiglitz, *Globalization and Its Discontents* (New York: W.W. Norton & Co., 2002), p. 172.
41. Ibid., p. 178.
42. "Don't Call It a Cartel, but World Aluminum Has Forged New Order," *Wall Street Journal*, June 9, 1994.
43. "Aluminum Makers Are Expected to Post Sharp Profit Increases for 3rd Period," *Wall Street Journal*, September 29, 1995.
44. Stiglitz, *Globalization and Its Discontents*, p. 175.
45. "Company, President Face Charges of Rigging Bids," 70 *Antitrust and Trade Regulation Report* 458.
46. Eric Norton and Martin Du Bois, "Justice Department Closes Antitrust Probe into Aluminum Pact," *Wall Street Journal*, May 16, 1997.
47. "Don't Call It a Cartel," *Wall Street Journal.*
48. Final Report, International Competition Policy Advisory Committee to the Attorney General and Assistant Attorney General for Antitrust (February 28, 2000), p. 166, www.usdoj.gov/atr/icpac/finalreport.htm.
49. *United States v. Brown University*, 805 F. Supp. 288 (E.D. Pa. 1992).
50. Robert Pitofsky, Harvey J. Goldschmid, and Diane P. Weed, *Trade Regulation* (Westbury, NY: Foundation Press, 2003), p. 275.
51. Gavil, Kovacic, and Baker, *Antitrust Law in Perspective*, p. 96.
52. "Roundtable Conference with Enforcement Officials," *Antitrust Law Journal* 68 (2000): 614.
53. *Nash v. United States*, 229 U.S. 373, 376 (1913).
54. ABA Section of Antitrust Law, *Antitrust Law Developments* (Chicago: ABA Publishing, 1975), p. 236.
55. 15 U.S.C., chapter 1, § 15.
56. "Court Approves Record Settlement and Over $220 Million in Counsel Fees," *Antitrust and Trade Regulation Report* 86 (Jan. 9, 2004): 5.

Chapter 9

1. Robert H. Bork, *The Antitrust Paradox* (New York: Basic Books, 1978), p. 408.
2. Frederick M. Rowe, "The Decline of Antitrust and the Delusions of Models," *Georgetown Law Journal* 72 (1984): 1511, 1569.
3. D. T. Armentano, *The Myths of Antitrust* (New York: Arlington House, 1972), p. 279.
4. Abe Fortas, Foreword to A. D. Neale and D. G. Goyder, *The Antitrust Laws of the United States of America*, 3d ed. (Cambridge: Cambridge University Press, 1980), p. v. (emphasis supplied), quoted in Daniel J. Gifford and Leo J. Raskind, *Federal*

Antitrust Law Cases and Materials, 2d ed. (New York: Anderson Publishing Co., 2002), p. 1.

5. Robert H. Bork, *The Antitrust Paradox* (New York: Basic Books, 1978), p. 409.

6. Thurman Arnold, *The Folklore of Capitalism* (New Haven, CT: Yale University Press, 1937), pp. 211–12.

7. Richard A. Posner, *The Problematics of Moral and Legal Theory* (Cambridge, MA: Harvard University Press, 1999), p. 229.

8. *United States v. Microsoft Corp.*, 253 F.3d 34, 72, 74 (D.C. Cir. 2001).

9. Robert W. Crandall and Clifford Winston, "Does Antitrust Policy Improve Consumer Welfare? Assessing the Evidence," *Journal of Economic Perspectives* 17 (2003): 3, 4.

10. Milton Handler, "Reforming the Antitrust Laws," *Columbia Law Review* 82 (November 1982): 103.

11. Gary Hull, ed., *The Abolition of Antitrust* (New Brunswick, NJ: Transaction Publishers, 2005), p. ix.

12. D. T. Armentano, *Antitrust Policy* (Washington: Cato Institute, 1986), p. 74.

13. Ibid., p. 13.

14. Phillip Areeda and Louis Kaplow, *Antitrust Analysis*, 5th ed. (New York: Aspen Law & Business, 1997), p. 12.

15. "Muris Discusses Methods to Improve Economic Foundations of Competition Policy," *Antitrust and Trade Regulation Report* 84 (January 17, 2003): 34, 35: "In conclusion, Muris observed that there is 'much to do to assure that antitrust avoids the mistakes of its past.' "

16. Eleanor M. Fox and Lawrence A. Sullivan, *Cases and Materials on Antitrust* (St. Paul, MN: West Publishing Co., 1989), p. 738: "The decision in *E.C. Knight* was a defeat for antitrust."

17. Lawrence A. Sullivan and Warren S. Grimes, *The Law of Antitrust: An Integrated Handbook* (St. Paul, MN: Thomson-West, 2000), p. 10, quoted in Daniel J. Gifford and Leo J. Raskind, *Federal Antitrust Law Cases and Materials*, 2d ed. (Cincinnati, OH: Anderson Publishing Co., 2002), p. 27.

18. Thomas J. DiLorenzo, *How Capitalism Saved America* (New York: Crown Forum, 2004), p. 135.

19. Ibid., p. 155.

20. Arnold, *Folklore of Capitalism*, p. 211.

Index

Alcoa. *See* Aluminum Company of
America (Alcoa)
allocative efficiency, 34–38
aluminum cartel, 92–93
Aluminum Company of America
(Alcoa), 58–59
American Bar Association, 32
American Bar Association's antitrust
law section, 17–20, 24–25, 35, 36,
42, 56, 60–61, 72
antitrust, 1–2, 27–28, 100, 101–2
analysis, 4, 28, 37, 40–42, 53
definition, 4–5
dynamic nature, 10, 29, 94
law school indoctrination, 20–22
litigating, 23, 96–97. *See also* lower
court decisions; Supreme Court
decisions and opinions; *specific
cases and companies by name*
Antitrust, 18
antitrust community, 1, 2, 100–102
camaraderie, 24–25
decisionmakers and, 17, 21
development, 17–20
government service and experience,
16–17
language. *See* antitrust vocabulary
law school indoctrination and, 16,
20–22
self-righteousness, 22–25, 92
skills required, 15–17
antitrust doctrines, 5, 11–12, 101–2
mergers, 64–65, 71, 73
tying arrangements, 86
antitrust goals, 4, 23, 31–34, 38
efficiency, 11, 36–38
enforcement goals, 23, 31–34, 38. *See
also* the Chicago school rationale
fairness and equity, 11–12, 38
innovation and technological
progress, 38
justice, 11
undistorted competition, 48
Antitrust Law Developments (5th ed.), 18,
88–89
types of regulated industries, 27–28

Antitrust Law Journal, 18
antitrust laws, 1, 36–38, 100
as common law statutes, 10, 55–56
definitions, 3–4
legitimacy/illegitimacy, 12, 22
modernization, 20, 86
National Committee to Study the
Antitrust Laws, 15
See also Clayton Act; Sherman Act;
statutes
antitrust literature, 3, 21–22, 28–29
Antitrust Modernization Commission
Act, 20, 86
The Antitrust Paradox, 42
antitrust proceedings, 56–61
antitrust vocabulary, 6, 10–11, 15–17,
22–25, 24, 103
Appalachian Coals case, 28–29
Areeda, Phillip, 4, 6, 48–49, 55, 75,
77–78
Armentano, D. T., 49, 50, 91, 101
Arnold, Thurman, 1, 42, 99–100
AT&T consolidation, 89

baby food merger case, 69
Baker, Jonathan, 65, 77
barriers to entry, 7, 16, 44, 52–53, 61
the baseball exemption, 28
Baxter, William, 35
Bell South consolidation, 89
Bergson, Herbert, 15, 26
Black, Hugo, 90
Boeing Co., 70
Bork, Robert, 12, 33, 34–35, 42, 57,
76–77, 79, 80
Brandeis, Louis, 5
Brown Shoe case, 7, 8, 64
Brownell, Herbert, 15
Brozen, Yale, 33–34
Burger, Warren, 64
buyer-side market power, 61–62
buyer's freedom to sell, 37, 83, 84
See also exclusive dealing; tying
arrangements

119

cartels, 29, 87, 90–94
the Chicago school rationale, 34–38, 42, 66
Clayton Act, 3, 5, 28, 31, 47, 101
price fixing and, 87
the Robinson-Patman Act and, 32–33, 35
section 7. *See* merger prevention
tying and exclusive dealing, 75–78
Clinton administration, 25
coercion
mergers and, 48–50
tying and, 75–76, 77
collusion, 90
Commentary on the Horizontal Merger Guidelines, 8, 41, 42–43, 66, 68, 69–71, 89
Committee on Antitrust Policy of the Twentieth Century Fund report, 19–20
competition, 4, 5–8, 61–62
competitive advantage, 7
competitive losers pressing government action, 56–59, 61–62
different meanings, 30–31
fair, 28, 101, 102
foreclosing rival opportunities, 75–78
lessening, 8, 66, 73, 78, 87
market entry and, 44, 67. *See also* barriers to entry
New Deal policy toward, 29–30
potential, 7, 29
procompetitive and anticompetitive conduct, 9, 53, 61–62
reconciled with social justice, 52
undistorted competition, 48
U.S. policy, 27–31, 32
Concentrated Industries Act, 33
concentration concerns, 33–34, 36, 38, 42, 66, 67–68, 73
Congress, enactment of antitrust laws, 3, 47
consumer welfare, 12, 31, 34–38, 90, 91, 101, 102
contracts
freedom of contract, 5–6
sanctity of contract, 101
tying arrangements, 23, 77–83
contracts in restraint of trade. *See* price fixing
corporate greed, 102
Crandall, Robert, 12, 49, 90
Curt Flood Act, 28

Demsetz, Harold, 33–34
DiLorenzo, Thomas, 49, 102
Douglas, William O., 63–65, 81, 89

economic efficiency, 7–8, 50, 59, 66, 89
economic theory, 12, 100, 103
the Chicago school rationale, 34–38, 42, 66
market power, 2, 10, 11, 23, 38, 39–42, 46
educating society on antitrust, 2, 10, 12–13, 101, 102–3
Eisenhower administration, 15, 25, 31
enforcement, 1, 27–28, 31, 99, 103
goals, 23, 31–34, 38. *See also* the Chicago school rationale
New Deal antitrust enforcement, 29–30, 31
See also merger prevention
English common law, 55, 99
Epstein, Richard, 91
evils of antitrust, 2, 99
government protection from evil, 5, 7, 10–11, 13, 22–25
See also exclusive dealing; mergers; monopolization; price fixing; tying arrangements
exclusionary conduct, 53–55, 59, 81–83
exclusive dealing, 23, 27, 35, 75–76

Federal Trade Commission, 6, 31, 34, 102
Microsoft case, 8–9, 58
Sherman violations hearings, 48
See also Commentary on the Horizontal Merger Guidelines; merger prevention; mergers
Fortas, Abe, 90, 99
Fortner case, 83, 84–85
Fox, Eleanor, 4, 47, 49, 51–52, 75, 77, 81, 87–88
Frankfurter, Felix, 81
free markets, 27–28
Freyer, Tony, 87
Furth, Fred, 36

garment industry, 31, 32
Gavil, Andrew, 54, 65, 77
General Dynamics case, 64
General Mills Inc., 68–69
General Motors, 32, 34
Gifford, Daniel, 34, 47, 75
Globalization and Its Discontents, 91

government protection from evil, 5, 7, 10–11, 13, 22–25
Griffith case, 81
Grinnell case, 51–52

Hand, Learned, 58
Handler, Milton, 100–101
Hart, Phillip, 33
Harvard Law School textbook definition, 3
horizontal mergers, 7, 29, 35, 42–43, 65–72
    See also Commentary on the Horizontal Merger Guidelines
Hovencamp, Herbert, 37, 55, 76
Hull, Gary, 101

IBM, antitrust case, 32, 34, 56–58, 87
Illinois Brick case, 16
In Defense of Industrial Concentration, 33
Industrial Reorganization Act, 33
International Competition Network, 25
International Competition Policy Advisory Committee, 25
Ivy League Cartel, 93–94

Jefferson Parish case, 80–81
judgments, subjective, 6, 12, 46, 103
Justice Department, U.S., 6, 35
    Alcoa monopoly complaint, 58–59
    antitrust division policy, 95
    IBM case, 32, 34, 56–58
    Merger Guidelines, 8, 65–73
    Microsoft case, 9, 58
    Sherman violations hearings, 48
    See also Commentary on the Horizontal Merger Guidelines; merger prevention; mergers

Kaplow, Louis, 4, 6, 48–49, 55, 75, 77–78
Kintner, Earl, 78–79
Klein, Joel, 10
Kovacic, William, 65, 77
Krattenmaker, Thomas, 83

labor unions, 27
language of antitrust. *See* antitrust vocabulary
law professors and law schools, 20–22
lawyers and law practices, 10–11, 16–17, 23–24

    See also American Bar Association's antitrust law section
Leary, Thomas, 68
lessening competition, 8, 66, 73, 78, 87
    See also merger prevention; mergers
Levy, Robert, 80, 82–83, 90–91
Lopatka, John, 56–57
loser competitors, 8, 56–59, 61–62
lower court decisions
    exclusionary conduct and tying, 81
    mergers, 64–65, 69
    predatory overbidding, 61–62

market analysis, 40–42
market control, 23
market distortions and imperfections, 28, 100
market division, 35
market dominance, 23
    codes of responsibility for dominant firms, 54
    Standard Oil, 48–50
market efficiency, 11, 37
market power, 1–2, 5, 10, 13, 23, 27, 39–42, 73, 81, 100, 101
    assumptions and predictions, 11–12, 38, 43–46, 51–52, 70–71
    buyer-side market power, 61–62
    economist definition, 38
    imagined and unverifiable, 44–46
    market definition and existence, 42–44, 46, 67–68, 70–71
    proxies, 42
    subjective decisions and, 45, 46
Market Power Handbook, 18, 44, 52–53
market shares, 42
market structure, 33
markets, 100–102
    definitions, 42–44, 46, 52, 67–68
    metaphoric label, 8, 10, 16, 27
Marvel, Howard, 90
McDonnell Douglas Corp., 70
McGee, John, 33, 50
Merger Guidelines, 8, 65–73
merger prevention, 7–8, 32, 33–34, 35, 40–41
    enforcement, 63–72
    unpredictability, 68–72
mergers, 27, 29
    advance notice, 8, 35, 71, 73
    arbitrary decisionmaking, 8–9, 11–12, 72–73
    barriers to entry and, 7, 16, 44, 52–53, 61

coercion and, 48–50
competitive advantage, 7
concentration concerns, 33–34, 36, 38,
    42, 66, 67–68, 73
conglomerate mergers, 7, 10–11, 35,
    66
economic efficiency, 7–8, 50, 59, 66,
    89
fear of corporate consolidation, 5, 8,
    13, 39, 73
horizontal mergers, 7, 29, 35, 42–43,
    65–72. See also Commentary on the
    Horizontal Merger Guidelines
lower court decisions, 64–65, 69. See
    also specific cases and companies by
    name
market power assumptions and, 45,
    51–52, 70–71, 73
partial divestitures, 70–71
potential competition, 7, 29
price cooperation and, 88–89
reciprocity/reciprocal dealing, 7, 10,
    23
rule of law and, 72–73
Supreme Court decisions, 7–8, 63–65,
    66, 72
vertical mergers, 7, 35, 66
Microsoft case, 8–9, 58, 85, 100, 103
Miller, James C., 35
monopolies, 6, 27–34, 34, 102
creating, 7, 39. See also mergers
market power assumptions and, 45,
    51–52
successful competitors, 56–59, 61–62
monopolization, 10, 37, 40
case examples, 56–59
combination offers. See tying
    arrangements
conduct and outcomes of antitrust
    proceedings, 59–61
defining, 47–55, 60
the elements of the offense and,
    51–52
exclusionary conduct, 53–55, 81–83
government support and, 50–51
model jury instructions, 60–61
proof of monopoly power, 60
See also specific cases and companies by
    name
monopoly power, 52–53
Muris, Timothy, J., 4–5, 69

Nader, Ralph, 36
National Committee to Study the
    Antitrust Laws, 15, 25

National Industrial Recovery Act of
    1933, 29–30
Netter, Jeffrey, 90
New Deal, antitrust enforcement,
    29–30, 31
Nixon, Richard, 32
Noerr-Pennington case, 16
normative rules for judging conduct,
    20, 37, 50–51, 53, 60
Northern Pacific case, 79–80

O'Connor, Sandra Day, 81
the Oil Trust, 49
oligopoly, 10, 33–34
O'Neill, Paul, 91–92

PepsiCo, 68
per se rule, 5, 16, 64, 76, 84, 87–88, 91,
    94–96
Philadelphia National Bank case, 64
Phillips Petroleum Corp., 69
Pillsbury Co., 68–69
Pitofsky, Robert, 69
Posner, Richard, 12, 34, 35
potential competition, 7, 29
predation, deliberate, 35
predatory bidding, 23, 61–62
predatory buying and selling, 23, 62
predatory pricing, 23, 35, 38
price discrimination, 27, 32–33, 35, 87
price fixing, 35, 87–90
    Appalachian Coals case, 28–29
    efficiencies and, 90–96
    treble damage actions, 96–97
price gouging, 47
price increases, market definition and,
    43–44
Procter & Gamble, 89

Quaker Oats Co., 68

Raskind, Leo, 34, 47, 75
reciprocity/reciprocal dealing, 7, 10, 23
reform/repeal of statutes, 1, 9–13, 100,
    101
    the Chicago school rationale and,
    34–38, 99–100
    "The State of Federal Antitrust
    Enforcement—2004" report, 32
regulated industries, 27–28
    concentration concerns, 33–34, 36, 38,
    42

*Regulating Big Business: Antitrust in
Great Britain and America
1880–1990*, 87
regulations and economic controls, 12,
102
antitrust as alternative to, 27–28
Microsoft case, 9, 58
relevant market, analysis, 40–42, 53
religious faith, antitrust as, 1, 3–5,
12–13, 25, 36–37, 102
See also antitrust community
Robinson, Anthony, 90
Roosevelt, Theodore, 15, 42, 56
Rowe, Frederick, 32, 43, 46
Rubin, Robert, 93
rule of law, 1, 2, 11–12
mergers, 72–73
rule of reason, 5–6, 16, 76

Salop, Steven, 53, 83
Schwinn case, 84, 90
Sherman Act, 3, 5–6, 9, 10, 12, 28, 31,
32, 34, 47
criminal sanctions, 55–56, 95–96
market power and, 40, 41
price fixing and, 87–88, 95, 96
tying and, 77, 84
violations, 48, 51
small business, protecting, 7, 31–32, 33,
90
social justice, competition reconciled
with, 52
Socony–Vacuum case, 29
Sproul, Michael, 90
Standard Oil, 5, 9, 27, 39, 47–50, 56, 63,
94, 101, 103
Standard Stations case, 81
"The State of Federal Antitrust
Enforcement—2004" report, 32
statutes, 1, 99, 100
definitions, 3–4
judicial inquiry and judgments,
40–42
vagueness and discretion, 5–8, 55–56,
95–96
See also Clayton Act; enforcement;
reform/repeal of statutes; Sherman
Act
Stevens, John Paul, 41, 76, 81
Stiglitz, Joseph, 91–92

Sullivan, E. Thomas, 55, 76
Sullivan, Lawrence, 4, 47, 49, 75, 77, 81,
87–88
Supreme Court decisions and opinions,
7–8, 12, 28–30, 38, 62, 95, 99
mergers, 7–8, 63–65, 66, 72
monopoly power, 52
price fixing, 88–89
on Sherman Act's deficiencies, 55–56
small business and, 90
Standard Oil, 48
tying and exclusive dealing, 75, 76,
78–85, 86
Warren Court decisions, 7–8, 8, 29,
64–65, 71, 73
*See also specific cases and companies by
name*

Telex case, 57–58
Tosco Corp., 69
trade restraint, 5–6
See also price fixing
the trust, 47–48
tying arrangements, 35, 58, 75–77
charged as monopolization, 85–86
contracts, 23, 77–83
modernizing doctrines as to, 86
sales on credit, 83–85
tie-ins, 80, 85

United Shoe Machinery case, 81
U.S. Steel Credit Corp., 84–85

vertical mergers, 7, 35, 66
Von's Grocery case, 7

Waller, Spencer, 17, 18–19
Warren Court decisions, 7–8, 29, 64
merger doctrines, 64–65, 71, 73
small business and, 90
Weyerhaueser case, 61–62
White House Task Force on Antitrust
Policy, 33, 36
Whitney, Simon, 50
Winston, Clifford, 12, 49, 90
Wyzanski, Charles, 81

About the Author

Edwin S. Rockefeller graduated from Yale College and Yale Law School. He has a master's degree from Johns Hopkins' School of Advanced International Studies. Following graduation from law school, he spent two years with the Central Intelligence Agency, three years in the U.S. Army Judge Advocate General's Corps, and four years on the staff of the Federal Trade Commission.

From 1961 to 2001 he was in private law practice in Washington. His clients included Canada Dry, General Motors, Jantzen, Kellogg, Norton Simon, Puritan Fashions, and Weyerhaeuser. He argued a case in the Supreme Court involving the granting of discriminatory advertising allowances and lost. He defended General Motors against an FTC charge of monopolizing its inventory of "crash" parts and won. Although the commission decided every question of fact and law against him, after five years of litigation, the commission dropped the charge because, as a practical matter, it could not force GM to sell parts without choosing its customers.

Mr. Rockefeller has served as chairman of the Section of Antitrust Law of the American Bar Association and as an adjunct professor of law at Georgetown University Law Center. Since 1961 he has been chairman of the advisory board of the Bureau of National Affair's *Antitrust and Trade Regulation Report*.

His previous publications include the following:

Antitrust Questions & Answers (Washington: Bureau of National Affairs, 1974).

Desk Book of Federal Trade Commission Practice & Procedure, 3d ed. (New York: Practicing Law Institute, 1979).

Antitrust Counseling for the 1980s (Washington: Bureau of National Affairs, 1983).

Cato Institute

Founded in 1977, the Cato Institute is a public policy research foundation dedicated to broadening the parameters of policy debate to allow consideration of more options that are consistent with the traditional American principles of limited government, individual liberty, and peace. To that end, the Institute strives to achieve greater involvement of the intelligent, concerned lay public in questions of policy and the proper role of government.

The Institute is named for *Cato's Letters*, libertarian pamphlets that were widely read in the American Colonies in the early 18th century and played a major role in laying the philosophical foundation for the American Revolution.

Despite the achievement of the nation's Founders, today virtually no aspect of life is free from government encroachment. A pervasive intolerance for individual rights is shown by government's arbitrary intrusions into private economic transactions and its disregard for civil liberties.

To counter that trend, the Cato Institute undertakes an extensive publications program that addresses the complete spectrum of policy issues. Books, monographs, and shorter studies are commissioned to examine the federal budget, Social Security, regulation, military spending, international trade, and myriad other issues. Major policy conferences are held throughout the year, from which papers are published thrice yearly in the *Cato Journal*. The Institute also publishes the quarterly magazine *Regulation*.

In order to maintain its independence, the Cato Institute accepts no government funding. Contributions are received from foundations, corporations, and individuals, and other revenue is generated from the sale of publications. The Institute is a nonprofit, tax-exempt, educational foundation under Section 501(c)3 of the Internal Revenue Code.

CATO INSTITUTE
1000 Massachusetts Ave., N.W.
Washington, D.C. 20001
www.cato.org

LONG ISLAND POETS

an anthology

featuring works by

PHILIP APPLEMAN • JANE AUGUSTINE • GEORGE BRADLEY
EDWARD BUTSCHER • MARYANN CALENDRILLE
SIV CEDERING • GRAHAM EVERETT • BARBARA GUEST
MICHAEL HELLER • DAVID IGNATOW • YAEDI IGNATOW
KENNETH KOCH • NAOMI LAZARD • HOWARD MOSS
STANLEY MOSS • DAN MURRAY • ANSELM PARLATORE
SIMON PERCHIK • ALLEN PLANZ • ANNE PORTER
FAIRFIELD PORTER • GRACE SCHULMAN
JAMES SCHUYLER • ARMAND SCHWERNER
HUGH SEIDMAN • HARVEY SHAPIRO • R. B. WEBER

Edited by Robert Long

The Permanent Press, Sag Harbor, NY 11963

Library of Congress Number: 86-061 406
International Standard Book Number:0-932966-72-1 (Paper)
0-932966-73-X (Cloth)

Manufactured in the United States of America

THE PERMANENT PRESS
RD2 Noyac Road
Sag Harbor, NY 11963

Acknowledgments

JANE AUGUSTINE: "Anti-Cycle for the New Year" is reprinted by permission from *The Atlantic Review*, New Series, No. 3, 1980 (London, England). Copyright © 1980 Jane Augustine.
"The Stars" originally appeared in *Montemora* #3, Summer 1977. Copyright © 1977 by The Montemora Foundation, Inc. Used by permission of the author.
PHILIP APPLEMAN: Selections are reprinted from OPEN DOORWAYS, Poems by Philip Appleman, by permission of W. W. Norton & Company, Inc. Copyright © 1976 by W. W. Norton & Company, Inc.
EDWARD BUTSCHER: "Middle Age Summer" originally appeared in The East Hampton *Star*. Copyright © 1985 Edward Butscher.
SIV CEDERING: "On the Shore," "On Some Such Morning" and "Fata Morgana" are reprinted from LETTERS FROM THE FLOATING WORLD: SELECTED AND NEW POEMS, University of Pittsburgh Press, 1984. Copyright © 1984 Siv Cedering.
"Sea Drift" Copyright © 1985 Siv Cedering.
MICHAEL HELLER: "Coral Stanzas" originally appeared in *Bluefish*. Copyright © 1985 Michael Heller.
"On the Beach" and "At Albert's Landing" appeared in KNOWLEDGE, Sun Press, 1980. Copyright © 1980 Michael Heller.
"Two Swans" appeared in FIGURES OF SPEAKING, The Perishable Press Ltd., 1977. Copyright © 1977 Michael Heller.
DAVID IGNATOW: All selections appear in NEW AND COLLECTED POEMS, 1970–1985, Wesleyan University Press, 1986. Copyright © 1986 David Ignatow.
YAEDI IGNATOW: "The Offer," "Equations," "Praise," and "Limbo" appeared in THE FLAW, Sheep Meadow Press, 1983. Copyright © 1983 Yaedi Ignatow.
KENNETH KOCH: "Fate" and "The Boiling Water" appeared in THE BURNING MYSTERY OF ANNA IN 1951, Random House, 1979. Copyright © 1979 Kenneth Koch.
NAOMI LAZARD: All selections appeared in THE MOONLIT UPPER DECKERINA, Sheep Meadow Press, 1976. Copyright (c) 1976 Naomi Lazard.
HOWARD MOSS: "Notes from the Castle," "The Long Island Night," and "Aspects of Lilac" from NOTES FROM THE CASTLE. Copyright (c) 1980 Howard Moss. Reprinted with the permission of Atheneum Publishers, Inc.
"Bay Days" from BURIED CITY. Copyright (c) 1975 Howard Moss. Reprinted with the permission of Atheneum Publishers, Inc.
"In Traffic" from RULES OF SLEEP. Copyright (c) 1984 Howard Moss. Reprinted with the permission of Atheneum Publishers, Inc.
STANLEY MOSS: All selections appeared in SKULL OF ADAM, Horizon Press, 1979. Copyright (c) 1979 Stanley Moss.
ANSELM PARLATORE: "Woman of the Late Fall Run" originally appeared in *Cincinnatti Poetry Review*. "Portrait in Veiled Waters" appeared in *Vegetable Box*. Both Copyright (c) 1986 Anselm Parlatore.

Introduction

Editing this anthology, or, to be more precise, assembling it, has been a great pleasure. To have the opportunity to read, and re-read, the work of these writers in the context of the environment of the South Fork has been illuminating. What these poets have in common is a connection to this particular landscape, the weather and the special light of the Island's arm that reaches from Riverhead, the crossroads of Long Island, into the ocean at Montauk Point, where all dissolves into the ocean air.

Some of these writers live in this area full-time; others divide their time. The late Fairfield Porter, great painter and friend to poets, important critic and very fine poet himself, split his year between Maine and Southampton; James Schuyler lived in the Porters' house on South Main in Southampton, on and off, for a bit over a decade. Yaedi Ignatow and the painter Josh Dayton (an engraving of his faces our last page) both grew up in East Hampton, went on to live elsewhere, and now spend most of their time here. Kenneth Koch migrated to New York from Cincinnati by way of Harvard, and now spends a lot of time in Bridgehampton. And so on.

I've lived in East Hampton for fourteen years now, not counting brief spells in Manhattan, where I grew up. I've come to know most of the poets in this anthology personally over that time; some I've met only briefly; a few I have yet to meet. Drawing up a list of poets to invite to contribute to this anthology was easy; the difficult part came in leaving people out, for the area is rich in talent. Originally, we had planned a modest collection of 150 pages or so; as you can see, those plans went by the boards as it became apparent that so many fine poets had created so much good work that related, directly or indirectly, to the environment of the South Fork. Finally, we had to stop inviting writers to contribute, for pragmatic reasons, and this is why many deserving poets have been left out.

5

The writers represented here cover a broad spectrum of styles, manifold approaches to the poem. We have poets in their twenties and poets in their seventies. The most recent recipient of the Yale Series of Younger Poets Award (George Bradley) is here, as well as a distinguished former recipient (Hugh Seidman). We have a Pulitzer Prize winner (James Schuyler), a National Book Award recipient (Howard Moss), a Bollingen Prize recipient (David Ignatow) and others whose awards and distinctions go on and on. Our cover art is by the renowned painter Robert Dash, who lives in Sagaponack.

The idea of asking each writer to contribute a statement on the relationship of his or her work to the immediate environment came to us early in the planning stages of this book; the response has been fascinating. One way to approach this anthology might be to read only the statements, in sequence: they cast a unique light on each author's work.

What we wanted, in short, was an eclectic collection of poetry written by very different artists, held together by theme and quality. It's wonderful to read different writers' approaches to the same subject. Michael Heller and Hugh Seidman both place poems at Albert's Landing, a bay beach between East Hampton and Amagansett, and the poems couldn't be more dissimilar. Trees, birds, light, sand, sea, even the trip East from Manhattan supply these poets with raw material, vehicles for the speech of poetry (Note the Long Island Rail Road's appearance in Anne Porter's "On the Three Hour Train Ride," the flowers in Howard Moss's "Aspects of Lilac," the birdie in David Ignatow's "Little Friend."

It is our hope that this anthology can be read front to back as a serial of visual facets of the South Fork of Long Island, and that, at the end, one will have experienced the kind of guided tour of the region only poets could lead.

Robert Long
September 1986
East Hampton

6

Contents

Introduction   5

PHILIP APPLEMAN   11
Westhampton Cemetery   12
The Tennis Player Waits for What Waits for the Tennis
   Player   14
Red Kite   14
East Hampton: The Structure of Sound   15

JANE AUGUSTINE
Anti-Cycle for the New Year   17
The Stars   20

GEORGE BRADLEY
Walking Sag Beach   23
Six of One   26

EDWARD BUTSCHER
After Great Pain   29
At Play in the Field   30
Middle Age Summer   31
Hand Lane: Literature   32
Cleaning the Garage   32

MARYANN CALENDRILLE
Black Mail   35
In the Big Country Dreams Stay Alive   36
See Jane Run   37
Tomorrow in a Bubble   37
New Moon, or No?   39

SIV CEDERING
On This Shore   41
On Some Such Morning   42
Sea Drift   44
Fata Morgana   45

GRAHAM EVERETT
Pulling the Days Together   48
Early May   49
Day/Night   49
Near Thanksgiving   50
January   50
Families at the Shore   51
Here   51

BARBARA GUEST
Clouds Near the Windmill   53
Sag Harbor, the Tchekov Letters   54
Lawn Bumps   55
Hohenzollern   58
from Wave (ii and iii)   59

MICHAEL HELLER
At Albert's Landing   63
On the Beach   65
Two Swans in a M̲ ᵼdow by the Sea   67
Coral Stanzas   068

DAVID IGNATOW
A Cloud Creates   69
Behind His Eyes   70
My Own House   71
from Leaving the Door Open:
  #1   71
  #31   72
Respected Graves   73
Autumn   73
Little Friend   74

YAEDI IGNATOW
The Offer   76
Blackout into Sunlight   76
Equations   77
Forest   77
Limbo   78
Praise   79

KENNETH KOCH
The Boiling Water   81
Fate   87

NAOMI LAZARD
Walking with Lulu in the Wood   92
Stray Dogs   93
Stepping Out with My Big Cats   94
The Angels Among Us   95

HOWARD MOSS
The Long Island Night   99
Bay Days   100
In Traffic   101
Notes from the Castle   102
Aspects of Lilac   103

STANLEY MOSS
Homing   106
Clouds   107
Potato Song   108
Clams   109
The Seagull   109
The Meeting   110
The Branch   111

DAN MURRAY
June   114
July   115
August   115
Theory   116
Passamaquoddy Sunrise   116
Constellation: Rorschach   117

ANSELM PARLATORE
Mecox Motel   120
Mecox Nunnery & Saint Dominic   121
Woman of the Late Fall Run   122
Portrait in Veiled Waters   123

SIMON PERCHIK
"The pale stone . . ."   127
"Like a warden . . ."   129
"I should wear gloves . . ."   130
"The mirror . . ."   131

ALLEN PLANZ
Woodknot   133
Mako   134
Scalloping Northwest   135
Midwinter   135
Inquiline   136

ANNE PORTER
In a Country Hospital   139
Leavetaking   140
On the Three Hour Train Ride   141
Four Poems in One   142

FAIRFIELD PORTER
The Reader   145
The Morning Train   146
September   146
At Night   147
A Painter Obsessed by Blue   148

9

GRACE SCHULMAN
Blessed is the Light   151
Easy as Wind   152
The Marsh   152
The Swans   153
Images of Gravity   153
The Island   155
Songs of Our Cells   156

JAMES SCHUYLER
Empathy and New Year   158
Poem   161
In January   161
The sky eats up the trees   162

ARMAND SCHWERNER
Tablet IX   165
Tablet XXIII   167
Tablet XXV   168

HUGH SEIDMAN
Eurydice   171
Albert's Landing   173
O Tree   173
The Immortal   174

HARVEY SHAPIRO
At the Shore   178
July   179
Battlements   179
Riding Westward   180
Montauk Highway   181
The Bridge   181

R. B. WEBER
Peconic Autumn Day   184
November. Over the Hills   184
late   autumn   afternoons   185
Weathers   185
ocean beach house   186
Behind these lids   186
August dusk: Sag Harbor   187

Notes on Contributors   188

© 1980 Thomas Victor

PHILIP APPLEMAN

Living and Writing on Long Island

My wife and I are both native Hoosiers, and I've taught for thirty years at Indiana University; but fifteen years ago the magnetic tug of Long Island caught us both, and we've been coming here ever since, renting houses for a summer or a year at a time in Amagansett, Northport, West Hampton, Sag Harbor, and East Hampton. Now we've built our own house on the ocean beach at Sagaponack and are here most of the time, year-round. It's a long weekly commute from the eastern tip of Long Island to my job in Bloomington, but fortunately not an impossible one.

Places always work their way into my poems: Indiana maple trees and limestone quarries; New York City's cheery hassle; and out here the wild swans in the sound, gulls on the bay, bluefish in a feeding frenzy, gravestones

11

weathered by two hundred years of salt air, stately lawns, beaches and tennis cousrts. The images that constantly cross the eye eventually cross the page.

But more important to me as a poet are the writers who live here or gather here in the summer. The first person to call us when we arrived in 1970 was Galen Williams, who asked us over to meet her husband, Bill Cole, and Michael and Eleanor Goldman, and later David and Rose Ignatow, who took us to see Si and Mickey Perchik—and so on, until, in the course of a few weeks, we'd met this whole nest of singing birds.

Some writers may like isolation; I prefer the company of other writers, artists, and editors, people who speak a familiar language, whose work interests me, and who are both keen and generous in their comments on my own writing. I learn from them and I enjoy that learning. In that respect, Bloomington and Sagaponack are not so different: I learn from my friends wherever I live. That's more important to me than the difference between Indiana robins and Long Island seagulls.

Westhampton Cemetery

founded 1795

for Jim and Tanya

No place for elegies, in these stern
stones, bleached
by the misty light that haloes gulls
and weathers the gray shingles
of the Hamptons—no elegies, but grace:
   Blessed are the dead
   which die in the Lord: my flesh
   will rest in hope.
No place for elegies in this austere
devotion to joy, the faith
of the departed:
   They do not die nor lose

their mortal sympathy,
nor change to us, although
they change.
No elegies for Mehitable, wife
of Enoch Jagger, died
1799 in the twenty-fifth
year of her age;
for Warren Goodall, drowned at Fire Island,
1832;
for Jennie McCue, died 1871,
agred three years, nine days—no
elegies, but grace:
   Precious in the sight of the Lord
   is the death of His Saints: we sorrow not
   as those which have no hope.

But for the backs that wearied out
these scars in the pale earth,
and for sailors at the aching capstans,
for fishermen scanning
the ashy sky—elegies,
yes, for all
of these—for bonneted girls
stooping till sundown in the itch
of potato fields, new widows walking their roofs
for the overdue whalers,
maids in the faded Hamptons
staring at hope chests—elegies,
chiseled in mossy stone:
   From sorrow, toil and pain
   and sin we shall be free.
This misty light is an elegy
for the living:
bleaching our blood to water,
scaling our bone to chalk,
fading every morning song
to the minor of farewell.

The Tennis Player Waits for What Waits for the Tennis Player

In the slippery swelter of asphalt,
in a blistering backhand return,
you wait every June, every August
for that stabbing of fate in the elbow,
that first sharp knifing of fact;
and because it comes with a certain
smug angle of the sun,
and because it comes with a bird
turning transparent as truth,
and because it comes with a cry
like preaching in the wind—
you know you are becoming
one of the pure, pale
Others; and you call back
all the grubby friends
of childhood, and command them
to surround your skin with singing.

Red Kite

Onto that long snowing of sand
the sea had nudged another derelict,
red as the rising sun in smog, and sheer
as butterflies, kite string and all,
ready to fly.
And it would have been a perfect
gift from the green tide, if
I hadn't, that day, in the idle-
ness of beaches, chucked
a stone at a silver
foraging fish—
and hit him, dead
center.
He leaped,

in a twisting flash of belly-white
so much like human pain I caught my breath
an ugly moment—then
the fish swam on, as graceful as before.
It was only that one
numbing
moment,
the terrible lifetime wait
as the fishflash in the air
meant quick or dead—how can I put it—
annihilation
hung there in the wind,
and a kite from the sea bled
red pain across the sky.

East Hampton: The Structure of Sound

Bedrooms ease their shingles
into the yawning gardens:
the silence sucks at my eardrums
and my skull flowers open like popcorn.
Perpetual Sunday morning:
the quiet spreads out like a meadow.
I loaf and invite my soul,
and it sprawls in the shade like a toadstool.

Mondays, Manhattan is shapely
in the perfect circles of sirens,
the shrill music of taxis
making symmetries, patterns, and bounds:
jackhammers chisel my brain
to correct community standards
as the dawn comes up like thunder
out of Brooklyn, the shaper of sunrise.

15

JANE AUGUSTINE

The Sea, the East End and My Poems

The east end of Long Island, especially in its quiet wintry guise, is the locus of my writing, quite simply because I do my writing here. The little house off Three Mile Harbor Road near Maidstone beach which Michael Heller and I have shared for years and have rehabilitated together is our home—for me the place I feel most *at* home and settled in, as distinct from our New York city apartment, which is a transportation hub, the point I take off from. East Hampton therefore makes me think of other homes, with my children in my first marriage, and my childhood by San Francisco bay, whose ocean fogs carry the same salty whiff that comes in with the mist from the Amagansett shore. At home here both coziness and spa-

16

ciousness feed my memory and meditation; a fireplace
helps as much as oakwoods and a vista over the bay. I live
in the East Hampton without tourists; though its summer
green is lush and gorgeous, its everyday life of work, of
fishing and boats, water and sky is what lures me. My
poems are my everyday work, in so far as possible, the
work of going both more deeply and more widely into the
human condition which perches precariously between air
and earth.

Anti-Cycle for the New Year

(i)

Dark days,
    thin snow on the roofs

graying, he described me

      too long a mother:

        no cycle
of return to
    before that

(ii)

Light snow on the airfield
   —take it lightly

the great engines grind

    lift my sons off
      our common ground

    in a long curve
      opening

(iii)

Poets praise motherhood
    especially
    if they are fathers

and move on to
    less burdened women

    no new start for me;
    only the old

effort to juggle loss
      against
        the continual gift

    wrapped in tissue
    that gets thrown away

(iv)

I strip the tree whose little lights
the shivering tinsel multiplied—
hopes, joys

When I was a child I thought I'd die
after Christmas. I thought rightly:
nothing ahead but comedown

I lit a tree for my sons, who fly
east, who will wing back my way,
but it's not my symbol

this cut convention drying in a corner,
seduction clung to—
           now I lean
towards plain day. I stand

at its uncurtained window

(v)

Pity these cycles
beginning again:

the woman betrayed by lovers
will once more encounter brutes;

18

connoisseurs who find little to suit
their tastes will find less;
the writer of radical protest
will find the middle class more obtuse;
the taciturn poet at parties
will find the girls mute—

all will come beg me to tell them
they're right because they are wronged

and my cycle starts. I'll be drawn
into murmuring sympathy—yes,
I support your plausible lie:
external forces exist
and are vicious—
                    again I'll be drawn
into failing to say what I know
what I constantly say to myself
as a charm against panic
    the world's selfmade
    observe! observe!

                    (vi)
The long curve of the year
    empties

We're out of bread:
    must get more
    at the I.G.A.
    —they're out of our brand
        and the price is higher

Supplies come through
    on odd timetables

We rotate on a bent
    axle-tree
    —thus the Sahara
        once a polar icecap

you can see the bend itself
    on the non-stop jet
    to California

19

the mind in its long passage
      over the winter Rockies

  its momentary lights
    a pattern
    on the night airfield:

gray snow

going back to water

The Stars

              (i)
In the mind's midnight
the fixed stars ride

tonight I gaze at the space
between them

              (ii)
a red star invisible
until it falls—

and then for a moment
flaring

I long to see it stay
—a comet, a signal—

but only its exploding gave it
that luminous trail

of fire

              (iii)
at midnight
two darknesses:

confusion
and illimitable space

in the west
a star-sickle to slash through;

overhead the dipper
swings from Arcturus' peg

pours out what it
cannot contain

what does not
contain it

(iv)

in the northeast burns
yellow-white Capella
star of the first magnitude

in the meadow grass
its slow imitator
ignites   goes out   goes on

(v)

o stars you live in the dark
as I do

I lie down on the bony ground
to stare up

my body letting go—

o diamonds fall into my eyes
become my seeing

clear and indestructible

© T. Charles Erickson

GEORGE BRADLEY

Writing about Long Island's South Fork came as a conscious decision on my part. Place, of course, is fertile ground for poetry, and especially for American poetry. The psychological freight carried by a location—the geological and historical record embodied by a landscape—is often large enough to be a subject in itself, and whatever the subject, landscape makes a good beginning. Until fairly recently, though, I had found foreign places more receptive to treatment than the places I was more at home in. I suppose that in landscape, too, I prefer the poetry of hypothesis. It was reading other poems about Long Island that prompted my own. I found, naturally, that you don't have to go very far afield to move into the unknown. An examination of even the most familiar facts and features becomes an abstraction in no time at all.

Walking Sag Beach

1.

It's never exactly itself, the beach,
For all its aura of eternity,
Its infinite sands and unceasing waves,
Never an impassive instant unmoved.
The obdurate end of Montauk Point, thrust
Like an accusing gesture out into
The gigantic motion of the Gulf Stream,
Is ground imperceptibly into grains
The currents distribute with largesse
Over several hundred miles of coast.
From Napeague to Nags Head, the shoreline twists
And twitches on the continental shelf
Like rivulets against a windowpane,
A serpentine saga of shifting bars,
Of lots washed away, to the great distress
Of real estate agents and frustration
Of Army engineers, as the best laid
Bulwarks come undone of a winter's eve;
And so if Sag Beach remains a landscape
We identify as home—the grand curve
The shore takes towards Wainscot in the east,
The long march west to New York City's smog,
Its nightly nimbus and daily haze—still
What we recognize, year on year, is change.

2.

From June to August, as the weather wills,
An ocean of humanity will swell
This shore; turned out in tricot triangles,
Symbolic fig leaves fit for paradise
On earth, the gamut of generations
Comes to celebrate an old religion:
Sunshine and the body's enlightenment,
Complete immersion in the acts of life.
A girl offers her breasts up to the sky

23

As old men, living vicariously
On the heat, shift their seat and shade their eyes;
Small children run in circles, and a dog
Digs in the sand, while lovers hand in hand
Stroll by on parade; mothers call the kids
For sandwiches and soda; someone shouts,
Someone bats a ball, someone flies a kite.
All summer long the crowd proclaims the rites
Of spring, basking in its own contentment,
Dining at the table of idle hours
While nature's little sword of Damocles,
The nesting tern, cries murder overhead,
And schools of frenzied fish consume their way
Through regions of delicate light and shade,
A site of bitter draughts and foundered dreams,
The restless medium in which we wade.

3.

Walking along the water's edge, the world,
Or parts of it, comes to our feet, as bright
Bits of plastic, a lobster pot, skate eggs,
A doll's head rocked up from the ocean's arms,
A rusted oil drum, one oar, shark's teeth,
Nylon line, unbiodegradable
Shards of styrofoam, a broken bottle
Worn smooth as stone in the tumbling shingle,
A horseshoe crab, a toy boat, shells, bones, weeds,
Detritus from all walks and swims of life,
Are chewed like a cud in the churning sea,
Turned like thoughts, and then regurgitated,
Spat up like Jonah salvaged from the deep,
Strewn in evidence anyone may read,
That we and what made us and what we make
Are grist to a mill, curious remains,
Flotsam bobbed off from some colossal wreck.
Who ever found himself beside the sea,
Ever heard its muffled drumbeat or watched
Its vast expanse stretch miles away beneath
An empty heaven, without suffering

His own alteration, discovering
Leviathan in a dogfish, himself
Annihilated in a burst of spray?

4.

Though the beach appears sheer desolation,
The sun and sand a desert by DeMille,
And though the sea, bearer of so much life,
Can't bear ours, yet this contiguity
Of *mer* and *terre* is where the comedy
Of living is carried out in earnest,
The biological hysteria
At its most acute in confrontation;
Where opposites react, where volcanoes
Boil up from the waves and coral reefs add
Their small increments to geography,
In borders, frontiers, no-man's-land, where
Elemental forces meet and move, there
Something forms, something grows out of itself,
Becomes a particular in process,
An aspect of enormous spectacle.
So the sage in us would have us see it,
And so we would see ourselves, as partial
To this sun, part and parcel to this sea.
A beach is a quandary, food for thought;
Our desert spaces are interior,
Wasted space of small possibility,
Death Valleys of moribund conception.

5.

Walk to the step-off on Sag Beach and you
Have reached a place where you cannot proceed,
Where you are offered endless evasions
On each hand, but of progress make no more
Than you could make walking the ocean floor
Or waving your arms to fly off to Spain.
There comes the point where you go no further,
Where you reach the end of your world, alone
As the last man must someday be, with space

25

Soaring off to the distant horizon
And all that color floating in your brain—
Azure, cerulean, gun-metal blue—
As if the sea and sky sluiced right through you,
Poured into your eyes with a pounding sound
Like breakers crashing in over the bar,
As if you could feel an ocean sweeping
Your mind as the sea does this crumbling shore,
Shifting your configuration, bearing
You away and adding chance accretions,
Changing you once and forever and yet
Leaving you recognizably the same,
The way the beach seems the same one morning
When you come to see what the night has done,
Come to stand awhile in the undertow
And gaze again off into nothingness,
Left with hardly a thought to call your own,
With the breeze and cries of the birds, filled
As if with waves by ideas of the sea.

Six of One

Of course, it may well be that the mind is of finite
Capacity as it is of finite space, so that
There comes a time when it will not hold any more
And whatever facts, figures, and nagging thoughts
We continue to cram into it, what with night-school
And the learning of something new every day,
Must be balanced, must be given room enough,
And that this is what the meticulous mechanism
Of memory and its forgetfulness is for.
In this event, all the subconscious area left over,
The millions of brain cells swarming and hiving,
Buzzing like bees under summer sun, occupies itself
With things that can't quite be called thoughts,
Things like emotions, like interminable boredom,
Sitting vast in the mind but too vacuous to be

An idea, instead just a gesture, or a sort of sense,
And therefore is the piece of mind given to thought
A mere fraction of the whole, more like a baseball,
Probably, than a melon, i.e. we haven't really
Come all that far since the days of the dinosaur,
Terrible lizard. It would stand to reason, then,
That the precious little bundle of nerves is crucial,
That increments of intelligence make worlds of
   difference,
But in truth our own discrepancies don't matter much,
Since the professor may be absent-minded, the idiot
May be a savant, and since many of us are dumb-lucky
Or too smart for our own good. Thus, although no one
Seriously believes it of himself, all of us are born
Equal to one another more than we know and equal
To little else, neither the love of women, held
In the tremulous hands like something fragile, nor
The love of language, words turned on the tongue;
And thus the poem arises out of a chance accumulation,
Out of a mind that perhaps achieved optimum content
Months or even years ago, say one morning in winter
When the sky was so blue and steam rose off the ocean
Into the other element of air.

© Linda Chen

EDWARD BUTSCHER

With painful candor, Wallace Stevens complains somewhere that places always meant more than people to him,
which tends to confirm, I think, the basic narcissism and its
bottom void of insecurity that generates art. For the poet,
place is essential. It is no accident that I have passed most
of my life in Flushing, Queens, where I was born and
raised. Nor is it an accident that I have adjusted so readily
to the East End, since the area replicates, in village am-
bience and New England architecture, the Flushing I once
knew (or imagined) as a child.

As for the impact on my poetry, it is there, of course,
ready fodder for ravenous lyric machinery, especially in a
sense of the past restored and the past under siege by
urban imperatives. Our move to Amagansett ten years ago
led directly to *Amagansett Cycle*, which structures its lyric
versions of a divided self upon the natural carnage and

historic perspective the town offers. In addition, as "After
Great Pain" suggests, a chunk of my heart is now buried
out here, taking possession of our roots.

After Great Pain

The path dividing the old cemetery
is straight and neat until it curves
out of sight, reverses field,
leaving as it began,

the hole by the side of the road
equally true to its rectangle self,
despite the wheel of hunched figures
violating shaft space,

a pine planted every so many feet
with a regularity that fences out
the backyard chaos where children
scream for milk and freedom,

when the casket is placed on green
straps (vectored by a silver frame),
cold cherry wood stroked slick enough
to slide off the sun's back.

The small crowd sags and sways and smear
salt lips before resuming a ragged arc
around the rabbi and his anchor book,
keening *Kaddish* in tongues.

After a hidden machine gently denies
swellings of narrow secrets without
smoke or surprise, fists of unsure dirt
strike hard, shatter the last

ceremony we may impose upon a scene
where composition must always rule,
the retreat down a mourner aisle

hurried as a bride's escape.

At Play in the Field

The lawn-mower had only three wheels
and stumbled, now and then,
into treacherous patches
of sand that scabbed
the entire backyard.

I loved the fingers of sweat that
slid under my unhinged shirt,
tickled my heaving chest
as I pretended to labor
like a farmer.

On the porch step, sagging in rain,
I witness myself, hands full
of cats, staggering across grass
with drunken self-indulgence,
an obese stranger.

When machines die, if not carted off
in the night, they often refuse
to yield their private parts
to fire, field, or flood,
gaunt in their
own image.

I remember lying on top of a big girl
across my grandmother's neat bed,
hands searching endless leaves
for swells of snow, bloody
underbrush between us
like porcine springs.

Breath slows, at last, to a monotone,
flanks of down at rest against cold
callouses, and the field is dis-
assembled,
                becomes a puddle
of savage scarlet.

Edward Butscher

Middle Age Summer

I freed the pampered shoots from plastic cells,
pale roots still squared and wet,
then fingered, patted them
gently into place,
boxed anew
like a bonsai tree
or an Oriental girl child
straining for a fiery breast,
where light divides itself
into a balance
of blindnesses,
leap after leap, paint peeling
off the whale sky
in strips
of white excess.

I planted marigolds in the highest sun,
lemon drops and honeycombs,
my sweat and brain
in exact accord
for once,
naked hands spading deep
again and again
(on my knees)
to cup and overturn
the rich black bottom
of grave and bed,
where relics
of old couplings
have long since slept.

I dug much deeper than the marigolds demanded
until Italian soil was breeched, its rusty
amulets rubbed for luck before
discarded: Hamlet's marble
skull, dense and smooth,
and a baby sister's
lithe skeleton (light as a web)

31

pinwheeling
into raucous gulls overhead
that center all darkness:

my hands cannot hold them,
save them, hardening
under their loss
into the fall.

Hand Lane: Literature

At the lip of the abstract
where a chrome sky
sheds arsenic
grins
    against backless space,

I seem myself:

what lolls (tongue-lewd)
among folds of corpulent foliage
when her loins have forked oceans,
unyielding while yielding:

what stiffens inside her,
entering its own grave
to cannon
      a cloud
          across the moon
              like a scar.

Cleaning the Garage

Another season come and gone,
another scene shifted beyond sight
as I lift the picnic table into light
and watch sullen spider eggs

gasp for breath, an end
to the crystal chains
coupling predator
and prey.

The clouds explode under my broom
in ominous cones that announce
the advance of victim armies,
flakes of fly wings, husks
of dismembered angles
scattered in ticker
tape at my feet,
dancing down
ice stairs.

Sweaty and happy when the floor
lies white and bare before me at last,
frozen into a stage for absent
witches to shadow, lawn
furniture paling in spring
air, arms and legs taut
as Tudor kings caught
at the neap tide
of stone.

I swing the head free of its stick
body and pretend the Babe has returned,
launching myself at a high curve
ball with exaggerated style
that collapses the realm
where fall never fails,
tasting dust ashes,
the wooden O's
our father loved
too well.

© Carle Gravey

MARYANN CALENDRILLE

Living the Life of Luxury

A person can jot down a poem almost anywhere: while waiting along with 20 other people, shopping carts chock full, behind the only cashier on duty at the A&P at 5:30 p.m.; while trawling for bluefish on a very slow day on Gardiner's Bay; while sweating out the summer in a tiny fourth floor walk-up in New York's Hell's Kitchen.

I've done it in these places but perhaps have done it best while sitting quietly behind a humming typewriter: the sun setting brilliantly on the pond outside my window, the wind blowing lightly. I've noticed the absence of screaming ambulances, traffic noise, radios. Here, where it's quiet enough to hear myself think, I feel my best work gets done. (I also find it productive to maintain a positive attitude about the place in which I live.)

It's this quiet, backed by the rushing ocean, colored by seasonal geese, suffused with the white haze of sun off the water, that sets the gears in motion, that establishes a rhythm. Here there is space enough to concentrate unimpeded by steel and glass and cement structures towering over your cranium already crushed by the incessant chatter of a million voices, although those ingredients cook up another kind of inspiration.

But here, the rolling farm land, dunes, waves, help draw a poem out, pull the imagination one stanza further in long islands of thought.

Black Mail

This letter, a cold wind in August says she's dead.
Those days lost like rare wine gone rancid.
She writes from a country of shattered moons
Where blades of grass ooze drops of blood,
Where air's too thick to breathe.
She opens the holes in her dress:
Blue steam pours through,
Ribs bang like shutters in a storm.

The one clue she left, a bit of fingernail,
I see it fits my own hand. A spot
Where the ink swam loose silhouettes
The pigeon-toed girl we tied to a bush
Her tears, her almond eyes.
Our mothers called and we raced up the hill
Screaming a small fear from our lungs.

With wet hair pressed flat to my head
Like a hand holding back a river
I run down steps that domino behind me.
Her face turns to ash as fast
As a summer sky turns thunderous.
I leave the house, its blossoming flames.
The wind pulls a voice from my throat,
A voice that burns your name on my tongue.

In The Big Country Dreams Stay Alive

In the dark swarming the past sits on a log,
Slips into a puddle I kick a pebble into
An owl lifts the shadow from my back.
Car lights along the lake drive
X-ray my legs. We're closed
Says the voice of the road
And all the cab doors, elevator gates
And revolving hotel entrances swing silence
On all the times I've been through them,
Tagging after you or leaving you behind.

These are fairly young woods of stunted oak
Already wind bent and rooted in damp sand.
Blueberries and sumac above the twelve foot
Pond full of murky clumps, turtles
And currents of deafening blue bands
That years and years of weed wave through.

Last summer floated our patched raft past midnight
Sails when at least my arms hung mosquito bait
And yours draped through the dripping sky
Motioning toward some far-off catch
Some unexpected bird song or thought
Just beyond my finger almost reaching your toe.

These nights, frog cries, dirges from the swamp
Animate our dark rooms, call out our names
As tiny stars pop in the sky. Your eyelids,
The undersides of beach shells, close.
Now ready for the nights of wolf chase
Or the meeting with the brother you never knew.

See Jane Run

The combo of velvet and vanilla proved dangerous.
I could see the stars were sick.
A black muck at night smells like her hair,
Sticks to my feet. The window glows
Like a gown she wore, slick and blue.
Dark sheets. She'd say no more.

In her house, there are no chairs
Just arms, golden and stringy like honey.
I wear flannel, pull her close to my heart
Feel a water fountain gurgling inside my skin.
She twists my ear, some kind of handle.
Drowning in sweat, I'm deaf to all but fish melodies.

She broke this town's back. Left us with something
We couldn't fix. A blonde humor goes cold fast.
Bob pulls his weight around like a dog,
A lounge chair, a busted dream no one sweeps up.
He presses himself between streets looking for her
Some old-boy talk, religious adventure.

I swam in her hair, left my wallet on the bus
Past the diner she worked. Swivel stools
Shining like her teeth, spinning like her hips.
Her kiss rode a breath of Budweiser.

Godiva this, Godiva that. I dip my fingers in her skin
Sharp as a pineapple. I'd walk through monsoons to see
    her.
The price of wanting. Tranquil as quinine,
See Jane slip through the glass.

Tomorrow in a Bubble

You sashay in in summer whites
As I'm about to leave cinema verite.
Our shoes tangle a few paces ahead of ourselves

Perhaps off screen in a quiet dark place
Where I'm sure you'll tell me all I want to hear
And I'll blow the secret that's been eating me for weeks.

But the adrenalin rush is so great
It flings me off camera, awake
Staring at the ceiling, at the note you left
Half in French, half hopeful.

How anyone could possibly live
Three miles from Versailles I'll never know,
But I want to live there with you, naked
On a crushed velvet sofa
While you breakfast, butter and tea
Leaf the Italian ski magazines
With the ingenue rubbing her eyes.

I've inventoried your khakis, corduroys, boxer shorts:
White with fields of tiny green clover.
The faded polo shirts, your blue book bag.
I've traced every feather of conversation
Landing on my hair, earring, or breast
For a clue to follow you on a dare.

Through my monstrously clumsy breath
Your footsteps silent in the hall,
This is a love song to the one
I've never seen before, and probably never will:
The train I'm on is late
And your plane took off 15 minutes ago.
Now that ocean, swelling between our toes.

To the one who won't claim each raised eyebrow,
Each upward tilting sentence,
"This is the way the Americans do it, no?"

No, that's not it at all. We're all aliens
With a sore spot like the one you hit, Bingo!
Smack on the kisser. With one smile too many
I only meant to hook you, then throw you back.
I'm casting into an empty pool of sunlight.
The way your eyes shine:
That's what I want to remember.

New Moon or No?

With shining certainty, the smallest pressure,
Your fate is sealed behind her face. Beyond recall.
Speak seriously to her, feel safe.
The purpose of morning she agrees
Shows no symptoms but a very catching figure.

We speak of her only among friends
Listening and wondering. Always
The satisfaction of gazing at lovely shoulders.
The small thought that returns again and again
Like the chorus between swift acts.

Someday when you say goodbye to this body
Your purpose will be called perfect vision.
In a dream you will lick the wet lips of heaven.

Meanwhile, the bold spill of the future is on your tongue.
Here, everyone is a holiday.
She sends you to Paradise
Yet you don't like the wallpaper.
You want perfume, the sun
Rising in all the unexpected places.

What gets lost in translation
Is that the world is better than both of you.
And it's here to stay.
Rain will come like a blessing:
Citrus and spice, a common inspiration.
The fortune teller marries the mailman
But you miss the wedding, off
On ideal travel. How foolish can you be?
Left in Paradise and looking for the way out.

SIV CEDERING

Did I begin to write poems with a seascape after I moved to the East End of Long Island or did I move here because of the seascapes growing in my poems? Perhaps I can dismiss the chicken and egg question by stating that I believe a person who has known and loved one landscape has it within herself to transfer that attachment to another kind of landscape.

Born inland, by the Arctic Circle in Sweden, it might seem strange that I feel at home by the Amagansett shore and in the small villages out here, and that my new poems have adopted a coastal landscape. "On This Shore," which refers to an ocean crossing by a balloon that ascended from The Springs, was written before I moved out here. So was "Fata Morgana," which is set on a mythic shore. But my new work is made of real waves and real sand, dune grass and scallop shells.

Not until I recently was asked if the landscape has influenced my writing did I realize that it had. The word *topic* comes from the Greek word for *place*. Maybe this is the reason why the landscape that surrounds me surfaces in my work, perhaps not as topic, but as the embodiment of the spirit that insists that the poem becomes a poem.

On This Shore

Listen.
It is by this
shore
that the loon
whistles.

It is from this
shore
that the ball
floated
away,
and the child
followed.

It is above this
shore
that the balloon
drifted:
Oh, that colorful, joyous
flight of the aeronauts,
waving from the basket,
to then sink
miles off shore
and out of sight
on a night
when the sky was starless
and the equally starless sea
opened its arms
as if to forgive
everything.

Human sacrifice
is
old-fashioned.
We feel no need
to appease
the elements.
But the sea accepts
each offering
like old folks
who open their arms
to that prodigal
child. Disasters
are blamed on
the stars.

And we who walk
on this shore
are not more
aware
than any other couple
who happens to stop,
pick up a shell,
a polished piece
of glass,
a ball

and to point out
the loon, disappearing
in the deep
to reappear
again,
           and again.

On Some Such Morning

On some such morning
when the lake is only reflection,
a boy will come down to the shore

untie a small boat, climb in,
push out, and begin
to row.

Proud of his skill
he will let the oars fall
rhythmically, like wings,
as he moves out
across the clouds
leaving only the wake
that will still to be clouds
again.

On some such morning,
a man will come down to the lake
to see only some bird
breaking the reflection,
while he calls and keeps
calling, as the morning turns to afternoon,
and afternoon
to evening.

On some such morning, afternoon,
or evening,
when doves call and keep
calling,
a man will be dreaming.
The woman beside him
will feel his eyelids
flutter,

and in her half-sleep
she will not know
if it is her own heart, that of
a bird, or some breast feathers
ruffling.

And she will turn. Her hand will fall
against his chest, where someone is
rowing, rhythmically,
and someone is
calling.

Sea-Drift

On the first warm day,
when both the front door and the storm door
are left casually ajar
without thought of conserving fuel,
and the storm windows on the south wall are taken down,
and the Windex is out,
and a pile of old newspapers is waiting on the stoop,
and the chickadees are scattering the odor
of sun-warmed pine,
she takes the folded aluminum chair,
that has hung on a nail, all winter long,
and walks down the cement block stairs
to the strip of sand
that spans the narrow slope between ebb and tide.

She unbuttons her blouse at the neck,
rolls up the sleeves, sees a blue heron light
on the mud flat!—and that quick white flitting
with the sharp cry must be the supposedly shy
roseate tern already back! She adjusts
her chair, brushes back a strand of hair,
pulls up her skirt so the thin, white skin
of her knees can feel the sun.

In the shallows, diagonal lines of light
knot their flickering nets
over scallop shells, razor clams, the absurd scuttling
of an old crab.
What had she said, once upon a time, about swimming
out into the cold, when she grew old, out beyond
the surf, her strength, to grow numb, overcome
by some benign fatigue, to simply sink in the sea-drift,
a gentle accident, well-planned, executed
while she still could use her will, not to end
tied to a wheel-chair in a nursing home, half-blind,
or in a hospital bed, hooked to a tangle

of tubes? She unties
her shoes, places them neatly, side by side,
beside the chair on the beach, takes off her socks

44

and rolls them up into a ball, thinking
the swallows will soon be back under the eaves,
and the beach plum bushes will bloom, and the wild roses
on the dune.

The sand feels warm under her bare feet.
Even the water in the shallows has been heated
by the sun. Minnows scatter as she steps in
and laughs, feeling like a child on the first day of
summer, before knowing how to swim, standing
with a sand bucket and a new shovel,
ready for the splashing to begin,
while the still nameless birds
announce their return with
their crying, their song.

Fata Morgana

This is the Strait of Messina.
The images rise. They are real.
Castles in the air are inhabited.
The reflected evening light spills
Over windowsills. At dusk
Someone touches a light switch here
Or there, and vertical checkerboards,
With squares randomly lit, rise
In the night. What fool would dare
To explain the rules, or determine
Who is queen and who is knight?

This very tree, this very field,
The very woods beyond, all so richly
Green, on a summer day, are soft grey
In the morning. How could this be
So, if we believe in what we know?
Green is green. If we believe in
What we see, this very tree, this
Very field, the very woods beyond
Pull loose and rise, to float

Above the ground. What is the sound
Of an explanation? The line of vision

Bends. Distant lands appear or
Disappear. Who is the one viewing
The island we are floating on? Tell me,
Are we still below the horizon?
The color of your eyes is constant.
The answer to the question about hands
Is touch. Stay near. There is much
I do not understand. Though I do not
Fear the changes, I must know them
In your hair, your skin. The tide is
Coming in. Let's go down to see

The sun lose its roundness, grow
Squat and set, its reddest lip upon
The horizon—or observe the familiar
Disk breaking apart, one section rising;
The other slipping into the ocean
(A common illusion, this time of evening)
While we discuss some version of this little
Life and the baseless fabric of our vision.

© Elyse Arnow

GRAHAM EVERETT

My primal landscape, like the island's, is a topographical mix. There's the snap and crash of a tough oak broken across a hurricane-torn road, its sandy berm a signature. How frozen potatoes popped under our boots as we winter-trekked over countless furrows to the woods hunting rabbit and deer. How once inside these woods the light shone in cathedral-like shafts. Younger, we learned about our bodies in other woods—the far side of huge rows of blueberry bushes behind bulldozed oak and bramble. We danced naked on that palatial earth.

I recall a pasture, rye-green rolling where sheep once grazed. A ram lurked in centerfield of a 1957 summer baseball game, ready to butt our butts. Sheep-dung, sun-dried and kicked into heaps, marked the bases.

Later, having moved further east, we did sneak into the

47

chicken house and left eggshells hollow in the hens' nests.
Our poachers' jars filled with scrambled yolk and white.
More than once we stood wide-eyed before a bull and cow
rutting in a dawn-lit barn, our nostrils filled with pungent
dampness.

Another farmer, living closer to town, raised pigs. The
spring squeal of baby pigs getting fixed went on a day and
a night. Once, a bunch of castrated piglets died. They
weren't properly sulphured, or carefully cauterized. A crying I think I can still hear.

As this landscape finishes vanishing, singularities keep
occurring. A pond persists where a road was built, slowing
traffic each time it rains. How on foggy nights the old
houses dream themselves filled again with light and laughter . . .

Today, we have the landscape of the new island. The
spots of beauty—small and easily missed—hold on, sure of
something progress can not guarantee. I continue to mine
these spots, the ground under our feet, treading these
neighborhood sidewalks, the lost paths of this island's mor-
ained hills, as best as I can.

Pulling the Days Together

After our talking about trees,
how different they were last October,
how they make spring's wind visible
we walk thru bud and blossom, stopping
to note locust thorn, pine sap
or how downslope they lean uphill
growing sunward, fallen or steadfast.

Yesterday, on the cooler shadow-side
beech stayed wrapped in tight gold brown,
days behind oak and maple's abundance.

Come twilight, beneath leafy eyelet,
delicate in near full moon light,
we return midwood. A grape vine
lets us swing   thru clear air
—a moment,   hanging

Baiting Hollow, 1978

Early May

 Down the road nuclear protestors rally.
We're caught in our saturday chores—
nowhere to run. Evening, already
night
the garden   unplanted.

 That moon rising
holds the sky in eerie twilight zone blue. Young oaks
slow dance. That moon shrinks
smaller   the higher it rises
its incestuous grin a vernal high-tide.

 Under this moon the landscape is
bright enough to walk around in
—soon it'll be warmer and the neigh-
borly thing to do.

Day/Night

These mornings when Matisse
paints the sky his way
and someone with fog
is off by the woods—

tree and brush and field
are sprung green, caught

by yellow or definite gold.

Driving gets dangerous
the road swerves,
        near the shore
seasons pulse
all kinds of stars
            fade,   flare.

Near Thanksgiving

        Northwind whittles the last acorns down
out on the roadways streetlights, houselights
and such are wintersharp—this crispness
a sure sign of solar shift
and the rains that come

shower all leaf colors to the ground,
even yellow turns brown.

Late into the quiet of country night
thoughts of one hundred megaton soot
clog the air and alter the outcome
of a once recurring dream.

The third-quarter moon, mid-sky and
setting fast, brightens the rain
dropped leaves   driftless on front lawns.

January

Dumping hot coal ash
and what feels like warm breeze
skirts the windchill.
How short these minutes
out under winter stars,
ground covered with snow
iced over a week.

My city-friends, not knowing
cabin-fever, say they
envy all this. They grow
chilled to the bells ringing cross
county long before the chimes dim.

Families at the Shore

Dad is never first in, yet
swims out the furthest. The teens
scan the sand for deliverance
staring out across the water.

Mom floats on her back
a few stolen minutes,
dreaming. Water-wings
clutch the arms of the youngest
frolicking in the tide's change.

Sunlight lessens. Summer
flowers wild on eroded dunes.

Here

for Ray Freed

The fire whistles are wailing!

whatever's in flames, or false
alarm, has trucks from three
towns racing south.

In the night sky I can't see
any place lit up   barely the moon
in its first quarter shows thru

© Charles E. Manley

BARBARA GUEST

The typewriter, usually a little mist-bound, always the keys with their slow response, webbed in the Hampton damp. A variation on the city typewriter, it carries echoes of winter days in a still, snow-bound room, or of a summer fog settled on the keyboard overnight. The typewriter of the Hamptons, dwelling as it does by the sea, is never in a brisk condition, quick to the pulse; its life has not been nurtured near a rapid city sidewalk, but under the shadow of trees and low clouds.

Recalling my years in the Hamptons I remember lines of poetry and prose that were conceived on *Lanes: Halsey, Toylsome, Meeting House,* and now *Pleasant.* They each evoke an image that met me from the summer fields or sea, an ear of corn, sunflowers, snow, or summer haze turning into the abrupt clarity of September when, as I noted, "shadows are longer."

When I was writing the biography of the poet, H.D., I spent several years in a cottage in Southampton whose address was Meeting House Lane. During that period I was involved in a correspondence with persons peripheral and necessary to my biography, but whom I did not know and who lived mostly in Europe. I have never received such prompt return to my questioning letters as I did at that time. I became convinced, in particular as the British mail collected in my mailbox, that it was the address that fascinated and coerced my correspondents. The name of my street evoked those early settlers gathered in a small frame dwelling, colonists who had rebelled from the mother country, England, did it not? Meeting House Lane as such was an exotic address, with its overtone of purism. Correspondence is much slower to come to my numerical city address and I believe I detect a disinterestedness in my replies.

I know that in some mysterious natural way I must write differently here. For instance, absorption with weather lends its passage to my mood as does the controlling light. Sometimes I believe my poetry is untameable, conspiring with nature and its sovereignty. My work is tracked by country ghosts whose narrowed eyes are shielded by cover of shrub and seasonal ground. I observe with humility the great nearby sea, or its marginal inlets, that hold my life in their span. I am, I notice, in thrall, controlled.

Clouds Near the Windmill

Counting you one of us
              among the rushes
the difficult pebbles, these stones . . .
Quiet the water, it can do more,
we prefer it still and birds not chattering.
We like your voices because they have more portent.

We like the armor of your skin
the wisdom of your life line
hesitating from window to windowpane
and the exhaustion of your bare feet
climbing the sand.
                              Even as you turn
in the wind woodenly I catch a different sound,
enough to separate you from them
bringing, as you do, the bandages
from tree to wounded tree.

These are known as digestive moments
and the pear wearing its wrinkles
tunes down. Abiding calm
as light less curious now
and even less significant. That chair
it is moving closer to the pond.

Later we will watch the shadowless
birdwing and those straight lines
harsh without a tremor,
resembling pagoda field,
resembling stalks with your imagination.

The land is rutted with carriages,
they have their hoods pulled down.

Sag Harbor, the Tchekov Letters

A maritime history less blissful than orchards,
the chimes rush down
hill slopes where things rustle in their nets,
cold breaths. A giving in the left sleeve
where the wind meets,

"Remember the ship sails tomorrow." He wrote
of meetings at wayside stations, boarding
with victuals and wine, the pleasure of smoking
and smiling, mileage more like a novel,
cumbersome yet necessary for knowledge. Red, amber.

Being in the heart
of the candid, discreet and likeable conversings
while rasps of gulls over the harbor dun
the sad notes of near survival and sliding
of ropes into passages,

Acts responding to willow,
the blossoming willow leap no one caught,
on the sidewalk only a scatter,
    sea barrels sleep through their dying.

Lawn Bumps

The horseshoe print on the lawn
that started me down
on hooves
the carriage trade
a smart two wheeler running up the drive and Andrew
there at the wheel. No one had thought the horse's shoes
would dig so at the turf. And no one ever dreamed I
would return years later and uncover the leaves to find
those same prints, the ones the horses made when
Andrew took them up the drive in midsummer.

    "You seem such a stranger," she said,
    "when you look out onto the lawn, why
    don't you turn out the light? I'm sorry I
    was cross today at the shower. It was all
    those wild things under my feet with a sort
    of U shape and I kept stumbling over them.
    I think the shower should be put somewhere
    inside the house, even if we do bring the sand
    indoors with us, it's better than that funny
    smell out there and something running
    under your feet."

Because so much was said about being alive
and it was talked about boats and islands and
keeping cruisers drifting the way they were
                supposed to

A brick is replaced here and else. To replace
what is left of the curtains. As the windfolds
other things. Like where that is disturbed
                         and the stumbling towards it.

And the maritime uses of quiet exists when it was carried
down the lawn a kind of free booting as opposed to free
looting which was what it was supposed to be. A series of
inverted "U"s where the plaster had fallen and the
timbers showed like grain and there appeared an ivory
circumference like ears. A totality of expression in drips
and dabs also was uncovered until the margins were
released and the newspaper recovered.

A complex denuding of place once occupied
by house sitting on bumps. They were photographed
and afterwards the dance to the phonograph.

He arrived with his photographs. Actually stills.
We looked them over and remarked how much had
changed.
It proved our instincts to restore were correct.

Just possibly and with luck the house. The attic might
    remain
on top. Where the letter had said ma chère and a
    different
order was imposed like wisdom settling its accounts
although an opposite effect might be gained from the
    wind
arriving off shore. Someone might challenge
the wisdom of saddles being laid out to dry.

Units. The measure the glass takes to the handle,
nearly full. While birds in cry . . . on the veranda
the sounding of hurdles. Jumps. A neighing
as of wedding. Bells near the grass. An exclamation
with wisps lying near and some broken.
Yet the prints visible under the shifts of ice
where the key had been thrown. A winter court.

Usually the most stormy of us respond
Sometimes shipping in the harbor

Where the portrait hides.
Often waiting.

Housewifery, certain tricks with knives, the bay
   wind
Off setting them and their's of a kind

Wilfully as clouds whimper near bridges
Desiring to settle somewhere
Cause trouble
Bits and pieces fall apart

As generations in their disguises remove a few
We like least
What resembled those hooves

Meaning our apartness from that golden grasping
The mazes and the greenery
The permissiveness of growing
Into our variousness

Further explanations covering up the moss
Even a form of inter-marriage
Lending strength to the lawn
With its rudeness
Heavy ways a firmer tread

Brightness like calico was only piece work
Yet with remembrance the ruddiness
meant a lot to the corners.

Losing the trail was more trouble than finding the
   beginning
which stood there as house, but the tale of the hooves
went beyond all that, faster, with more rhythm to its
   slices,
loping off branches and unsmoking the parental tree
   there
in the wind sloughing about bringing tears to the eyes
and the need for further equipment to handle the seamy
adventures sewn into the cloth where it was whole,
evocative like scent in the upstairs drawer. Or the Keds.

            Decisive,

impregnable as temples their Indian temperament
obdurate as blue, a bright grazing
where warm draughts fell sideways on
elbow and hand like writing where there is order
of one kind
                Lawn bumps leading to

assurances with their partial payments—

        the river in the dark,
        people eating beside it under lights or lanterns,
        fishing at twilight,
        canoes setting northward with strangers
        interned in the futuristic cabins,
        "Excessive disappointments after the premiere"
           and
        "Animal behaviour the Balkans never knew"

the hooves bestowed their print

Hohenzollern

Asphodel isn't in the

     Gardening by the Sea

        but

Perdita is:

   "For you there's rosemary and rue; these keep
   seeming and savor all the winter long:"

The moon is there

   "shinin' through the trees"

Arrogance; savagery; loneliness   the moon

half sharpened a day later

     like asphodel first introduced

the same time or a day later than *The Winter's Tale*

daffodil moon

    'seeming'

Hohenzollern bloomed at me
today on Wickapogue Road
the princely banner high masted
over the dunes

potato dust settling
on the homestead sign

       Hohenzollern

formerly a tenant farmer cabin
outside the Henry Ford compound

       Hohenzollern

What glee! What ghoulish joyousness!

from Wave

ii

the eye tolls as burnished as bell
on coral the wave breaks or here
cold zone of equal blue and grey

      Tritons' throng appears

          where zephyrs
cast skyward by spume glance down
on islands of the deep mermaids
we'll never see   or hear   yet each

wave rolling brings in brightest
phosphorescence their hair

        a lyre
sweet voice of brine

    other secrets

in the tease and stress of wave song

                  Sun

multipowered it brushes

thins and splays
                    burns

wild-lidded over foam   in air   to touch
             Remembering the violence
we turn on house pillow and let
dolphins surmise us (dreams) the lap
of shore water enter our heads as ponds
forced from sea are inlets, we are
islets become soft   become grassy
turning   swaying   to each and yet

            the angry

                  it calls

Noon

     the crab walks

Night

     small fish

Rock and dawn
            Fog

iii

. . .

cricket and bird song about   alas

        until morning   the great sea and ledge

from which pines such low soundings   pines

that are green   and sea that is swelling

sea whose earth is sandy who in sleep

        changes as the pilot arm beckons

the arm we lie on shifts
                    early the stir
to cease from night close   to begin
to gather   to fall   as Wave
                    Bountiful and Bare

© 1979 Layle Silbert

MICHAEL HELLER

On the Poem and East Hampton

Not simply space, but space in which words can occur, take on the liberating spaciousness of the beaches and the skies. Maidstone on a wintry night encircled by lights of the North Shore, Shelter Island, the houses near Cedar Point to form metonymies of the stars and constellations. Near my house, so one guidebook has it, an immense clam pile left by Indians, also 'good' springs for the waters of which people came as far away as Connecticut. These necessary interminglings of natural world and human history spiked with the ironies of our being there, in my case, one of the 'summer' people who found intermittancies of staying on, who found useful the city—seashore antipodes, but even more the opening, the feel of immense good fortune by which the world and the poem interanimate each other.

At Albert's Landing
(with my son)

I.   The path winds. You are around a bend
Unseen. But your voice
Crackles in the walkie-talkie
You made me bring. "Here's a leaf,
A tree." The detail,
Not the design, excites you.
I don't know what to say.
After months in the city,
I'm feeling strange in the woods.

II.   Spongy ground.
Matted leaves
Beneath which lie
Dirt, bones, shells.
Late April: milky light
And warmth. Thinnest odors rise.
In the middle of one's life
More things connect
With dying, what's come,
What's over.

III.   It is said
That what exists is like the sky
Through which clouds pass. I suspect
That mine is a poetry of clouds.
Above me, some wispy tuft catches sun
In an interesting way. *The naked very thing.*
I'm glad of this, don't look
In the billowy mass
For the teased-out shape
Of a horse's head or a bird's wing.
Yet finding it now and then,
Unsummoned: some thought or image,
Recalling how each
Depends on each.

IV. Together we follow the trail's twists
Until the pond.
There, two white egrets
Stand against the high brown grass.
Intent watching
Is almost timeless, but some noise
One of us makes scares them off.
They rise over our heads, circle
Out of sight. Strange sadness
Grips me. The after-image
Of their shapes still burns.

V. Here we are in some fugal world.
Tree branches make a kind of tent.
And the squirrel, when he eats,
Looks like a little man. And here
You fling your arms out
Whirling around at the frightened
Skimming ducks. The duck's eye,
Like ours, must be its center. We
Are alone, rooted in our aloneness.
And yet, things lean and lean,
Explaining each other and not themselves.
I call you; it's time to go.

VI. Different as the woods are
This is no paradise to enter or to leave.
Just the real, and a wild nesting
Of hope in the real
Which does not know of hope.
Things lean and lean, and sometimes
Words find common centers in us
Resonating and filling speech.
Let me know a little of you.

On the Beach

I. My doctor tells me:
    With your skin, sunlight is dangerous.

    Western Man, I'm hurt, but go armed.
    A broadbrimmed hat, umbrella,
    Lotions which I am told stop light
    But draw flies.

    Sitting there, I read that Montale saw,
    A la Fellini, a monstrous woman
    Plump herself down onto crumbling sand
    And speak Truth.

    I try to stop truth from shade,
    Watching square yards of such flesh
    Baste itself with oil.

    Thou shall be anointed
    For glamour, youth, illusion,
    The thing to do.

    What I see is that the sun is bright
    And that perhaps suntans, while looking
    Healthy, are deceiving.

    Even here, amid these minor increments
    Of peril, one is consoled. In this
    Careless resort life of beaches
    Deceptions themselves are a kind of truth.

II. The philosopher tells us
    Mentally we are joined to what we look at,
    That seeing can haunt.

    If the wave is rough
    One sits it out, bathing
    In the shade or sun.
    It's as free as this other thing
    The mottled clacking teeth of empty shells
    Can hint at.

By the path's edge,
The infectious tick
Sits on the tip end of the dune grass

Like one's gaze,
Ready to be fed
Ready to install other infusions.

Above, seabirds wheel—
Not so much cruelness, but what is actual
In eye and beak.

Overhearing that line of Rilke's
"You must change your life."
I looked again at the sea's glint.

III.   Depending on the weather,
Yesterday's sandbar
Is today's dangerous shoal.

Yesterday's clam,
Today's 700 beats of a gull's wing.

The high rump of shingle
Where the sun fell, in the instant
When it fell for everyone,
Is also gone,
Dredged this winter to make
A boatman's channel.

It's not all mechanics, all improvement
Or all evolution.

Depending on the weather,
We play a funny game
On the beach.

My son follows me, stamping his feet
Deliberately into my tracks.

He says, I don't want to step on a sharp shell or
   jellyfish.
Laughs, Look, Dad, I'm crushing your footprints.

Two Swans in a Meadow By the Sea

High dunes falling away
To spongy ground; the water lying
In brackish shallow pools
A few feet from the surf

Broom and high grass hide a dozen birds
Which twitter. We take it in
As best we can. The sea's sound,
All the marvelous growth

No need to ask, to answer
Why sky and hilly tufts,
Noise of the cars on the road above

Are so composed to bring us, our eyes
Level with the sea
To where two white forms
Rest their lovely necks as though
In self-caress
Looking at each other

Coral Stanzas
—*After Mandelstam*

O City, o white filagree just below the grainy depths,
Can it be a reef which absorbs the star and moonlight,
O reef, am I flung, cast toward shoal, toward beach?
Is there water clear enough, soothes enough
Surrounding the far-flung branchings?

Bitumin pellicates fester in the vision
Falling like hell-snow, falling like hell-snow.
O into depths, more depths, your brother animal
Swims into the poisoned channels.

Brother animal, o white filagree, city of Venus
Light mote and tear duct festering in the hell-snow,
In the scurried depths.

© 1981 Layle Silbert

DAVID IGNATOW

The most important influence of East Hampton and the surrounding environment has been its distance from New York. At times I have felt trapped here, at other times grateful to experience the calm and quiet, yet at other times to experience the wonder of the trees, bays, and ocean. There has been no effort on my part, consciously, to write all of this into the poems. Rather I have found it necessary for me to resist it by reminding myself frequently of the tension, turmoil, and slaughter of people in the cities and in the Third World. However, I have gotten some of the scenery of East Hampton into my poems indirectly, when I was in need of metaphors, images, etc. with which to bring my concerns into focus on the page. I must admit, though, that some of the poems I've written reflect a certain calm and pleasure in the relief I find from time to time in living out here. It could be worse, especially so if I were not able to mix in New York City and travels throughout the United States. In short, East Hampton and its environs are ok in small doses. Too many vacationers lately. It ain't like it used to be.

A Cloud Creates

A cloud creates the face of a man who, happening to look up, recognizes it as his own. The face under stress of the wind begins to disintegrate into wings, and the man sees in himself the ability to fly. He stretches forth his arms and waves them up and down as he begins to circle and dip as a birdman would in the currents of the wind, and then the face vanishes and the wings drift apart, too, in shreds and patches.

The clouds darken, as they will; thunder rolls from their colliding with each other. Lightning flashes. He knows he is at war with himself, the reason for which he cannot go into at the moment.

There is no consolation, not until the rain ceases and the sun emerges and once more clouds arrive, white, brilliantly lit, and so for him full of hope. He has not attempted to sort out his, as it seems, random feelings since sighting the face. And though there is no order to his feelings, of that he is certain, he needs none, not while the sun rises and sets and weather prevails. It is from weather that he derives, and so he has no faults. He is without fault, he is of the weather.

Behind His Eyes

A man has been tied to a tree and thinks he is beginning to feel something of the tree enter his body. It is hard for him to discern what it could be, but he would like to grow tiny branches from his head, and leaf buds.

He loves standing still. He thinks he can feel the tree pressing up against him, as if it were trying to instill in him its nature and its seed. He is in a kind of trance about himself. Thinking, as he had sensed before, is no longer a function of thought but of action. That is because he has welcomed the possibility of tiny branches and leaves that now he believes are growing from his sides and from his head. He would laugh in pleasure but that he finds himself swaying back and forth as in a dance that could have been induced by wind.

He is very happy, very much the tree, and he has shed his alarm at having been tied to it in the middle of the woods and left to die. He can forget the reason for his captivity which he thinks of no longer as capture but as a piece of luck to have happened in the midst of this crisis in his life. He is free of crisis, and can celebrate by bringing forth more branches and leaves, and he straightens up from his now stooped posture of exhaustion to let new growth emerge more easily from his head and sides. He is alive and that is what counts, alive in a form he has always admired, and now it is his and he is glad, only to find himself growing more sharply stooped and losing memory of himself, as this last thought becomes the bark he has seen behind his eyes.

My Own House

As I view the leaf, my theme is not the shades of meaning
that the mind conveys of it but my desire to make the leaf
speak to tell me, Chlorophyll, chlorophyll, breathlessly. I
would rejoice with it and, in turn, would reply, Blood, and
the leaf would nod. Having spoken to each other, we
would find our topics inexhaustible and imagine, as I grow
old and the leaf begins to fade and turn brown, the
thought of being buried in the ground would become so
familiar to me, so thoroughly known through conversation
with the leaf, that my walk among the trees after complet-
ing this poem would be like entering my own house.

from: Leaving the Door Open

1.

He got his friends to agree to shoot him standing against
a stone wall, somewhere in the country on a deserted farm.
It was to resemble an execution, the plan cleared with the
police, at whose headquarters he had signed attesting to
his desire to be shot and, in clearing his friends, declaring
his death a suicide that they were to help him to—at the
peak of his strength.

Never to return to life in any form but that of earth itself,
since earth was not fearful or joyous. And then he was
followed, on inspiration, by his friends, one by one, each
fired on by a diminishing squad until the last left was shot,
as a courtesy by the police. Afterwards, the police shook
their heads, puzzled, grieved and somehow angry at those
bodies lying sprawled with outstretched arms and legs
against the ground, as if pleading with the earth to let
them in.

from: Leaving the Door Open

31.

Wherever he looks, standing still in the city,
are people born of coupling, walking in grey suits
and ties, in long dresses and coiffed hair,
speaking elegantly of themselves and of each
    other,
forgetting for the moment their origin,
perhaps wishing not to know or to remember.
They dress as if having been born in a clothing
    store.

They were born of men and women naked
and gyrating from the hips
and with movements up and down
and with climactic yells,
as if losing their lives
in the pleasure and so glad,
so wildly glad.

From this rises the child
from between the wet crotch, blood and mucous.
He stands upright and pronounces himself
humankind and steps from bed and clothes
    himself
in a grey suit and from the next room of birth
steps a woman in a long dress. They meet
in the corridor and arm in arm walk its length
in search of one room, empty of inhabitants
but prepared for them.

Respected Graves

I am seated on a chair resting upon a wooden floor supported by a concrete foundation poured and sealed into the earth that whirls in space without visible support. I am quite worried. This whirling sphere does not know its own future nor its past, and is traveling at a reckless speed into the dark. I hold my breath, expecting to crash at any moment with a star or comet, but I can't hold my breath for long, and I begin to breathe in trepidation.

And here I thought I could take pride in my ancestral beginnings, the history of my tribe, their complications, their rise and fall, as if they had been the real beginning. My lordly Indian killers, god keepers, makers of cloth and slave runners, all who endured their life's darkness are traveling with me in the dark in their respected graves.

Autumn

(For Wendell Berry)

A leaf lies shaking
at my door, about to be
blown away.
      If I should
bring it into the still
air of my room, it would
lie quietly on the windowsill
facing the tree
from which it fell.

Little Friend

Little friend, when do you rest?
You are standing as though idly
in the grass, your head turning
slowly in one direction, then in another
without alarm when, suddenly, you crouch,
flutter your wings and leap into the air
as though to escape an attack
or as if in memory of one to which
you still respond, so deep has been your fear.
And now you're safe upon a branch
above my head from which I sit
secluded, not to trouble you again.

But then you sail off quietly
to visit branches and parts of ground.
I lose sight of you, just as another
like yourself lands close
to where you stood and looks
in both directions first, before it bends
its head to feed. Off it flies
with something in its beak. I step out
from hiding, reminded of my hunger.
Later, I turn to read the news of state
and individuals and wonder what
the bird is doing at this moment,
now that it has eaten.

© Christopher Conforti

YAEDI IGNATOW

I've grown up in the country. For two years I lived in the city and I began to write poems about paranoia; but in the countryside around me I see the ancient symbols of moon, tree, sun, the animals as messengers and something in me echoes to the symbol in these things. This is what I love about the country. The natural isolation away from city distractions activates our race and historic memory which is rooted in symbols.

In the Koran, many suras speak of the sun as symbolic of man's spirit and the moon as a symbol placed within our nightly view to remind us of the soul. Just as the moon can only be seen clearly in the darkness of the night sky, the soul can only be seen clearly in the darkness and silence of private meditation. This is the solitude from which poetry springs.

75

The Offer

Shall I leave some money around the house for you?
my mother asked me over the phone.
Yes, I said, please leave some bills
scattered around the bathroom
in case I should get an urge
for currency on the toilet;
and around the livingroom,
as though money
had fallen through cracks in the roof
from the trees above the house.
Please leave the money
all over the house
as if someone had had a fancy
to dance alone with their money,
happy for the pleasure
it has brought,
raising it
above their heads.
All over the house,
hot with green dollars.

Blackout into Sunlight

I didn't know
it would happen at the mirror—
wiping the noxema off my face,
my fingers making wide strokes in the jar;
the cream sweeping into white cliffs,
the deep blue of the jar behind them.
I was seeing something real in my mind.
The world got off me in front of the mirror—
a passenger rushing from a train
and when I struck my head
on the bedpost
which tree
was it
I was running toward
wanting to feel the sun coming through its branches?

Equations

My left door won't open.
I hear fish under my wheels.
For four days I have water on the brain.
There seems to be an answer in the clear liquid,
amenable, able to flow
through strangely shaped spaces—
I know there is a wisdom in transparency
as in the mathematic perfection
of my cat moving so slowly
I can see the lines extending off her
to points in the universe
which hold her perfectly.

Forest

Green is a code, saying itself, unable to stop—
blissfully in love with its secret.
A bird whirs by me, wrapping up the air.
I gather courage
and say
the bird deep inside myself.
I say her movement, her eyes, the body
and the little feet.
As I move past the word suspicion disappears
and she answers
landing closer.
I say things over and over, not knowing
where else to start:
branch, eye, feather, moving toward each meaning
so the forest may begin to recognize me
as someone who knows
without the word.

Limbo

This is the life
I remember from pictures,
looking down from heaven.
It looked so lost down there;
dark and hopelessly tiny.
Nothing has surprised me
except my body,
which feels more each day
like a glue factory;
using whatever I find
to make sense out of fragments.
What is the substance
people seem so sure
this life is made of?
I hear their mouths,
as though full of cotton
mumbling like the beginning
of thunder rolling backwards.
Life is people standing on narrow beams
in millions of positions
till they find the one
to get out of this world.
They end up free, I hear,
sidestepping death—this side of it,
floating down a blue river,
belly to a darker sun.

Praise

Now
here in the kitchen
there is something in the air
sending phrases
to my tongue like flutters of an eyelid.
I cannot write fast enough and yet
I cannot even write it.
Heaven has descended
(a shower)
sending shafts of light
raining down, like a thousand
trails of falling stars—though
so near the heart I send praise
into the salad before me
falling together.

© Sharon Guynup

KENNETH KOCH

I worked on "The Boiling Water" over a period of four years. I began writing it in 1975, in early summer, when I was living in a house I rented on Millstone Road, about a quarter of a mile down from the intersection of Millstone with Scuttlehole Road, and next door to the house I later bought and spend summers in now. Some friends from out of town came to visit (a short visit, not an overnight one) and I put some water on to boil for tea. I went in from the deck to the kitchen a few times to see if the water was boiling yet, and, when I saw that it finally was, it seemed, rather suddenly and absurdly, to be a dramatic event. "How serious this must be for the water!" I thought, or something of the kind; and I had the suspicion this might lead to something in a poem. So it did, though the poem took a long time to write. I ended up thinking a lot about "seriousness." I put in a tremendous number of examples, most of which I later took out. My work on the poem began and ended on Millstone Road, though I was writing it also in New York City and in France. Some of its details come directly from Long Island, such as the tree waving in the wind, the hurricane (of 1976), the fly, and the bee; and the tree, full of pink and whitish blossoms, which was an apple tree in the yard between my house and the fields. The duck in the poem is not a Long Island duck but a duck I saw in Normandy. These are things that were there while I was writing the poem. Others, like the Cordillera of the Andes, were from before, and remembered; some, like the match factory, just imagined. "Fate," which I wrote in a few hours in New York City in 1977, is about an afternoon conversation with friends after I came back from Europe for the first time, in 1951, when I was twenty six. Its composition has nothing to do with Long Island, though the people who appear in the poem do. Toward the end of the poem I mention another afternoon soon after this one, in which Larry Rivers proposed that he and I and Jane Freilicher take a house for a month or so in East Hampton; at that time I hadn't visited that part of Long Island, and, in fact, didn't know quite where it was.

The Boiling Water

A serious moment for the water is when it boils
And though one usually regards it merely as a
    convenience
To have the boiling water available for bath or table
Occasionally there is someone around who understands
The importance of this moment for the water—maybe a
    saint,
Maybe a poet, maybe a crazy man, or just someone
    temporarily disturbed

With his mind "floating," in a sense, away from his
    deepest
Personal concerns to more "unreal" things. A lot of
    poetry
Can come from perceptions of this kind, as well as a lot of
    insane conversations.
Intense people can sometimes get stuck on topics like
    these
And keep you far into the night with them. Still, it is true
That the water has just started to boil. How important
For the water! And now I see that the tree is waving in the
    wind
(I assume it is the wind)—at least, its branches are. In
    order to see
Hidden meanings, one may have to ignore
The most exciting ones, those that are most directly
    appealing
And yet it is only these appealing ones that, often, one
    can trust
To make one's art solid and true, just as it is sexual
    attraction
One has to trust, often, in love. So the boiling water's
    seriousness
Is likely to go unobserved until the exact strange moment
(And what a temptation it is to end the poem here
With some secret thrust) when it involuntarily comes into
    the mind
And then one can write of it. A serious moment for this
    poem will be when it ends,
It will be like the water's boiling, that for which we've
    waited
Without trying to think of it too much, since "a watched
    pot never boils,"
And a poem with its ending figured out is difficult to
    write.

Once the water is boiling, the heater has a choice: to look
    at it
And let it boil and go on seeing what it does, or to take it
    off and use the water for tea,

Chocolate or coffee or beef consommé. You don't drink
    the product then
Until the water has ceased to boil, for otherwise
It would burn your tongue. Even hot water is dangerous
    and has a thorn
Like the rose, or a horn like the baby ram. Modest hot
    water, and the tree
Blowing in the wind. The connection here is how serious
    is it for the tree
To have its arms wave (its branches)? How did it ever get
    such flexibility
In the first place? and who put the boiling potentiality
    into water?
A tree will not boil, nor will the wind. Think of the
    dinners
We could have, and the lunches, and the dreams, if only
    they did.
But that is not to think of what things are really about.
    For the tree
I don't know how serious it is to be waving, though
    water's boiling
Is more dramatic, is more like a storm, high tide
And the ship goes down, but it comes back up as coffee,
    chocolate, or tea.

How many people I have drunk tea or coffee with
And thought about the boiling water hardly at all, just
    waiting for it to boil
So there could be coffee or chocolate or tea. And then
    what?
The body stimulated, the brain alarmed, grounds in the
    pot,
The tree, waving, out the window, perhaps with a little
    more élan
Because we saw it that way, because the water boiled,
    because we drank tea.

The water boils almost every time the same old way
And still it is serious, because it is boiling. That is what,
I think, one should see. From this may come compassion,
Compassion and a knowledge of nature, although most of
    the time

I know I am not going to think about it. It would be crazy
To give such things precedence over such affairs of one's
    life
As involve more fundamental satisfactions. But is going
    to the beach
More fundamental than seeing the water boil? Saving of
    money,
It's well known, can result from an aesthetic attitude,
    since a rock
Picked up in the street contains all the shape and
    hardness of the world.
One sidewalk leads everywhere. You don't have to be in
    Estapan.

A serious moment for the island is when its trees
Begin to give it shade, and another is when the ocean
    washes
Big heavy things against its side. One walks around and
    looks at the island
But not really at it, at what is on it, and one thinks,
It must be serious, even, to be this island, at all, here,
Since it is lying here exposed to the whole sea. All its
Moments might be serious. It is serious, in such windy
    weather, to be a sail
Or an open window, or a feather flying in the street.

Seriousness, how often I have thought of seriousness
And how little I have understood it, except this: serious is
    urgent
And it has to do with change. You say to the water,
It's not necessary to boil now, and you turn it off. It stops
Fidgeting. And starts to cool. You put your hand in it
And say, The water isn't serious any more. It has the
    potential,
However—that urgency to give off bubbles, to
Change itself to steam. And the wind,
When it becomes part of a hurricane, blowing up the
    beach
And the sand dunes can't keep it away.
Fainting is one sign of seriousness, crying is another.
Shuddering all over is another one.

A serious moment for the telephone is when it rings,
And a person answers, it is Angelica, or is it you
And finally, at last, who answer, my wing, my past, my
Angel, my flume, and my de-control, my orange and my
    good-bye kiss,
My extravagance, and my weight at fifteen years old
And at the height of my intelligence, oh Cordillera two
And sandals one, C'est toi à l'appareil? Is that you at
The telephone, and when it snows, a serious moment for
    the bus is when it snows
For then it has to slow down for sliding, and every
    moment is a trust.

A serious moment for the fly is when its wings
Are moving, and a serious moment for the duck
Is when it swims, when it first touches water, then spreads
Its smile upon the water, its feet begin to paddle, it is in
And above the water, pushing itself forward, a duck.
And a serious moment for the sky is when, completely
    blue,
It feels some clouds coming; another when it turns dark.
A serious moment for the match is when it bursts into
    flame
And is all alone, living, in that instant, that beautiful
    second for which it was made.
So much went into it! The men at the match factory, the
    mood of
The public, the sand covering the barn
So it was hard to find the phosphorus, and now this
    flame,
This pink white ecstatic light blue! For the telephone
    when it rings,
For the wind when it blows, and for the match when it
    bursts into flame.

Serious, all our life is serious, and we see around us
Seriousness for other things, that touches us and seems as
    if it might be giving clues.
The seriousness of the house when it is being built
And is almost completed, and then the moment when it is
    completed.

The seriousness of the bee when it stings. We say, He has
    taken his life,
Merely to sting. Why would he do that? And we feel
We aren't concentrated enough, not pure, not deep
As the buzzing bee. The bee flies into the house
And lights on a chair arm and sits there, waiting for
    something to be
Other than it is, so he can fly again. He is boiling, waiting.
    Soon he is forgotten
And everyone is speaking again.

Seriousness, everyone speaks of seriousness
Certain he knows or seeking to know what it is. A child is
    bitten by an animal
And that is serious. The doctor has a serious life. He is
    somewhat, in that, like the bee.
And water! water—how it is needed! and it is always
    going down
Seeking its own level, evaporating, boiling, now changing
    into ice
And snow, now making up our bodies. We drink the
    coffee
And somewhere in this moment is the chance
We will never see each other again. It is serious for the
    tree
To be moving, the flexibility of its moving
Being the sign of its continuing life. And now there are
    its blossoms
And the fact that it is blossoming again, it is filling up
    with
Pink and whitish blossoms, it is full of them, the wind
    blows, it is
Warm, though, so much is happening, it is spring, the
    people step out
And doors swing in, and billions of insects are born. You
    call me and tell me
You feel that your life is not worth living. I say I will come
    to see you. I put the key in
And the car begins to clatter, and now it starts.

86

Serious for me that I met you, and serious for you
That you met me, and that we do not know
If we will ever be close to anyone again. Serious the
   recognition of the probability
That we will, although time stretches terribly in between.
   It is serious not to know
And to know and to try to figure things out. One's legs
Cross, foot swings, and a cigarette is blooming, a gray
   bouquet, and
The water is boiling. Serious the birth (what a
   phenomenon!) of anything and
The movements of the trees, and for the lovers
Everything they do and see. Serious intermittently for
   consciousness
The sign that something may be happening, always,
   today,
That is enough. For the germ when it enters or leaves a
   body. For the fly when it lifts its little wings.

Fate

In a room on West Tenth Street in June
Of nineteen fifty-one, Frank O'Hara and I
And Larry Rivers (I actually do not remember
If Larry was there, but he would be there
Later, some winter night, on the stairway
Sitting waiting, "a demented telephone"
As Frank said in an article about him but then
On the stairs unhappy in a youthful manner, much
Happened later), Frank, John Ashbery,
Jane Freilicher and I, and I
Had just come back from Europe for the first time.
I had a bottle of Irish whiskey I had
Bought in Shannon, where the plane stopped
And we drank it and I told
My friends about Europe, they'd never
Been there, how much I'd loved it, I
Was so happy to be there with them, and my

Europe, too, which I had, Greece, Italy, France,
Scandinavia, and England—imagine
Having all that the first time. The walls
Were white in that little apartment, so tiny
The rooms are so small but we all fitted into one
And talked, Frank so sure of his
Talent but didn't say it that way, I
Didn't know it till after he was
Dead just how sure he had been, and John
Unhappy and brilliant and silly and of them all my
First friend, we had met at Harvard they
Tended except Frank to pooh-pooh
What I said about Europe and even
Frank was more interested but ever polite
When sober I couldn't tell it but
Barely tended they tended to be much more
Interested in gossip such as
Who had been sleeping with whom and what
Was selling and going on whereat I
Was a little hurt but used to it my
Expectations from my friendships were
Absurd but that way I got so
Much out of them in fact it wasn't
Causal but the two ways at once I was
Never so happy with anyone
As I was with those friends
At that particular time on that day with
That bottle of Irish whiskey the time
Four in the afternoon or
Three in the afternoon or two or five
I don't know what and why do I think
That my being so happy is so urgent
And important? it seems some kind
Of evidence of the truth as if
I could go back and take it? or do
I just want to hold what
There is of it now? thinking says hold
Something now which is why
Despite me and liking me that
Afternoon who was sleeping with

Whom was best and
My happiness picking up
A glass Frank What was it like Kenny
Ah from my being vulnerable
Only sometimes I can see the vulnerable-
Ness in others I have ever known
Faults with them or on the telephone
The sexual adventures were different
Each person at work autobiography all
The time plowing forward if
There's no question of movement as there
Isn't no doubt of it may I not
I may find this moment minute
Extraordinary? I can do nothing
With it but write about it two
Hundred forty West
Tenth Street, Jane's apartment,
Nineteen fifty-one or fifty-two I
Can never remember yes it was
Later or much earlier
That Larry sat on the stairs
And John said Um hum and hum and hum I
Don't remember the words Frank said Un hun
Jane said An han and Larry if he
Was there said Boobledyboop so always
Said Larry or almost and I said
Aix-en-Provence me new sense of
These that London Firenze Florence
Now Greece and un hun um hum an
Han boop Soon I was at Larry's
And he's proposing we take a
House in Eastham—what? for the
Summer where is that and
Already that afternoon was dissipated
Another begun many more of
Them but that was one
I remember I was in
A special position as if it
Were my birthday but

They were in fact as if my
Birthday or that is to say Who
Cares if he grows older if
He has friends like
These I mean who does not
Care? the celebration is the cause
Of the sorrow and not
The other way around. I also went
To Venice and to Vienna there were
Some people I drove there
With new sunshine Frank says
Let's go out Jane John Frank
And I (Larry was not there, I now
Remember) then mysteriously
Left

© Alexander W. Suchenko

NAOMI LAZARD

I leave my apartment in New York City whenever I can in order to be closer to animals in a natural environment. Some people have the need to live with animals. I am one of those people. I have been writing poems about animals almost from the first moment I began to write poetry. By this time there are dozens of animals who have found their way into my poetry; cats, dogs, seals, wolves, wolverines, beavers, and many others including, of course, birds. One question raised in my years of analysis has never been answered: "Why do I identify with animals?" I can't answer this question. I only know that I do. Maybe the answer is to found in the poem *Stepping Out With My Big Cats*. Easthampton for me is the place of animals.

91

Walking with Lulu in the Wood

The wood is a good place to find
the other road down to that hollow
which rocks a little with the same
motion as my soul. Come on, Lulu,
follow me and be careful of the rain
washed leaves. But you were always gentle.
I'll be quiet too, and we won't disturb
the raccoons or any of the other animals.
I want to talk with the god here, Lulu.
This is a grove where he must be hiding,
and here is a pool for a small water god
to swim in. Let's talk with the god, Lulu.

The sun makes a great splash and you
are the one who is hiding in the tall grass
just the way you used to. Lulu,
you are the color of sand in a certain light,
like the shadow of light. The sun
is embracing me; the shadow also
means death. It is the god's word
in the language he speaks. He says
you are small again, that you have chosen it.
He says your reflection will be in the pool
forever, a blue resemblance, a startled joy.
He says this is your world now, this night
of tall trees, this cave of silences.
He says he loves you too; he watches you sleep.

Is the grove real? Is this your heaven, Lulu,
that you have let me enter? This glade,
the winter ivories?—the season you missed
by dying in the fall. Are these your jewelled
stones, your curled up animals, your grass?
And your god, the secret splash in the water
that you always seemed to be listening for?
Is it the god's way—the mouth in the wood,
the opening to paradise?

God of animals and children, separations, loss.
Goodbye. Goodbye, sweet girl, again.
The days pass like oranges tossed
from hand to hand. Then one will drop
and it will be my turn. Wait for me here.
I hope to be fortunate, to come back and share
this winter wood with you, the dark hallow,
the snow-dusted face of the god.

Stray Dogs

At three o'clock the field is white,
a front tooth spit out by the moon.
That's where the grass will grow;
beyond is a blur of dark wool.
My eyes are held open by wires, my body
is stiff on the unyielding sheet.

In a matter of years it will be morning.

The dog sleeps, is sleeping
near the sea. Ringed with rocks
and the voices of fish, the dog sleeps
alone in the opalescent night.

The dog dreams before dying, before
falling down to the fish, of a woman
in a blue bikini and a man
with a couple of humorous chins.
You, lumpy and hot beside me,
stoic and hot; at my feet in a mingling
of breath and flesh, the dog
roped round the neck, licking the salt
from my legs. We all sailed together
in a boat chug-chugging toward light,
to a mythical island, white as foam.
I cried, "They are going to abandon him!"

Somewhere in the future, in the morning,
your words repeat themselves,
"We can't stop for an unknown dog."

My bed sails across the Aegean
to the holy islands again. White houses
signal from the beach, white sheets
are shining in a windless sky.
I have watched the sheep with their heads up
and their mouths open. The bleached grass
is frightening. I've seen the dog
sprawled out in the shade of a rock.
I gave him my lunch but he was too unhappy
to eat. He never opened his eyes.

My bed moves in the storm of the sea,
the shore recedes between the waves.
We are still sailing together
in our uncertain boat that toils
back and forth among the islands.
Now and then we catch sight
of a house with a little steel trinket
above, that hopes to turn in the right wind.

The starving dog is our witness.
The crust of water is breaking.
We are falling, through waves
and a thicket of fishes
into the swollen dark.

Stepping Out with My Big Cats

And now in the dark shell of night,
in secret, I cast off from the shore
of my life. It is cool in this dark.
They are near me, my big cats, taller
than I am, my cougar, my leopards
and their cubs. They have come
to take me away down the branches
and plains of their memory. I walk
with them in step with their eyes
and their purring. Tonight
by a trumpet of moons we are bright

as chains linked together, moving
softly in and out of the mist.
I am quiet as moss, safe in the nest
of our walk. My big cats rub
the trees as we pass. They show
their teeth and I smile back.

Nothing and no one I have known,
no mystery of breath or glance,
leads me to this peace. Here in the grace
of an hour with them I can enter
my life's resting place. My big cats
give it all back to me again,
the brilliant mane of the wind,
the silence broken by sighs of the dew
spotted leaves. I touch their fur,
I see the world with their startled
and watchful eyes. This is the world
I want. This is the end of the dock
where I jump off out of my life.

The Angels Among Us

Outside the window the night burned
by lights, the ice trellis blooming,
white armature of dreams.
And there, moving darkly, one after one
over the horizon, the beautiful herds
lowering into distance.

The waves break over my head.
It is time to sail right out of the window
into the wake of the animals
who are leaving their paw prints to follow
in the snow. They are not far
from the north wind now,

keeping pace, nuzzling together.
The wind is the form of their speaking.

It is the night and the force
of these buildings that loosen
the tongue of the wind.
They are calling to me:
across marshland, savanna, tundra
and thicket, their language borne
on prayer and dust. I must answer
the beaver, who, hearing her babies crying,
gnaws her own flesh through to escape,
leaving a paw behind. The blood
on the trap is the edge of my dream.

Felines and rodents of woods and rivers
run across my body on whispering paws.
Even now they go quietly, disturbing no one.
As I fall in the slow revolution
of dreams, I am traced by a bullet,
I am cut by the hunter's knife.
I hear slaps of the trap. My cries
inhabit the rooms of sleep.

I struggle to wake with my eyes
against locked eyelids and madness.
They are calling to me, a sister,
come from the same endless labor
in the same primeval mud. I stand still
with my ears back, light and listening
with the wolves and the wolverines,
the minks, the otters, the beavers.
I spring on all fours. We are all
one now. In my dream I can dare
to lay my own throat bare to my enemy
as the wolves do.
                            It is too late.
I think of the lamb and of milk.
They are shaving the head of the lamb.
We are flying to the limits of the night

from my own kind. Here, lungs on fire,
rung over rung inside the heart's glacier.
Here, where the dead bones glitter
in the magic center of the dream,
I see a sign. A flicker of stars,
pale and fluttering as a baby lamb.
I name them: the constellation
of animals—the angels among us.

© 1986 Nancy Crampton

HOWARD MOSS

The poems of mine included in this anthology are all direct or indirect expressions evoked by the landscape of the East End, and sometimes the result of small events: the transplanting of two lilac bushes, being caught in traffic, and so on. I was brought up on the other end of Long Island but the idea of living anywhere without an ocean in one direction and a bay in the other would be strange to me. (Two bodies of water framing an island are invisibly repeated, most of the time, in New York City where I live in the winter.)

The East End is full of surprises one never gets used to. I know a house which looks out on Vermont. Standing at its window or on its small terrace one sees cows, barns, horses, a silo, and small mountains in the distance (the Shinnecock Hills). At another, I can look 200 feet straight

down at the ocean, and out to where fishing boats are
strung out in a line. At my own house, there are trees and
the illusion, still, of deep woods—at least on one side,
though nothing is disappearing faster than acre after acre
of oaks, and the privacy provided by a solid screen of trees.
(But acres are no guarantee of silence.)

And then, what could be more different from the Main
Streets of East Hampton and Sag Harbor, each a testi-
monial to a distinct way of life and an aesthetic notion—the
studied elegance of a New England village green, the
bustling life of a port? Each is being encroached upon by
the boutique and the shopping mall. The sedate and the
maritime are both struggling to hang on to the authentic,
to ward off the increasing threat of the suburban.

I owe a lot out here to the stars, the birds, to random
drives through the countryside, to the bays and the
beaches, to the surprising bucolic wonders of North Haven
and Shelter Island where, just last week, the ospreys were
back, nesting.

The Long Island Night

Nothing as miserable has happened before.
The Long Island night has refused its moon.
La belle dame sans merci's next door.
The Prince of Darkness is on the phone.

Certain famous phrases of our time
Have taken on the glitter of poems,
Like "Catch me before I kill again,"
And "Why are you sitting in the dark alone?"

Bay Days

1

The clouds were doing unoriginal things
With grandeur yesterday, moving paintings
From here to there, slowly dispersing
Gangs of angels. Today there's nothing,
Nothing but a camera taking nothing.
Summer. Weather. Nothing could be clearer.
It is a perfect day, with no cloud cover.

2

The birds' gradual declensions stop.
The darkness takes the longest time to darken.
Sums of stars add to the overhead.
A city of hunches thickens and grows thin,
Appears and disappears across the water,
Depending on the light's strange gift for
    hanging
Scenery. And then for taking it down.

3

Each night, the outlines of that city form
Films of the ideal, illuminations
Of crumpled battlements whose rising argot
Is faintly heard above the motorboats;
Here, the night philosophers break camp
Down to a single-minded tent of parting.
The fire's out. The animals are gone.

4

Currents, always running, gauged to light
And wind, the depths varying the colors:
A copper milky green, and ink-splash blue
Turned tinsel. A vain castle's sinking
Into its sewerage system. A particle of sail,
Hurrying to meet its particle of sun,
Shakes the whole slack surface into speed.

5

Decisive laboring: the song recital
The rain was trying to compose this morning
On what the sun had glossed as marginalia.
References to happiness are obsolete
According to the gloomy view this evening,
Which says existence is the only share
Of ardent joy that's ever in our power.

6

I tried today to make of the wild roses
An untimely bouquet. Opening, falling,
They never last long—in short, they're dying.
Now I am thinking of taking to drinking
Earlier than usual. Gin. And something.
A potion of petals. They're thorns by evening.
Wild roses in the trash can in the morning.

In Traffic

Even if the highway had been moved to dance,
the stalled traffic, stuck in a line,
choreographed into something interesting—
Chevettes flying sideways in a field,
or up, up into a cloudless sky
where so much space cries out for movement—
still the Real would be on to us again
on this narrow trap of a road adorned with
a diner, a garage, and a nursery,
its trees struggling to produce more leaves.

How gradual spring is here! How impatient
all of us are to be getting home,
as if home were some sort of transfigured instant.
We're stymied, as usual, by the unknown—
a broken-down truck up ahead, an accident,
a Harvester dragging gigantic claws

too wide for one lane, or an animal
refusing to budge—and we begin to wonder
who we all are: the anonymous
taking on interest, the way a tree
stands out suddenly, exempt from its species.

Nothing is really dancing except
an insect or two, whose lives will be smashed
against a windshield once we begin
to move, which we're beginning to do;
a truck full of trees is carting its garden
away toward somebody's landscaped Eden,
and we're picking up speed, single file,
driving past ponds displaying their steadfast
green, through towns too pretty to be.

Notes from the Castle

The sunlight was not our concern or even
The pane it shone through, and no one was going
Down for the mail, and the four lettuces
The gardener brought as a gift seemed to be
A calculated bounty, so that early on
We knew we were going to be stuck with ourselves
The rest of the day, the vicissitudes
Marching in rows from the forest, the balms
Not arriving till nightfall. On the prowl
Since morning, the wind had a touch too much
Of motivation, an annoying way
Of exactly ruffling the same oak leaf
As if it were practicing a piano trill;
All day, repetitive birds, far off,
Were either boring themselves to death
Or, drunk on instinct, doing their thing:
Ritual dances, territorial rites—
The whole imperial egg. What nests
Ambition is weaving in us is hard
To say: after the flat occasion,

The unshared sphere, each childish wish
Grows hopeless finding this is what the world is.
For this, the recommended cures are useless:
A cheery hello to the disaffected
At breakfast? A soupful of tears at dinner?
You could spill the whole silly story out
To one more demanding, ill-tempered beauty
You happened to meet at the A. & P.,
And still every greedy shopping cart,
First overstuffed and then abandoned
In the parking lot, would leave in its wake
Some human need, ignored, half-starved . . .
Torn between having nothing to say
And saying it, whole diaries got down:
How terrible to have dressed beautifully for the rain! . . .
I was launched on New York's bisexual muddle . . .
And so on. And always the hoped-for redeemer
Turns up and turns with a country stare:
The girl in the lime linen shorts, the boy
With blond corn-silk tow hair, the heart
Speeding up until they speak: the dross
Of cars, the sportsman's life, and money;
And so, believing that you had come
To rest among the innocent soldiers
Of sleep, you had merely stumbled on
Another temporary battlefield
As never-lasting as the shine of water.

Aspects of Lilac

By the turn of the driveway, two lilacs have called
Attention to themselves, not by an excess
Of bloom but by an attenuation
Of design: altered shadow on gravel.
Gone for good are those understated
Cases I rescued from worthless soil:
Ripped-off dusty miller from the beach,
Or, struck by overdoses of rain,

103

Spoiled spotted-leaf geranium. Worse
Is the thud of birds that kill themselves
By flinging their bodies with force against
Glass windows and doors as if this were
Some sort of morgue for feathered things.
The deaf and dumb would find all language
Futile here; nature is silent—
But underneath the silence, struggle.
While powder-puff clouds are showing off
Quickening shapes against more stately
Clouds behind them, an ant has dragged
A fly across the threshold, a mealy
Bug fastened its sticky jaws
Into the crotch of two green stems,
Chewing the asparagus fern to scruff.
Last night the moon had a Byzantine flare
Of lemon gold like the goldleaf halos
One sees in the early Italian masters—
Venice, in fact, comes to mind, the palazzos'
Sandcastle, ice-cream feats, effects
Childish but pleasing, of spun-stone heights,
While a rat stands gnawing a lettuce leaf
At the edge of one of the canals. And sex
Like a frog jumps onto the screen at once,
Its spiritual and degraded aspects
Equally keen. In fall, when the first
Earth colors harden and oak fire starts
Its flame and rust, memory dotes
On the old clichés of the unexpected.
Desire never knows the end of the book
Any more than the leaves of the lilac dug
Up in the woods, brought home, and planted
Can tell us whether its roots next spring
Will burst into purple or white cascades.

STANLEY MOSS

No poet is rooted in Long Island in the sense that Cavafy, Valery, Lorca or Amichai are rooted. Dig a few feet in Long Island, you strike salt water or a crab's claw pointing way back, no old civilization, no layers of human history, mostly geology and botany.

I once lived in a village South of Barcelona whose generations of fishermen, sailors and peasants had out of necessity, love of life, and fear of God named eighteen different winds. We have our Northeasters, our hurricane named "Gloria," but any association the name Gloria may have had to the Holy Virgin or Elizabeth the First, has largely been sloughed off. I am told that Yiddish has twenty-seven words for genius. I take consolation from the "Montauk Daisy," the "Long Island duck" and our potato.

I was born on this island, I've been counted in its elections and my speech bears its distant tribal imprint. Alas I

105

can't get lost in its thousands of square miles of faceless suburbs, nor in its woods, dunes or cranberry bogs.

On this island I was given up for dead, I teethed, had teeth pulled, wet my bed and was house broken, I split my tongue in half, learned to read and write. My parents are buried in its sand, I wrote my first and most recent poem here. But home is mostly internal and where the people I love are, a wide geography, not necessarily where the landscape is most familiar.

In Long Island the poets are good friends but loners. I know of no Long Island poet who is church going or Synagogue attending. We have a Zen master behind his privet, but I believe no local poet seeks his teaching. On the South Fork more than a few are called to the contemplative life by flights of honking geese. The word is out that something is more important than man. Perhaps the young mother singing her rock and roll lullaby to her new born child has the same idea. Every seashell knows, poetry like theater should impose itself on the audience not the audience on theater or poetry. Again and again, the ocean opens its sacred scrolls.

Homing

On a bright winter morning
flights of honking geese
seem a single being,
—when my kind comes into such formation
I watch for firing squads.
I never saw a line of praying figures take flight.
On an Egyptian relief I've seen
heads of prisoners facing the same direction,
tied together by a single rope
twisted around each neck
as if they were one prisoner.

I reach for a hand nearby.
An old dream makes me cautious:

as an infant, howling and pissing across the sky,
I was abducted by an eagle,
I remember the smell of carrion on its breath,
I was fed by and kissed the great beak . . .
Now a ridiculous, joyous bird
rises out of my breast,
joins the flock, a spot on the horizon.
I am left on earth with my kind.
They tie us throat to throat down here,
unspoken, unspeakable.
Again the honking passes over my roof.
A great informing spirit kneels overhead,
gives the mind a little power over oblivion.

Clouds

Working class clouds are living together
above the potato fields,—tall white beauties
humping above the trees, burying their faces
in each other,—clouds with darker thighs,
rolling across the Atlantic. West,
a foolish cumulus hides near the ocean
afraid of hurricanes.
Zeus came to the bed
of naked Io, as a cloud,
passed over her and into her as a cloud,
all cloud but part of his face
and a heavy paw, half cloud, half cat
that held her down.
I take clouds to bed that hold me
like snow and rain, gentle ladies,
wet and ready, smelling of lilac hedges.
I swear to follow them like geese,
through factory smoke,
beyond the shipping lanes and jet routes.
They pretend nothing—opening, drifting, naked.
I pretend to be a mountain

because I think clouds like that.
A cloudy night
proclaims a condition of joy.
Perhaps I remember a certain cloud,
perhaps I bear a certain allegiance
to a certain cloud.

Potato Song

Darkness, sunlight and a little holy spit
don't explain an onion with its rose windows
and presentiment of the sublime,
a green shoot growing out of rock,
or the endless farewells of trees.
Wild grasses don't grow just to feed sheep,
hold down the soil or keep stones from rolling,
they're meant to be seen, give joy, break the heart.
But potatoes hardly have a way of knowing.
They sense if it is raining or not,
how much sunlight or darkness they have,
not which wind is blowing or if there are crows
or red-winged blackbirds overhead.
They are unaware of the battles of worms,
the nightmares of moles, undergound humpings—
they do not sleep or wonder. Sometimes
I hear them call me "mister" from the ditch.
Workers outside my window in Long Island
cut potatoes in pieces, bury them, water them.
Each part is likely to sprout and flower.
No one so lordly not to envy that.

Clams

Ancient of Days, bless the innocent
who can do nothing but cling,
open or close their stone mouths.
Out of water they live on themselves
and what little sea water they carry with them.
Bless all things unaware, that perceive
life and death as comfort or discomfort:
bless their great dumbness.

We die misinformed
with our mouths of shell open.
At the last moment, as our lives fall off,
a gull lifts us, drops us on the rocks, bare
because the tide is out. Flesh sifts the sludge.
At sea bottom, on the rocks below the wharf,
a salt foot, too humble to have a voice,
thumps for representation, joy.

The Seagull

When I was a child, before I knew the word
for a snowstorm, before I remember
a tree or a field,
I saw an endless grey slate afternoon coming,
I knew a bird singing in the sun,
was the same as a dog barking in the dark.
A pigeon in a blizzard fluttered
against a kitchen window,
—my first clear memory of terror,
I kept secret, my intimations
I kept secret.

This winter I hung a grey and white stuffed
felt seagull from the cord of my window shade,
a reminder of good times by the sea,
of Chekhov and impossible love.

I took comfort from the gull, the graceful shape
sometimes lifted a wing in the drafty room.
Once when I looked at the gull I saw
through the window a living seagull glide
toward me then disappear,—what a rush of life!
I remember its hereness,
while inside the room
the senseless symbol
little more than a bedroom slipper
dangled on a string.

Beyond argument, my oldest emotion
hangs like a gull in the distant sky.
Eyes behind bars of mud and salt
see some dark thing below,
—my roof under the sea.
Only the sky is taken for granted.
In the quiet morning light,
terror's the only bird I know,
—although birds have fed from my hand.

The Meeting

It took me some seconds as I drove toward
the white pillow case, or was it a towel
blowing across the road, to see what it was.
In Long Island near the sanctuaries
where there are still geese and swan,
I thought a swan was hit by an automobile.
I was afraid to hurt it. The beautiful creature
rolled in sensual agony,
then reached out to attack me.
Why do I feel something happened on the road,
a transfiguration, a transgression,
as if I hadn't come to see what was,
but confronted the white body,
tried to lift, help her fly,
or slit its throat.
Why did I need this illusion,
a beauty lying helpless?

110

The Branch

Since they were morose in August,
not worth saving,
I paid to have the junipers torn out
trunk and root, the roots had enough strength
to pull the truck back down so hard
the wheels broke the brick walk.

Heaped in front of my house,
cousins of the tree of mercy,
the green and dry gray branches
that did not suffer
but had beauty to lose.
Damp roots, what do I know
of the tenderness of earth,
the girlish blond dust?
Rather than have the branches dumped or burned
I dragged them to the bulkhead
and pushed them into the sea.

I know the story of a tree:
of Adam's skull at the foot of Jesus crucified,
of the cross made of timbers nailed together
that Roman soldiers saved from the destroyed
    temple,
that King Solomon built from a great tree
that rooted and flourished
from a branch of the tree of mercy
planted in dead Adam's mouth,
that the branch was given
to Adam's third son Seth by an angel
that stopped him outside the wall
when he returned to the garden,
that the angel warned him
that he could not save his father
who was old and ill
with oils or tears or prayers.

111

Go in darkness, mouth to mouth
is the command.
I kiss the book,
not wanting to speak
of the suffering I have caused.
Sacred and defiled,
my soul is right
to deal with me in secret.

DAN MURRAY

Some of the poems here are quasi-mirrorings of various places, times, and events on the East End and expressions of a mutual belonging. My purpose is to keep seeing the place but not dissolve into the bucolic aspect of the local environment. The poems are intended to be observations and participations, intimate connections, rather than calculated self-assertions. They attempt to challenge the supremacy of logical principles.

Insofar as the East End includes Plum Island, Brookhaven National Laboratory, and various other scientific research facilities, some of these poems might be said to be the consequence of place. Otherwise, they are the result of an attempt to incorporate theoretical scientific concepts and to assimilate technological language into poetry. Because the poet and the physicist are more concerned with creating images and establishing mental or invisible connections than with describing facts, I wanted to see what would happen when I consciously attempted to synthesize science and poetry.

June

In green shadows, leaning
ferns are brothering
leaf & unfathered moss.

A shock of upright yellow,
profusion of blameless daisies,
one is my daughter.
Abundance.
In its quickness,
the fidgety dispatch of crickets.

Over the blue bay,
flecks of pepper
trail down the twilight sky:

a community of gulls,
beaks open like tongs,
banks around the sedge
on utter tongues of wings
& lands a family
of squatters on the water.

Just before dark,
the astonishing chime of stars.

July

Your neighbor's telephone
rings & the morning glories
bloom riper than carnival lanterns.

Piano song from a pavilion,
full-blown, drowns
in afternoon ocean breezes,
drifts to another ear.
Strangers stop on the beach
to pet your unleashed dog.

Fireworks burst in the night:
golden spidery chandeliers,
showers of copper filigree,
tan the faces in a crowd;
fountains of lime spray
& wiggle like sperm.

A boom echoes along the surf
& lingers in the spirals of shells.

August

Sitting on the porch I shuffle the cards,
days flicker by like a picket fence.
Over gin & dispersed dandelion,
& leaves fizzing chartreuse,
innocence goes to seed.

Sunset inflames the evening haze.
Moths twitch around the porch light,
pleading another dream.

It must be rest
the locusts crave all night.

Theory

I think of a man my son met
in the schoolyard with a knapsack
full of steakbones
petting an invisible dog.

Heels in the ground he walked it,
claimed the dog could cook & sew.

"Next time," I said, "he says to you,
'don't step on the dog,'
don't mock, I want you to be kind."

Ask if it bites,
take the risk & rub its ears.

Passamaquoddy Sunrise

Not awake yet, the sun begins
through fog, a still life:
a radiant melon on a quilt.

Eight minutes late,
I rise, try to meditate,
to choose with love, not need,
to weed illusions:
the magnetism of money,
the lustered petals of lips.

Webs of mist vanish from the valley,
an arrowhead glitters on the lake.
Pure spring water waits under pine,
but wild lupine & lilac distract me.

Ah, Lord, weave
surplices of Queen Ann lace,
propagate the daisy in purple clover.
Expand the rings the feeding bass
break on the gold of peaceful water.

This is what all night the rain
on the cold roof was praising,
this is the promise of sunset kept.

Constellation / Rorschach

The vanity of imposing reason
on the universe of personal events
is another form of tyranny.
Research, all dressed up in labs & grants,
gives an absolute stranger a familiar face.

Say Orion & his belt
& seven drunken sisters
are Russian, put vodka in the dippers.

Say anyone's missing father
can be found in a double-breasted blazer,
if you happen to be looking
through palm trees in Florida.
How interesting.

How about that Kant
holding up his socks
with wire gadgets & springs in pockets?

Mind cajoles Cordelia into her heart
on her sleeve if not in her mouth,
or Lear in the mazes of the spirit
in the black desert sky.

Filter in St. Sebastian, walking target,
magnetize the hyphenated stars
into a shower of arrows

& Orion could still be
a quarterback bullet-passing poems.
How charming that truth arrives
more or less than its description.

© Gail Besemer Parlatore

ANSELM PARLATORE

. . . these from the journal, dear Roberto, in trying to answer yr "how the area has affected the work?" Psycho-geotectonics, perhaps, or more probably the landscape as a vast religious flood plain metaphor. ". . the transcendental & apocalyptic perspectives of religion come as a tremendous emancipation . ." (Frye). Emerson's expositor or Carlyle's morality. Jeffersonian, really. &, of course, a Givernian obsession but not the water-lily. Rather, maybe, a combe of gnarled pitch/poverty pines in a swale. It haunts me. The dune. The mathematics. forces. geometry. a crisscrossing matrix . . North/South (Glacial & Marine Geology) & East/West/East (Coastal Hydrology). It's all vectors. Arrows to the heart. "Like the wind & the rain & the great glacier itself, the surf is the complicated end product of a long series of equations." (Rattray). Also Ammons: "the very longest swell in the ocean, / I suspect, / carries the

deepest memory." More importantly Neruda: "water
which dashes over beaches like daring hands beneath a
skirt." Tides & wind a spiritual & lusty stenography.
Lyellian gradualism. Sir Thomas Browne's East Anglian
Shore. Sir Henry Vaughan's West Country. Paterson.
Gloucester. Metcalf. Robert Morgan's Zirconia. Evolution
also as one of many central myths/motifs. But you know as
well as I the tradition. "The greatest writers have been at
least parochial, provincial in their rootedness." (Walcott). I
dunno . . But, yet . . "if we do not know our environment,
we shall mistake our dreams for a part of it, & so spoil our
science by making it fantastic, & our dreams by making
them obligatory." (Santayana). But this much I'm sure of: a
preoccupation with resolving things bio-muck with the
transparency clear & sweet. An impassioned microscopy.
Place translated into line break/length at sea level: line
break(s) & beginnings pre & post synaptic membrane tem-
plates of increased lung capacity . . not Olson Hokum but
the flatness keeps the line(s) out there in bird land . . . "I
think more of a bird with broad wings flying & lapsing
through the air . . I think I read my poetry more by length
than by stress as a matter of movements in space than
footsteps hitting the earth." (D. H. Lawrence in a letter . .).
I might ever be able to . . . ! Anyway, a fetish quality, I tell
ya, about these erotic post atomic & Newtonian, space age
pelagian georgics. Narcissistic reveries with depleation . .
(pleas) because of the loneliness . . . & the wandering.
Loci. Nidus. Place. Home. Woman. Fold. "the landscape is
The Woman & there is Woman in the landscapes." (de-
Kooning). The medieval Brigit shared the Muse boat with
another Mary . . this one with blue robes & pearl necklace
. . was the ancient pagen Sea-goddess Marian in drag . .
Marian, Miriam, Mariamne, (Sea Lamb) Myrrhine, Myr-
tea, Myrrha, Maria, Marina (no pun intended), Mecox!
Marah (Hebrew) = brine. We have plenty of that here.
Mecox as liminal utopia. And these too re: water/posey:
"the bottom of the sea is cruel"; (Hart Crane) "nature must
include the void as its ultimate ground"; (Molesworth) "the
sight of unenclosed water is barely tolerable" (Francine du
Plessix Gray) "And the sea itself is there/behind the last

house at the end of the street"; (Simpson) "algae of long
past sea currents are moved"; (Ezra Pound in letter to
Perdita Schaffner in condolence upon hearing of H. D.'s
death) "how can water that doesn't chase the moon speak
to the imagination?"; (Barth) "the tide marsh, its twin
diurnal ebbs & floods continuously reorchestrating the
geography"; (Barth) "the places where water comes together with other water. Those places stand out in my
mind as Holy Places." (Raymond Carver.) But the longing/
loneliness defines the geography & the coordinates.
Melvillian wilderness. Geoffrey O'Brien recently sd,
"Melville was mad enough to believe that the groves &
harbors the words make are real, that the imagined world
opens into actual spaces. He entered those spaces, felt out
their recesses—those "wondrous depths, where strange
shapes of the unwarped primal world glided to & fro" . . .
An expeditionary geopoetics. Language as primordial
mud. Eroticism of annihilation. Even if in a Virgilian he-
roic. But, finally, this: reality should, ultimately, be non-
local. Like Bell's Theorem, the atom's measured attributes
are determined not by events happening at the actual
measurement site but by events arbitrarily distant, including events outside the light cone.

Mecox Motel

The axioms chelated & dendritic
at the surf's edge, a lace archive
of tangled foam & chasms
vacancies in the stranded
lattice discreet but grieving

a rubble in the veldt:
beyond the slender pinnacles
the sun's blind tenderness

moisture of the stain spreading
sleep's blotter, the dark ravine

her ankle on the sheet
annihilation's exotic particles
in an immune cascade
the swish-groan of their benediction
unbinding the wind, precipitating
unknown & intricate salts.

Outside the window facing the bay
an echelon of geese over the peat bog
echoes of peasant stories

their dark lust a Medieval Church Latin
braiding & unbraiding the DNA's language

a rhapsody, the storm, now a long way off.

Mecox Nunnery & Saint Dominic

In Water Mill the last glacier still moans
it can be heard in the nuns' evening prayer

as the candles melt, their wax
beads flowing down the meridians
over chains of amino acids
proteins electrifying the organic matrix

scallop shells, desperate for mineralization.

She leaves the prayer hall of Villa Maria
& out in the flushing wetlands of Mecox Bay

in the clumps of undulating cordgrass
culls young finfish from their mudholes
as they feed on minute phytoplankton & zooplankton

the larvae of shellfish, brought in with the tide.

Shorebirds, windbirds, gather around her
they peck at the fiddler crabs caught in the Spartina
  grass.

She runs her pale fingers through the mud
over the lenses of sand in the inter-tidal marsh

121

feels the cool, aerated spring water from the glacial
    font

the headlands, that has drained across the outwash
    plain
from Seven Ponds, Mill Pond, Mill Creek, Hayground
    Cove
Calf Creek, Burnett Creek, Sam's Creek, to the Ocean.

Her hair loosens in the cross winds of the dunes.

At the Seapoose her mouth fills with roses
& her secretions rush in & out of the bay.

She ignores the litter of angels
filling all her floating orbs

the tumescence of the estuaries

& returns to town, to the derelict windmill
whose sails baffle the continuum.

She climbs the tailpole, her habit caught
in the spindles, the pinion gears
slides out onto one of the blades

as it methodically slices the sky
the moist, gleaming membrane of the spheres

& stares at a comet's tail. It vanishes
in the tapestries of Saint Dominic.

Woman of the Late Fall Run

The fall moons have been blood streaked
full & luscious they continue
to suck through the nets
& embrace their aftermath
lazily as they spin on their axes.

Mats of oily baitfish hug Flying Point Beach
mature eels slither out at Mecox

geese point out over balmy Wickapoque
& the marauding, migratory schools of blues
the plump bass, scallop the shore
glisten in the wash of night fire.

She knows all this & accepts it
sweeps her garments through the sky
scattering the star clusters at her waist.

She grabs a fish, slides her fingers up
under its edematous gills, lifts
& kisses the phosphorous spent there.

She is like a ghost in a membrane
& then she is the membrane
fading out of the ecliptic
into higher tidal latitudes
where she is always cybernetic & loved.

It's she who hears the groans of antler replacement
& radio star scintillations. Her juices provide
this gusty supersonic plasma flow
a lunar wind filling interplanetary space
entwining Mill Pond & Mill Creek
spilling out into Mecox Bay

as she drags the tense, burning
lunar magnetic field lines along
& slowly out into the Ocean
trapping huge bass, causing a rip
in the tide, a careless, deadly gesture.

Portrait in Veiled Waters

Even with the ice & wind
the night herons continue to stare out
across Mecox Bay
the lanterns of the eelers & crab boats
no longer flickering
in the moon's gnarled reverie.

These nightbirds perch invisible
tightening their balance
on the porticoes of sleep
with the coots & fish hawks
water witches, filling
the deserted piazzas & basilicas of Mecox

they never cease gnawing
the surface knobs of its viruses.

This winter, the fiddler crabs, mud snails
& periwinkles remain
in the swales between the dunes
with the trailing arbutus
black pine, berries

& a new pale white parasitic vine.

We're all expecting the storm
of the equinoxes & winter solstice
it will build up the dunes.
The shifting sand will increase the heather.

Years back, on the farm of John Hand
the shifting dunes buried
the abandoned whale boats
& fish wagons along the old beach road.

John Jagger's beach lot
is still under the ocean
& the meadowlands
back of the beach at Sam's Creek
now are in danger. Only last week
a few dune houses toppled
into the surf during a storm

& the old route down past
Mrs. Berwind's bungalow is gone.

But it's calm far & deep off the beach
at Mecox where very little changes.

Along the purple spine of the planet
The Mid-Atlantic Ridge
run the rivers of the sea
warming the basins, troughs, & canyons.

A long seamed, sloping flank of the continent
descends out there to abysmal plains
of boundless silence: past the marbled canyons
glistening with tunicates
& out beyond the Continental Shelf
in the crevices of memory
where our breath filters the dark waters.

Huge starfish prowl slowly
over this mantle seeking mussels.

The chitinous lances of mantis shrimp
pierce the chambered light

bivalvular siphons weep perpetual
vortices of swirling plankton

& in all the candelabras of sponges
all dreams become nocturnes.

The sea-cucumber's parasols of red tentacles
float in this darkness
cooling all the caverns & recesses
of the moon snail's presbyteries.

Here the ocean buffers
all rapid changes in mute piety
the only sound, a grading
of microstructural increments
within a molluscan shell
a growth of the prismatic layer.

There is a solitude in the coherent matrices
within the prism
as the electron-dense lamellae
at the terminal boundaries
lull over each other
dragging all the organic strands
laced with hinged filaments of amino acids
& protein linkages
across & down into the sunken canyons
down the eons, to comb
the rich bottom oozes

down where evolution takes all its time.

© Russ Coughlin

SIMON PERCHIK

Since I don't begin a poem with any pre-conception, it's natural that the images at hand creep into and guide the work. Stars, suns, moons, waves, sand, trees, leaves are the symbols I find both powerful and appropriate for the ideas that eventually will emerge.

Moreover, my work has almost no narrative or exposition. I leave that to prose. The power, if it comes at all, comes from those primordial symbols so prevalent on the East End.

And perhaps that's why I and my neighbors are writing. To get it all down before Eden itself is tainted.

*

The pale stone under my rib
expects an answer
thinks there's a breath
filled with milk

—I sleep on this stone
as a convict will touch a key
melting in his shirt pocket
—I don't turn

or drag it off like a splinter
or ladder.
I can't get up.

My side won't dry.
I leave marks on the road
on the bedsheets, stare at the smoke
as if I recognize a voice

—in this road
the gravel act as guides
through their own mass-grave
the torn-from-its-throat
that can't get up—this stone

expects a number, rounded off
easy to remember
how many come each night to breathe
through the cracks in the road.

It knows I'm looking :fathers, mothers
sisters, sons
still blacken the sky
—who can find them
under this dark, swept

under the wide roller brushes
by a chimney sweep
who once closed a door—he yells
get off the street
no one's here to take the blame

—he even talks in reich
in roads that never heal
—too much is under the ground

and the stone that can't get up
crawls into traffic
into the fumes
into his house and children
who love him, who listen
side by side to the story
how one night some nut
who wouldn't let go
wouldn't let anyone touch a small stone
he kept calling his sister, his mother

his father—side by side
as bricks will stand around a chimney
that licks the dirt
with hot, small mouths.

There is no chimney
except the soft cries :stones
that for the first time
felt a gentle hand.

They were reaching for their mother's breath
—it takes a small breath :a child's voice
under the dripping grates
no one in all the world would hear
except this stone, that stone
that one   : cinders

to pave this road
as charcoals hand in hand
drifting over the last breath they heard

over this stone
that managed to stay pale
that thinks the moonlight
which hardly touches it
will give it an answer.

I tell it *yes*. Sleep under me.

*

Like a warden at the evening meal
I body count :these stars
have something to hide—only at night

my phonograph again that *Angel Eyes*
as the maze engraved in a tire
filters, each nail till the sting
circles higher and higher, ropes dangling.
All these knots. The set

healing on my floor, trussed
taped, glued, its top caked open
—what's to escape :that song

is on its third engine.
I'm used to my room going black
spin blind as if the fuse
blew itself up taking the sky with it

and I count without looking up
one, and wait. It takes a while.
But at least who else, what else, how else
one is there. I never reach *two,* the sun

plunges once its black hood is untied
and lights everywhere broken, my *Angel Eyes*
Angel Eyes, Angel Eyes reeling
snarled :its treads worn down
to almost a whisper.
I can't even see the pieces.

Escape from what!
The claw I thought would puncture
licks the wound, singing, singing :*Angel Eyes*
prefers its blindness

—even I wait in the trenches
in the cliffs falling from her mouth
from the sky not yet worn through
from the cone

coiling tighter and tighter above its prey
its road on a map

on a song dead weight :the stillness
steadied by something hid
that outnumbers her voice, *one*
and *Angel Eyes.*

*

I should wear gloves, these white pages
unpacked from their pad, laid out
as a surgeon would your snapshot
till only the closed lips can be seen
and my table begin to tremble
—who can work this way
not know your lips won't move.

I need glasses, that new lens
urged in the journals, my eyes
would enter your skin
go at your heart
while the dead, writes the inventor
just by a blink toward the door
and under that faint breeze
everything breathes again
—you rise from your photo
as once turning from a mirror
you crowed, *Not bad, eh!*

There was
except now everything needs enlarging
no page is wide enough
—even my pulse falling off
before it dries into a word
into a question mark at last at rest

—I should practice grammar
let these sheets read
how their blood too will clot
become that small and smaller
just the right cut and your lips

fly! I should huge fans
surround your picture and in my arms
the pages louder and louder
work this way.

*

The mirror a convict holds out
and between two bars
sees the long, steel corridor :the sun

aches too, hunting down the light
that escapes each evening, hides
a few hours, a few clouds, the cold
the lifetime—what did you expect

holding out your hand
as a dorsal fin will deflect
and everything swerves to the floor
—I'm drowning
so close to your lips

and my heart held out
still looks down the hall
the dust covered breasts
no longer thirsty for lips
or hands almost on fire

—a small mirror shares my room
with an electric switch
with light that kills on the spot

and what did you expect
holding out the sun
till it finds my window
covered with morning frost
and how the curtains warmed your shoulders
and kisses and yes, birds and oceans too
are hiding somewhere from my arms.

ALLEN PLANZ

One is the fate of one's place. The East End is great because it's mostly water. And that's the North Atlantic out there.

Woodknot

1

A hard thing to break
   is scartissue. Ligaments
     & tendons
   snap with bone, twist thru muscle
but this torque gnarled with wire & horn
   gives way only to fire,
     & that last.

That 1001b blueshark we cut up for chum—
   everything went cheerfully
thru the meatgrinder but the liver casing:
     I ground & ground
     while it writhed
   unscathed in coils of steel

   & plopped on deck. I picked
     it up thinking
     of the glint
in the slack skin of a scar knotting my arm.

2

Woodknot: a shadow never strays from it,
   voice of a shadow
     heard only in flames, in
resinous steam.
          Up north it tells
   where streams draining ponds
point downcountry, toward home.
     Offshore
   the barometer in its grip
         falls faster
   than celldoors close or termites
     eat celluose to tinder.

Even the hardest texts
   fracture
in the stress of their own making.

3

Thumbjoint
cantilevered into arthritic archways,
    winch clutch suddenly unfreezing,
        chainsaw
    shying away from a cedar hip in deadly
        abrupt recoil:

these things I can take
        only in rest
    that rust
in which I hear myself snoring,
        by which I keep tuned
all the scars crossing my voicebox
        but one
torchcut by my captain spinning the wheel.

Mako

Cleaning Mako shark stoned in firelight
I catch fire from a brainstem
where blood is darkest in my hand,
dark as the underwaters it hurtled from
blind to the flying gaff.
I have killed & I have slaughtered
in no name but my own & still I raise
the great head to the sky, prise open
the jaws to show rows of teeth
staggered like a tank trap, & feint
left in a circle at a school of stars.

In a ring of trees underlit by fire,
my knees in guts cascading from the carcass
uplifted in my arms, I lurch keening
for the moon that drags me out to sea,
moon I never dreamed but
as a bloodred disc occulting in my heart . . .
now this bloodlord of the sea I feed on fire.

Scalloping Northwest

1

Centuries ago
the indians said animals
no longer talked to them
and both entered the fur trade.

Working six weeks into scallop season
I stop speaking and enter that silence.

2

Even the slenderest water
is thicker than air. Erecting itself

on the skittery rasp of the cullboard
a crab holds out a bubble

on the drawtrap of its jaws.

With my next breath
a rock in the fog
lifts its deadrise a boat's length away.

Midwinter

at Cedar Point
I saw a half mile off
six dogs
take down a doe
they'd driven again thru the glare-ice
and again into the surf.

Disemboweled
when I got there
but not dead,

and it is dirty work too
leaning idly

with a trident
over a shoal
to spear
dogfish against gravel

then both on one shaft
twist wildly away

Inquiline

There is one more mess in East Hampton   this
    morning
        you & me at our worst
"in the world's most sophisticated resort"
talking rehab & rebellion   land value prepped against
        vigorish   foreshortening the seaward lawns
the kickoff martini in the sculpture garden   color
    vodka
            washes out if it can

at our worst
        lying about money. Drugged
                yet mean
enough to cut one dead   this elegance
that says, beyond words, what they are
        drives us crazy, love
as we play it, i.e. fuck or fight! class
            against class in
the only underworld left late in the century.

Seasonal
        survival. From pop to punk, key home free
all summer. Next to the wafflehouse, the swallowfields.
Next to you
        me, waiting in line
welfare unemployment high tech shoplifting uplifting
            lubricious
        my tool throws me seagreen
                out the window. Look

    at it this way
quantisized and discontinuous next
      we got the berries
& you have a breakdown. Child
now you know ward doors closing behind you
      Child, had
we'd been elsewhere in the suburban underclass
    style says we'd of made it style says
Hey!
    move it out move it down

& it all lies down in the county this morning
    at least, clean it up
you at your worst
    moving out of the hospital, out of the county
& I must hustle the best of them,
the gofers, Jake & the Sconzo family.
      I do my best. You
    look cool, you too! with the best of them
& the best of ourselves
      at worst leaving too early.

ANNE E. PORTER

All I think and feel about this place is only in the poems I've written. Only another poem could say more, and whether I ever write that poem or not I don't know.

In a Country Hospital

Somewhere in this brick building a woman in labor
    groans,
The morning is still dark.
But the robins' clamor has started, and the ground-fog
    is rising,
(I had to get up to look.)
Two lamps at the hospital gate
Paint the green hedge with falseness
And the morning star is shining,
High, clear, fresher than dew
In the transparent wilderness overhead.

Soon day will come, with her plain clattering gold
And linen piled on carts, and smells of ether and
    coffee
Filling the wards and corridors, and the lamps and the
    star will go out.

We can hear the cries of the new-born, and a man
    coughing without relief,
We can hear sparrows rilling up out of the coolness
    into the eaves
And chirping there, loud and excited, as if it were their
    marketplace

We can hear the roar of the mile-away Atlantic floating
    beyond the town,
Beyond the wheat and potato-fields and the beach-grass
    and the dunes
Beyond the brackish ponds where the swans nest,
A shimmering mountain of praises, of crystal and
    thunder.
And to us, whose sweaty gowns stick to us,
Who are all twisted, who are all aching,
This Friday morning the blessed Eucharist was brought.

Leavetaking

Nearing the start of that mysterious last season
Which brings us to the close of the other four,
I'm somewhat afraid and don't know how to prepare,
So I will praise you.

I will praise you for the glaze on buttercups
And the pearly scent of wild fresh water
And the great cross-bow shapes of swans flying over
With that strong silken threshing sound of wings
Which you gave them when you made them without
    voices.

And I will praise you for crickets.
On starry autumn nights
When the earth is cooling
Their rusty diminutive music
Repeated over and over
Is the very marrow of peace.

And I praise you for crows' calling from tree-tops,
Speech of my first village,
And for the sparrow's flash of song
Flinging me in an instant
The joy of a child who woke
Each morning to the freedom
Of her mother's unclouded love
And lived in it like a country.

And I praise you that from vacant lots
From only broken glass and candy-wrappers
You raise up the blue chicory flowers.

I thank you for that secret praise
Which burns in every creature,
And I ask you to bring us to life
Out of every sort of death

And teach us mercy.

On the Three-Hour Train-Ride

First we pass a farm
And see dark wings flare up
Out of a patch of grain

We see the water-loving willows
With their slim leaves
And the tall rushes in the swamp
Their fleeces filled with light

Here's a wide inlet
Perfectly still
Glazed with the tender colors
Of the morning sky

And here's a fisherman
With his rod and creel
Standing alone
Thigh-deep in water

His spirit
Will outlast the earth

And here's an acre of crushed cars
And there's a refuse-heap
That's white with seagulls

Here blindfolded with boards
Is an abandoned factory
In a field of yarrow

Here closer to the city
Some small pleasure-boats
Dance at their moorings
In the dirty river

King David says
We're thirsty

For God
For the living God

When will we see His face?

Four Poems in One

At six o'clock this morning
I saw the rising sun
Resting on the ground like a boulder
In the thicket back of the school,
A single great ember
About the height of a man.

Night has gone like a sickness,
The sky is pure and whole.
Our Lady of Poland spire
Is rosy with first light,
Starlings above it shatter their dark flock.

Notes of the Angelus
Leave their great iron cup
And slowly, three by three
Visit the Polish gardens round about,
Dahlias shaggy with frost
Sheds with their leaning tools
Rosebushes wrapped in burlap
Skiffs upside down on trestles
Like dishes after supper

These are the poems I'd show you
But you're no longer alive.
The cables creaked and shook
Lowering the heavy box.
The rented artificial grass
Still left exposed
That gritty gash of earth
Yellow and mixed with stones
Taking your body
That never in this world
Will we see again, or touch.

We know little
We can tell less
But one thing I know
One thing I can tell

I will see you again in Jerusalem
Which is of such beauty
No matter what country you come from
You will be more at home there
Than ever with father or mother
Than even with lover or friend
And once we're within her borders
Death will hunt us in vain.

FAIRFIELD PORTER

from Fairfield Porter's letters, courtesy of Mrs. Fairfield
   Porter:

(on October:)
". . . It's really beautiful here this month. There are warm
   pink days alternated with very blue-black ones, with
   white sun . . ."

(on June:)
". . . The cold here has delayed the season all of one
   month, but the slowness holds the beauty, and on cold
   north wind days the sky is extra blue. I sat and
   observed the apple trees in bloom."

(on November:)
". . . This is the first time that I have thought that
   November after the leaves have fallen may be one of
   the best times of year on Long Island. That is, I like the
   way the trees don't block the light anymore."

(On "regionalism," from a letter to poet and art critic
   Claire Nicolas White:)
"I don't want to be forced to consider the question, which
   I never think or care about, of some sort of Long
   Island regionalism—that is forcing a false issue. It has
   nothing to do with me, only with temporary fashions in
   journalism. We moved here because I wanted to be in
   connection with New York as a painter. It seemed a
   place that, if we couldn't afford to keep on going to
   Maine, would be a place where, in the summer, one
   could swim in the ocean. If you try to make something
   of our living in Southampton rather than in some other
   place, you won't find much real material."

The Reader

You who read beautifully
Straight under the lamp in your chair
Brave in the face of encompassing sorrow
Witholding the tears induced by the course of the story
There are things that you know
Even if you have never lived them
Which I who have lived them
All the habits and the first occasions
Do not understand that I hardly know
Still not at their repetitions
As I did not the first time
Nothing is the same there is nothing to do differently
No way is surely right
And your voice at once sorrowful and unpitying
Is full of a hardness of knowledge resembling ignorance
Beyond my attaining
Lost or asleep in the encompassing event
And the story tells what you accept
That the missed event is unfulfilled

The Morning Train

When the morning train blows at the station
Where shining puddles remaining after rain
Reflect the autumn colors and new green
Already yellowed by the rising sun,
I remember a night of one car after
Another swishing through a film of water,
And a dead skunk squashed against the asphalt,
Spreading its perfume that fortells the frost.

The new air still includes an aching
Left from the effort of a dusty summer
Declining—always more a mordant green
Of branches moving in the windy dark,
Unable to let go their load of leaves,
Beyond a screen door that filters in the cold.

September

A warm wind
Blows all night
No clouds
Brilliant stars.
The barometer drops
On the outermost edge
Of a hurricane.
Rainy morning
The barometer shifts
As the wind wheels
To the north west.
In adjusting clouds
Colors multiply
Colors of shells,
Until the sun
Bursting through
Tears them apart

Again and again.
An intense light
Sucks colors out,
A blue-black day.
The north west gale
Rips whitecaps off
The bay turned
Dark purple-green:
"The wine-dark sea."
As night comes
The wind drops
Then stars again
Mars in the south
Brightest of all.

At Night

Out of the rumbling dark
We accumulate the shapes
Of other beginnings
The train stops for a moment
And it is almost the same—
Only a little different—
Green crescents floating
A place name like a flash card
Close to the eyes, big, definite and dim
There is no reason for mistrust
And the rumble resumes:
When it stops one wakens into silence
And the wetness of the air
The pavement firm and black
Black sky with geometric lights
Violet, electric; the smell of bushes
A barking dog, footsteps, the slam of car doors
A latching door, newspapers and boxes
The color of food on the colored tablecloth
And music, and musical voices.

A Painter Obsessed by Blue

No color isolates itself like blue.
If the lamps's blue shadow equals the yellow
Shadow of the sky, in what way is one
Different from the other? Was he on the verge of a
   discovery
When he fell into a tulip's bottomless red?
Who is the mysterious and difficult adversary?

If he were clever enough for the adversary
He should not have to substitute for blue,
For a blue flower radiates as only red
Does, and red is bottomless like blue. Who loves yellow
Will certainly make in his life some discovery
Say about the color of the sky, or another one.

That the last color is the difficult one
Proves the subtlety of the adversary.
Will he ever make the difficult discovery
Of how to gain the confidence of blue?
Blue is for children; so is the last yellow
Between the twigs at evening, with more poignancy than
   red.

A furnace with a roar consumes the red
Silk shade of a lamp whose light is not one
Like birds' wings or valentines or yellow,
Able to blot out the mysterious adversary
Resisted only by a certain blue
Illusively resisting all discovery.

Did it have the force of a discovery
To see across the ice a happy red
Grown strong in heart beside intensest blue?
In this case the blue was the right one,
As a valentine excludes the adversary,
That will return again disguised in yellow.

If it were possible to count on yellow
Dandelions would constitute discovery:

But all at once the sudden adversary
Like a nightmare swallows up the red,
To dissipate before the starry one,
The undefended wall of blue.

Blue walls crumble under trumpets of yellow
Flowers—one unrepeatable discovery—
And red prevails against the adversary.

© Claudia Ott

GRACE SCHULMAN

From my studio window, in Springs, I see trees whose names speak of life *(arbor vitae)* and death (hemlock). Their gestures recall human actions: branches of the Norwegian spruce are extended majestically, in command; those of the blue spruce hold votive candles, as in prayer. As strangers exchange greetings, hickories touch branches across the road.

Boldly, the trees flourish in acid soil near salt water bays. They are many, in number and variety, as are the birds: I see swallows and terns, cardinals and egrets, here or within a few minutes of my house.

The poems in this section were composed in this area, and show a tendency—which may be common, among poets born in the city, who regard nature as exotic—to see things of the natural world as metaphors for human deeds and principles. "The Marsh" deals with the distintegration of a marriage, portrayed in vines that are hooked into elms for survival, just as the people endure, "as if we knew life's law / was cleave or die." In "Images of Gravity," birds and plants, as well as people, demonstrate scientific laws; "The Flight" is based on a dream that is set in this area; "The Island" has to do with change and loss, drawn in the image of a spindly house built on sand.

I know that the landscape of East Hampton—of Springs, especially—has affected me in this way. I am uncertain, though, about the essential reasons as to why I work here. Perhaps only the poems know.

Blessed Is the Light

Blessed is the light that turns to fire, and blessed the
  flames that fire makes of what it burns.
Blessed the inexhaustible sun, for it feeds the moon
  that shines but does not burn.
Praised be hot vapors in earth's crust, for they force up
  mountains that explode as molten rock and cool, like
  love remembered.
Holy is the sun that strikes sea, for surely as water
  burns life and death are one. Holy the sun, maker of
  change, for it melts ice into water that bruises
  mountains, honing peaks and carving gullies.
Sacred is the mountain that grows compact, less porous,
  over time. Jagged peaks promise permanence but
  change, planed by rockslides, cut by avalanche,
  crushed, eroded, leached of minerals.
Sacred the rock that spins for centuries before it shines,
  governed by gravity, burning into sight near earth's
  orbit, for it rises falling, surviving night.
Behold the arcs your eyes make when you speak.
  Behold the hands, white fire. Branches of pine,
  holding votive candles, they command, disturbed by
  wind, the fire that sings in me.
Blessed is whatever alters, turns, revolves, just as the
  gods move when the mind moves them.
Praised be the body, our bodies, that lie down and
  open and rise, falling in flame.

151

Easy as Wind

Easy as wind that lifts white pine
and blows for flowers, showering rose
petals on cold marble statues,
we touch and separate.
                            I am familiar
with water burning the land,
turning catbrier to red-brown wire,
clinging to live. I have seen flame
waiting to burn, altering shadows,
striking rectangles beyond the trees.
Even the sea collects its powers and strikes,
baffling the sand's composure.
                            But now, suddenly,
wherever I look I see wind
I cannot see, touching nowhere, everywhere.

The Marsh

For years nothing grew
in acid soil
near my house
that stood on scant legs.
Then, year by year, I saw
sassafras and glasswort;
creepers curled around
bayberry trees,
tall stalks hunted soil
to live. Nearby, shadblow trees
with striated, gunmetal bark
lifted wiry branches.
Then fires of wind and water
burned the marsh;
only bare vines,
hooked into elms,
survived,

as we had, joined
together, in the house
on bulldozed sandy ground,
draggled, storm-blown,
still holding fast
to memories of dense grasses
and green vines
as if we knew life's law
was cleave or die.

The Swans

All day I have thought of the swans
that flew skyward, bellowing,
maundering at first,
immense and web-footed,
fanning tousled wings,
parting the stream
then surging through air.
I know you will pass and return,
your body tense, then writhing,
undulant, coiled in sleep,
your silver eyes mirroring my eyes,
your hands raveled and free,
that somewhere the swans have alighted
on lucent water,
their spiral forms
utterly denying
turbulent flight.

Images of Gravity

1.

Buoyancy:
The wind moves
a swamp reed
that the finch rides.

2.

Force:
Swallows
plummet like hail,
careening
over wild roses.

3.

Vector:
Bulrushes
gesture in wind,
dancer's arms.

4.

Density:
Gulls,
angular in flight,
stand pot-bellied.

5.

Weightlessness:
I've heard the albatross
sleeps on the wing
in the heart of a storm,
gliding
on currents it raises.

6.

Acceleration:
Dead
birds
fall
fast.

7.

Balance:
Fragile as a grasshopper,

my house stands
on spindly pilings.

8.

Momentum:
Waves crash
still rising
in vapor.

The Island

So slender
is the island
that I can see sun ignite the bay
and strike the ocean
at the same time.
Larks sweep the sky
soon to be scarlet;
beyond shadblow trees
presumptuous catbrier climbs
a pine tree, and tall stalks
sway like metronomes,
displacing patens,
claiming the marshland.

Here I find it strange
to find peace strange.
The island
is no more real
than the moon's singularity;
it will change
as a cloud's shape
alters in wind,
as storms move dunes
and sea-spray chops
their heather.

Surely as the ocean batters
the sand's composure

prodding the shoreline inland,
this land will change
just as the boat develops out of fog
and courses through water
to carry me
from my house
on stilts in sand.

Songs of Our Cells

In dreams I hear the songs I cannot hear:
leeches tap, earthworms and snakes
rattle their skeletons.
                              In these white pines
the thrush, the red-winged blackbird and the dove
sing in antiphony; under that earthly clatter,
I hear a canorous thunder and I know
I am inhabited by tiny remnants—
bits of viruses and organelles—
that go through evolutionary storms
with genes of fathers. Carrying the dead,
we are descended from a single cell,
waking to song.

JAMES SCHUYLER

The poems included here were all written in the Fairfield Porters' house on South Main Street in Southampton, where I used to stay in the sixties. Each is concerned with a view from a different window. In "Empathy and New Year" the man heard shoveling snow was the Porters' eldest son, John, and the man with whom I have a conversation about a snow picture coming back from the movies was Fairfield. The others, which, like many of my poems, are in a sense diary entries, seem self-explanatory.

Empathy and New Year

"A notion like that of
empathy inspires great
distrust in us, because it
connotes a further dose of
irrationalism and
mysticism."—LÉVI-STRAUSS

Whitman took the cars
all the way from Camden
and when he got here
or rather there, said,
"Quit quoting," and took the next
back, through the Jersey meadows
which were that then. But
what if it is all, "Maya,
illusion?" I
doubt it, though. Men are not
so inventive. Or
few are. Not knowing
a name for something proves nothing. Right
now it isn't raining, snowing, sleeting, slushing,
yet it is
doing something. As a matter of fact
it is raining snow. Snow
from cold clouds
that melts as it strikes.
To look out a window is to sense
wet feet. Now to infuse
the garage with a subjective state
and can't make it seem to
even if it is a little like
What the Dentist Saw
a dark gullet with gleams and red.
"You come to me at midnight"
and say, "I can smell that after
Christmas letdown coming like a hound."
And clarify, "I can smell it
just like a hound does."
So it came. It's a shame

expectations are
so often to be counted on.

New Year is nearly here
and who, knowing himself, would
endanger his desires
resolving them
in a formula? After a while
even a wish flashing by
as a thought provokes a
knock on wood so often
a little dish-like place
worn in this desk just holds
a lucky stone inherited
from an unlucky man. Nineteen-sixty-
eight: what a lovely name
to give a year. Even better
than the dogs': Wert
(". . . bird thou never . . .")
and Woofy. Personally
I am going to call
the New Year, Mutt.
Flattering it
will get you nowhere.

II

Awake at four and heard
a snowplow not rumble—
a huge beast
at its chow and wondered
is it 1968 or 1969?
for a bit. 1968 had
such a familiar sound.
Got coffee and started
reading Darwin: so modest,
so innocent, so pleased at
the surprise that *he*
should grow up to be *him*. How
grand to begin a new
year with a new writer

you really love. A snow
shovel scrapes: it's
twelve hours later
and the sun that came
so late is almost gone:
a few pink minutes and
yet the days get
longer. Coming from the
movies last night snow
had fallen in almost
still air and lay
on all, so all twigs
were emboldened to
make big disclosures.
It felt warm, warm
that is for cold
the way it does
when snow falls without
wind. "A snow picture," you
said, under the clung-to
elms, "worth painting." I
said, "The weather operator
said, 'Turning tomorrow
to bitter cold.'" "Then
the wind will veer round
to the north and blow
all of it down." Maybe I
thought it will get cold
some other way. You
as usual were right.
It did and has. Night
and snow and the threads of life
for once seen as they are,
in ropes like roots.

Poem

for Trevor Winkfield
December 26, 1970

The wind tears up the sun
and scatters it in snow.
The sky smiles and out
of its mouth drifts free
a milk tooth which of itself
glides under the pillow
of a cloud. The Tooth Fairy
knows where to look and when
to lock away the leaves
long since packed up and
left: "I'm southbound." Not
now, though this funny
fluffy winter rain coasts
down and coats the grass
dry and white, a corn meal
shampoo. "Brush it in,
brush it out." Easier
said than done. Things
take the time they take:
leaves leaving, winter
and its flakes, not less
though shorter lived.

In January

after Ibn Sahl

The yard has sopped into its green-grizzled self its new
  year whiteness.

A dog stirs the noon-blue dark with a running shadow
  and dirt smells cold and doggy

As though the one thing never seen were its frozen
  coupling with the air that brings the flowers of
  grasses.

And a leafless beech stands wrinkled, gray and sexless—
all bone and loosened sinew—in silver glory

And the sun falls on all one side of it in a running
glance, a licking gaze, an eye-kiss

And ancient silver struck by gold emerges mossy, pinkly
lichened where the sun fondles it

And starlings of anthracite march into the east with
rapid jerky steps pecking at their shadows

The sky eats up the trees

The newspaper comes. It
has a bellyful of bad news.
The sun is not where it was.
Nor is the moon. Once so
flat, now so round. A man
carries papers out of the
house. Which makes a small
change. I read at night.
I take the train and go
to the city. Then I come
back. Mastic Shirley,
Patchogue, Quogue. And for
all the times I've
stopped, hundreds, at their
stations, that's all
I know. One has
a lumberyard. The sun
puts on its smile.
The day had a bulge
Around three p.m. After,
it slips, cold and quiet,
into night. I read
in bed. And in the a.m.
put a record on to

shave to. Uptown in a
shop a man has blue
eyes that enchant. He
is friendly and inter-
esting to me, though he is
not an interesting man.
Bad news is a funny kind
of breakfast. An addict
I can scarcely eat my
daily crumble without
its bulk. I read at
night and shave when
I get up. That's true.
Life will change and
I am part of it and
will change too. So
will you, and you, and
you, the secret—what's
a secret?—center of
my life, your name and
voice engraved like
record grooves upon
my life, spinning its
tune between the lines
I read at night, a
graffito on the walls
of flowered paper I
see, looking up from
pages of Lady Mary
Wortley Montague or
a yellow back novel.
A quiet praise, yes
that's it, between the
lines I read at night.

© Dave Gearey

ARMAND SCHWERNER

I had a house in Springs for over 15 years. It was there that I experienced an intimacy with my woods, Accabonac waters, the birds—both visitors and permanent residents in my "aviary"—and my first vegetable gardens. I first clammed there and learned whatever I do know about salt-water fishing from the experiences with flounders, stripers, bluefish, snappers at Louse Point, weakfish and. . . . The appearance of the natural world in my poetry is deeply indebted to these intimacies.

KEY:
. . . . *untranslatable;*
+ + + + + + *missing;*
(?) variant reading;
[ ] supplied by the scholar translator.

TABLET IX

because the terror they* afflict me with is well-known

　　　　　*The Foosh? Old No-Name? The Fly? The Creep?

. . . . the fire which is palsy . . . . penis
because the raaling the goruck me lightthring paws ship
+ +
and what will you do when your words give out
when the dumb whose blood is paste in a hot mouth
. . . . + + + + + + + + + + + + + + + + + + purple foxglove*

　　　　　*one of the first mentions of the finger shaped plant,
　　　　　source of digitalis, the heart stimulant; intense con-
　　　　　sciousness? rise into awareness?

because the paste lightthring paws ship
because repulsives in sperm-offerings dry in a big cockshead box
　　　pintrpnit
because the sinuous fever snakes through my bone-ends makes
　　　me crazy
reminds my body of sacrifice, they follow they afflict they follow
and what will I do when my glue words dry and lightthring dust
　　　paws ship
they is *you* and *anyone,* dust sperm and a crush of mush brains pity
because the dumb follow in slow death the riven owl Old No-
　　　Name
and cry soundlessly like cut wheat and can only live shrinking
. . . . + + + + + + + + + + + + + + + + and yesterday
the fresh waters teemed with upturned lips of jelly
with tentacles and the tiny mouth
and yesterday the fresh waters teemed

165

with the fat upside-down jelly mouth trailing forests*

> *touching instance of close zoological observations:
> lines refer probably to the polyp and sexual medusa
> stages (upturned and downturned vessel shapes) of
> the coelenterates: hydra, jellyfish, obelia . . .

now the other world, this place, THIS IS . . . .
. . . .
THIS IS . . . . + + + + + + + + + ... + + + + + +
. . . . as they are leaving me as they leave, sperm
and tears go out, and pus goes out, and piss, and they leave,
everything's always going out, they . . . .
. . . . pattern (shoes?) for the [Sheol] of Pinitou
. . . . out like sweat, like earwax, like shit, nothing + + + + + +
+ + + + + + + + + + + + + foxglove . . . . holds
his long man . . . . this unexpected place THIS IS . . . .
hurtling turnaround lightthring paws ship cockshead alone for a
    toy
I walk when I walk
        when I walk I walk
            I walk when I walk, they . . . .
they follow they afflict they follow THIS . . . .
. . . .
. . . . loveliness

in the face of a bog	with jealousy
in the face of a creek	with jealousy
in the face of sometimes-wet-hard-thing*	with jealousy
in the ear of the last shallow breath	with jealousy
in the face of salad greens	with jealousy
in the guilt of clay ear-plugs	with jealousy
in the eyes of swell-shrink*	with jealousy
in the face of thin-thin-fat*	with jealousy
in the life of the round dance	with jealousy

> *approximations. Cognate fragments suggest that the
> reader may continue the list ad lib, with group re-
> sponse continuing.

when I walk, I walk, I must say I walk when I walk

I have that I have had that
no envy of Old No-Name gets to me I have these legs of laughter
everything always keeps leaving me, it is
never enough, I've surrendered the damp lips of speech
emptied these eye sockets, filled my ears with good clay, ground
    down
my fingertips I'm left like a dog to smell my way to the dream
THIS IS AN EMPTYING . . . . . . so much living . . . . . . forgiven
. . . . + + + + + + + + + + +
. . . . in the face of a creek reeds come back
+ +

TABLET XXIII

+ +
how I want to become transparent!
+ + + + + + + more sturdily in the world
. . . . of water
tractableness of roots twisting. . . . . much like water
doing their practice under the forest floor
in season laden with shoots from the tree-roots, com-
panions in the changing . . . . of the shadowed
    understory of the floor
there's a stillness in this upward-tending of the sap-laden lives
contains its opposite. how I want to become transparent
+ + + + + + the vibrating ochre atmosphere of my body . . . .
between the violence of the slow drying-up of the water-tubes
in the trees and the vivifying brown and rust forest + + + + + +
my dear love you are the green denominator of this liquid
    ambience, or
you have the specialness of a drop of water

not attached to anything . . . . is it stupid to say
You are not in a place, or
there is no place that contains you, not a place is special, all but
greening presence and movement and the plunge into the green
pain
I love you as if you had died and are here anew. the kitchen floor
is clean. in the kitchen the breezes of our separate
practices vibrate the upperstory of the forest leaves
to unforethought-of
song. you are practicing by giving away
your shoulds, this gift the cambium
of the forming will, the breeze plays, the entire arching forest
    plays
seeing you now after your death, I study, you
invested with such surprise
of movement, look, now, here,
gone, gone back to return . . . . in flights
in the vast forest mind . . . the narrow room yes become so vast so
hospitable o so hospitable to the hunt and catch of the waver of
    the minute
insupportable, and these gestures toward the available—
becoming in their green good time the very roots the tractable
filament-bundles the violence of our story in the stillness of its
    water

TABLET XXV

clearly I'm the swimming animal, the light
song or the dark song + + + + + + + + + simple . . . .
when it's hot I'm wet, I don't need to celebrate, to
strike two stones together, alone in this small getting older house
humbled by distractable eyes, quiet realm . . . . animal
what happened yesterday? the lettuce drains on the sill

colored liquids going up and down inside me......tracks......
......................without any time + + + + + + + + +
+ + + + + + + + + + + + + + + ...
river .... reaching around behind my left shoulder. never mind.
..........................reaching around into the hollow
behind my left shoulder, anything, there might be
water, a wasp, clangor lately, the thickness
of the vagina smell of another room, the great matters of my
    pictures
whose songs in my dreams look like my story, look like + + + + +
nothing, there's nothing after I cut down the frenzied objects
in the dance, nothing
to celebrate or hide from.................iron cinctures
in my shoulders, unnecessary to turn around, back
is back ....a phalanx of my teachers' changing voices
on the clay road and I lift my head up to the perennial sun, hot
red stone in a blue containing it, or back of it,
so it is there
I in my air here.........................these small
getting older thighs matted like the floor of the woods
with webs and fists of branches keeping their story
+ + + + + + + + + + + + + letting drop away
their story ....ah the ground yesterday
a vast invitation of voices, wet through by flooding,
alive with drone and crawl, track and shimmer of beings in love
with the hazy dust of water ....
....
....
....
....
....
.........................hazy ....

© William Suttle

HUGH SEIDMAN

Essentially, I've spent two summers on the East End. In 1977 I shared a house in Amagansett near the ocean. In 1985 I was in the woodsy Springs by the bay with two writer friends, although the rural illusion got ruined some mornings by the bulldozer and the banging, as the third of three brand new houses went up across the road.

And how interesting that nature and man should co-exist so forcefully, since whether one works out in the ocean or the bay, it is hard to forget the Hamptons' other major exercise—social swimming.

Thus, for instance, aside from catching the light in the late afternoon at Georgica Beach after a day at the type-writer, one of my favorite pastimes was a ride into town followed by a coffee and muffin at a nice white table in front of the Hackings Buttery on Newtown Lane. My theory was that I was bound to meet someone from past or present, since undoubtedly everyone passes down Route 27 sooner or later.

In fact, during that summer eight years ago, in a similar frame of mind, I ran into the person who is the subject of "Eurydice." I didn't have a car and a walk down the main street of Amagansett was grand adventure.

This year, however, I scooted around in a little yellow rented Datsun. Yet, too, what could compare to a quiet afternoon at home sitting out on the deck under a bright sky and the trees, listening to the wind rattling the leaves. Nice to keep in touch with all that, as another poem, "O Tree," might make clear.

So, I don't know if I qualify as a true poet of the region, but I have, as they say, been inspired by the place.

Eurydice

But still after seven years I met you again like a movie
by accident in the street:
a psychologist, a mother
still tall with small feet
still to be called beautiful
dark haired yet with one gray streak
as if the human had marred the human

But still it was hard not to smile
that lovers died or that death went on
like a life or that we
lived again before the blue steel
toy angel of your new daughter
who was yours and no man's
though I slept like a husband and wore your bone ring

And still the gulls glinted
and we fed the ducks and horse
on Amagansett's white beach
and still any wind blew the clouds
at the abandoned elevated road in the dusk on the
    Hudson
where the bulbs were screwed
as to the metal of some war

And still you asked what I thought
whatever I thought I thought

and your daughter played doctor
when nothing seemed wrong but that
you stood at the yellow chrysanthemum
I held on her birthday
like all that you must not take

Or as when a woman takes anyone
to return to men as you said
that I had you to have nothing
whatever you said I withheld
to dream myself barred with the dead
at my barred crib
on Spring Street and on Water Street and on Ocean
    Avenue

So that the abstract dark grew
particular as of no particulars
like the shadows on the floor
or like that man and that woman
who still woke to the dawn
from whatever had been mammal
to thirst with the first salt of the reptile

Whatever love raged as to cure
love's second failure from the personal
blasphemy of its metaphors:
like the sun as the great
black arachnid in the tree
to track men by their vibrations
or like the dark on the stone in its blast that had been
    a man

Though you wrote in my book: *for H against despair*
and the mystical blue of your eye
like a chip of the air
still sparked in the room
whether of the mind or actual
close, total, yet unfathomable
as the glitter that was the sea

Or as the terror and the awe
of your body as your body

of whatever sent us back to the underworld
whatever hope meant or to yield
that you hung up in the dark when I called
whatever the dark was that blew
up an image to the enormous shining
like some dead actress in some dark theater on the
    screen

Alberts Landing

And how shall we toil like the crab beyond repayment?
And how shall we not act in its conflict?
And what song shall last as long as the earth?
And how shall we be led to the dust?
And how shall the richest or the poorest come to
    bathe?
And for whom shall the beautiful be saved?
And who is so ugly or dumb that he knows no love?
And is the white sail free on its walled infinity?
And what is the context before the blank of everything?
And who shall stare fearlessly at the blue?
And what is the desire that is as simple as opening the
    eyes to see?

O Tree

O sentinel, magnet, north.
You set the poles and are the pole.
You ring nothingness

and grow toward nothingness.
Your blood climbs and the insects
inch your crevices.

And the rock attends you,
and you are like rock.
You are so solid yet the wind

makes you echo the sea.
You tremble, you undulate
beneath the watery light.

It shimmers and wavers.
It presses its weight.
Your edges burn so much,

but you are unperturbed.
And each creature comes
whose shadow stains the ground,

whose face is ablaze,
but you are unperturbed.
But under the last sun, that one,

that greatest sentinel,
when rose touches gold,
you yield, the soul opens.

You watch the sky, the stars.
You become a sky, a star—
or you change once more.

You become the shaggy friend,
the day's awkward dog.
You take the water of earth.

It ends in your living,
and you are its patience.
And always you rise over earth:

so naked, comic, anchored.
O hero, companion, technician.
O oldest and youngest.

How should I ever be lonely before you?

The Immortal

The ferry heaves past the buoys
the island spruce stand
straight to the universe

The dawn sea burns with phosphorus
I think the Milky Way's
immense dust

On a deck like this one
one hero had been chained
to steer the song

Many too have tried to clear
to be returned like his men
upon the body

For at that sky I can hear
your pitch beyond the current
so tuned to the lured

Or you were the Amazon
your nipples like flints
that spark under the hands

Your were the gold-eyed
soldier of the mammal
who wails for the hull of rib

Or then you grew archaic
like the arachnid
or the stark blind fish

Or you were nothing but the air
the blue metal shield
and what you knew I knew

Of the whole wind
as if you would always be
love past the human

Like the mud
and the mineraled knife
in your hair for the initiate

Where the light strikes rock
at the coast like a fact
of what belief assures

Though you are only a woman
come down to the dock
common as a goddess

As I stand like all heroes
where the precise bee
whines at the screen

Because in the world
all men have seen
she who rules the world

Strict as rock
like you who are always empty
like you who are always full

And the sun flecks the tide
and the cormorants glide
on the drafts of the air

And the trees are at peace
the trees are at peace
or so it is said

And so

"Harvey Shapiro, Saul Shapiro, Dan Shapiro, 1966"

HARVEY SHAPIRO

Looking through my work to suggest poems for this anthology I was surprised by how much this region, the eastern shore of Long Island, has given me. Surprised because I think of myself as an urban poet, in those uplifting moments of the early morning when I think of myself as a poet at all.

Yet why should I be surprised. I started coming out to the east end about twenty-six years ago, and have spent more vacations either on the north or south forks than anywhere else in my adult life. I began in 1953 by staying for some weeks in East Marion, at the home of the painter Stamos. For the next several years I took my summer breaks mainly in Peconic, in a shack-like house on a bluff over Long Island Sound. See my poem "The Bridge," which grows out of that experience and is dedicated to John Wissemann, a fine painter, born in Southold, who has spent his life teaching high school there.

177

Then for fifteen years I had a house in the dunes area of Amagansett. Some of my poems were written there. Some were written in my head, on the Long Island Expressway, during those interminable traffic jams (see, for example, "Riding Westward").

I started fishing on the north fork, catching porgies for breakfast in the Sound, to pan fry with my eggs. When I can, I still cast into these waters, as I cast for these poems.

At the Shore

1.

If my head is numb,
my heart, my genitals also,
I can guard my wallet
confidently in the subway
like a citizen.

2.

When the face that was beautiful
turns ugly in argument—
You always—
then it is I see that death will come
leaving me as ignorant as ever.

3.

The bugs batting against the lamp, the
    midges,
in an old house, in summer,
the peacefulness after voices are stilled
is like the still small voice we were
told to tune in to as children.

4.

If you could figure it out,
the domestic arrangements you fall into,
like beds or a summer at the shore.
You wake up facing a meadow,
beyond that water, beyond that an island.
On the other side of the island
you begin another life.

July

You poets of the Late T'ang send me messages
   this morning.
The eastern sky is streaked with red.
Linkages of bird song make a floating chain
In a corner of the world, walled in by ocean and
   sky,
I can look back on so many destructive days and
   nights,
and forward too, ego demons as far as mind
   reaches
Here, for a moment, the light holds.

Battlements

For H. R. Hays

These dark colors I place against
the blue heron at Louse Point. Summer
eternal, though after we go,
it may all be paved over.

Into the calm morning
steps the blue heron. The shore
oscillates like a nest to his leaving.

179

The old poet is brought down to look at the bay.
He thinks he has never done justice to anything
   in his poems.
Gulls crack shells on the macadam road.
Returning, held by others, he urinates by the
   car.

When you die, who will come out
to meet you if not the blue heron.

Riding Westward

It's holiday night
And crazy Jews are on the road,
Finished with fasting and high on prayer.
On either side of the Long Island Expressway
The lights go spinning
Like the twin ends of my tallis.
I hope I can make it to Utopia Parkway
Where my father lies at the end of his road.
And then home to Brooklyn.
Jews, departure from the law
Is equivalent to death.
Shades, we greet each other.
Darkly, on the Long Island Expressway,
Where I say my own prayers for the dead,
Crowded in Queens, remembered in Queens,
As far away as Brooklyn. Cemeteries
Break against the City like seas,
A white froth of tombstones
Or like schools of herring, still desperate
To escape the angel of death.
Entering the City, you have to say
Memorial prayers as he slides overhead
Looking something like my father approaching
The Ark as the gates close on the Day of Atonement
Here in the car and in Queens and in Brooklyn.

Harvey Shapiro

Montauk Highway

Murderous middle age is my engine.

The Bridge

for John Wissemann

John, the old bunker fleet at Greenport
Is a ghost. Many beautiful things are gone.
The masts, the dockside buildings
Float in your blue water colors,
Blue and black, in Brooklyn,
Where I seem to be giving up the ghost.
Artists of the region. All one island.
Whitman's crummy fish-shaped island.

Like you I do the indigenous stuff—
Crabs from the creek, blues from the September sea,
Poems from the tar roofs and the redbrick library
Where they house the prints—opening the Bridge!
Fireworks and exultation! Crowds moving
In a mighty congress back and forth.
While we, unmoving on the starry grid of America,
Stare failure in the face, our blazing star.

It was a dream of summer. From the cliffs above
The Sound—humming birds hovering, red foxes
At the door—at evening I could see the schools
Of blues come in, savaging the waters and the bait.
Everything I wrote was magic to me. Ancient days.
Believe me, John, they wear us down with shit and
   work.
But one pure line—still mine or yours
For the grasping—can take us to that farther shore.

181

R. B. WEBER

Clearly, the landscape and the waters have affected me strongly, as they have nearly everyone who writes many poems out here. The selections here reflect some of that natural "affect." Writing poetry in this part of Long Island almost ipso facto involves words about the sea, potato fields, bays, scrub oak thickets, ponds, pine barrens, marshes, various wild fauna, the whole nature mystique going back to Wordsworth in poetry in English. I suppose, however, that Hesiod and Virgil are the ultimate ghosts for the bucolic nature out here, although Emerson and Whitman and Frost are the more immediate American models. Anyway, I try to intensify awareness of the human roots in the natural world through my work concerned with it. And I usually *celebrate* the recognition of living on and *in* this part of the whole earth called the East End.

Meanwhile we are all beset by three dangers. The first two arise from the temptations of prettification and nostalgia. They are such easy, sentimental stances. We don't always remember that what we humans call "Nature" doesn't exist out there as a picturesque pictureshow for our entertainment. It is a multiform wonder, with heartless competitiveness and rapacious appetites, amid the luxurient beauties.

The third danger comes from the American cultural craziness that threatens the natural world itself, too much of which is still disappearing before our eyes, being ground away by the emerging Condo-and-Glitz Hamptons. The link between the money and social glitter out here and the debasement of the environment, through excessive development, makes me feel pessimistic about the future of the "fabulous Hamptons," at least as a place where the natural landscape will continue to matter very much. Some of that feeling has come out in poems not used in this anthology. So I won't go on any more about that now; perhaps next time, for another and different anthology.

Meanwhile, in a culture with a subnormal taste for poetry which demands that readers feel and think about their lives differently, with an abnormal appetite for the new, and with an extraordinary thirst for instant gratification, a surprising amount of sensitivity remains, along with a stubborn will to live thoughtfully and well. The best poems in this book will have a central place in the lives of readers with those virtues. For the poetry that matters constantly struggles to renew the language and, through that renewal, to help its readers perceive/think/feel with the nerve ends of their consciousness of what it means to be fully alive in communion with the rest of life, all of life.

Peconic Autumn Day

The sandbacks   the tinted trees
the mussel-knotted grasses,
double themselves in the bay,
a mirror of old Apollo
rolling across the future
already part of the past.
My head lattices the net
work of the rocketing
mallards, the scalding flashes
of gulls, a great blue
heron   racketing wings
against the winds, the sub
marine fishing casts of
cormorants, the loons
crying their divings, the baffle
heads   bulleting beneath,
a swan   balanced on its bill
in gastronomical
gymnastics, and the black
ducks   scooping. In the marsh
muck   slime   of smelly
sweetnesses   of clamflat
gasses, "all of the elements
conspire" inside this bonebox
this shapechanger   my head,
cozing with the living waters.

November. Over the Hills

The clouds unroll us a diorama
of the world. They roil in the wind,
an argument that fractures ratchets.
Amidst the tumbles   the house shrugs,
wraps its jacket of shingles tighter
around our shoulders. We yearn
as we lean   jumbled together   to learn
directions to another world whirled,
unfurled from the moil of the clouds.

late   autumn   afternoons

holding earth   the sun
light   strums the strings
of tree trunks   my body
their long   long   rising
notes of disappearance
(the darkness wells up,
the light buckets down).

Weathers

"The seventeen of us left under a waning moon,
the march was very tiresome . . .
The news seems to be diversionary."

The moon blues the beach.
The sea shines like dark lead,
only moving   moving   swells
slowly   and recedes.

Walking out here   on the edge
I know now the world is flat.
We can't quite see it go,
but the water cliffs off   out there.

And suddenly you skip   to stop
crunching the shells that pave our way
in these blue lights.

A short wind bites at our fingers
even together
making December in our pockets.

Hushed   the ocean   flutters
along the brittle edge of sand,
like small   blue   birds   with white wings
balance on telephone wires in a freezing wind.

"Today   Nato killed a little bird
with his slingshot   We enter
the era of the bird."

185

ocean   beach   house

the seagulls   and the terns
drifts   passing my windows
all day   the clouds   falling
flakes   by feathering
wings   the white and the dusk
grey   both   up and down
lighting the air   swirls
riding the devious winds
fleet   reflections   beating
turning   hollow   bones

Behind these lids

as I lie back
my eyes float
below the top of my face:
two deep closed wells,
boarded over now
I hear from the wind
at the edge of the windows,
muttering through the mesh:
from the south   it keeps
saying   **from the south.**

A long time ago
I saw what it said:
my eyes opened ponds
birds flew around—
snow geese   and loons,
sparrows and blue birds
crows and cardinals—
But now   who sees
what the wind says?
My eyes shutter shut.

R. B. Weber

August dusk: Sag Harbor.

Sutures of shadows lace the grass,
while across the street   some small   crazy
legged children   run around   and
around   playing   Indians   while
(woowoo, woowoo, woowoo, woowoo)
a robin sits on a branch above
preening the lice from its softfeather
breast   The small pumping legs
continue to run   bright   red
feathers   in shuttles from trees
to garden   and back again   until
a porch light   blinks on   a voice
and the robin   plummets a last flash.

Notes on Contributors

PHILIP APPLEMAN teaches at the University of Indiana. His books include *Open Doorways* (Norton) and, most recently, *Darwin's Ark* (U. of Indiana Press). He lives in Sagaponack, New York City, and Indiana.

JANE AUGUSTINE's poems have appeared in numerous magazines and anthologies. She has taught and read widely, and has been a New York State CAPS fellow. She lives in New York and East Hampton.

GEORGE BRADLEY was born in 1953 and grew up, for the most part, in Sagaponack. *Terms to Be Met,* for which he was awarded the 1985 Yale Series of Younger Poets Award, recently appeared. He spends most of his time in New York.

EDWARD BUTSCHER is a critic and fiction writer as well as poet. His *Sylvia Plath: Method & Madness* is well known. The poems in this anthology are from a forthcoming collection, *Child in the House.* He lives in Amagansett and New York.

MARYANN CALENDRILLE took her MFA at Vermont College, where she studied with David Wojahn, Mark Doty, and Jack Myers. Her poems have appeared in several magazines. She lives in Sag Harbor and teaches at LIU/Southampton.

SIV CEDERING, novelist, poet, and translator from (and into) Swedish, recently published *Letters from the Floating World: Selected and New Poems* with the University of Pittsburgh Press. She lives in Amagansett.

GRAHAM EVERETT's most recent collection is *The Sunlit Sidewalk.* His poems have appeared in many magazines. He is founding editor/publisher of Street Press and Backstreet Editions, and has published many Long Island writers. He lives in Sound Beach.

BARBARA GUEST's *Herself Defined* is the highly praised biography of the poet H. D. Barbara Guest's collections include *Moscow Mansions* and *The Countess From Minneapolis.* She lives in New York and Southampton.

MICHAEL HELLER's *Knowledge* appeared from Sun Books. His other collections include *Accidental Center*. He is also well known as a critic. He lives in New York and East Hampton.

DAVID IGNATOW's *Collected Poems 1970–1985* is about to be released by Wesleyan University Press. His other volumes include *Poems 1939–1969, The Notebooks of David Ignatow,* and *Open Between Us.* He has been awarded the Bollingen Prize and the Shelley Memorial Award. He lives in New York and East Hampton.

YAEDI IGNATOW's collection *The Flaw* appeared from The Sheep Meadow Press in 1984. She received her MFA from Vermont College in 1985, and has read and taught workshops widely. She lives in Southampton.

KENNETH KOCH's newest collection is *On the Edge.* His plays and books on teaching poetry to children are also well known. He lives in Bridgehampton and in New York City, where he teaches at Columbia University.

NAOMI LAZARD's collections include *The Moonlit Upper Deckerina.* Her poems frequently appear in *The New Yorker* and other journals. She lives in New York and in East Hampton.

HOWARD MOSS's *New Selected Poems* appeared recently from Atheneum. He was awarded the National Book Award for *Selected Poems* in 1972. He is the author of a book of satirical biographies illustrated by Edward Gorey, *Instant Lives,* as well as a play and several collections of criticism. He lives in East Hampton and in New York, where he is poetry editor of *The New Yorker.*

STANLEY MOSS has a collection out from Horizon Books called *Skull of Adam.* Former poetry editor of the original New American Review, he is editor and publisher of The Sheep Meadow Press. He lives in Riverdale and in Water Mill.

DAN MURRAY is a founding editor of Street Press and Street Magazine, and his poems have appeared widely. His collections include *Short Circuits* and *The Calendar Poems.* He lives in Riverhead.

SIMON PERCHIK's *Who Can Touch These Knots: New and Selected Poems* recently appeared from The Scarecrow Press, in its "Poets Now" series. He has published eight other collections, and his poems have appeared in hundreds of magazines. He lives in East Hampton.

ANSELM PARLATORE, editor of *Granite* and now of *Bluefish,* lives in Southampton. His collections include *Hybrid Inoculum* and *The Circa Poems.*

ALLEN PLANZ is a licensed captain as well as a poet and teacher. He lives in Sag Harbor. Among his books of poems are *A Night for Rioting, Wild Craft,* and *Chunderhara.*

FAIRFIELD PORTER's *Collected Poems* has just been published by Tibor de Nagy Gallery, with an introduction by John Ashbery. His paintings are in museum and private collections the world over; *Fairfield Porter: Realist in an Age of Abstraction* was published by Boston Institute of Fine Arts a few years ago. He lived in Maine and Southampton.

ANNE E. (Mrs. Fairfield) PORTER lives in Southampton. Her poems, as yet uncollected, have appeared in many magazines, most frequently in *Commonweal.*

GRACE SCHULMAN has a house in East Hampton. Her collections are *Burn Down the Icons* and *Hemispheres.* She is the poetry editor of *The Nation.*

JAMES SCHUYLER was awarded the Pulitzer Prize for *The Morning of the Poem.* His other collections include *The Crystal Lithium, Hymn to Life,* and, most recently, *A Few Days.* He lived in Southampton for about a decade.

ARMAND SCHWERNER's well-known Tablets are included in *sounds of the river Naranjana and the Tablets I-XXIV* (Station Hill Press). He lives on Staten Island and had a house in The Springs for over fifteen years.

HUGH SEIDMAN won the Yale Series of Younger Poets Award for his first book; his most recent, *Throne/Falcon/Eye,* appeared from Random House in 1982. He has spent summers in East Hampton. He lives in New York.

190

HARVEY SHAPIRO's six books of poetry include *Lauds and Nightsounds* and, most recently, *The Light Holds* (Wesleyan). He lives in Brooklyn, and has spent many summers in East Hampton. For eight years, he was editor of *The New York Times Book Review;* he is now deputy editor of *The New York Times Magazine* and is a *Times* literary critic.

R. B. WEBER's collections are *Laurie's Songs, Poems from the Xenia Hotel,* and *The Fishing Print Poems.* He teaches at LIU/Southampton and lives in Flanders.

ROBERT DASH (cover art), the well known painter, is represented by Hirschl and Adler Modern in New York. He lives in Sagaponack, and his essays on gardening are well-known to readers of the East Hampton *Star.*

JOSH DAYTON (etching) was born and raised in East Hampton. He is represented by Bologna-Landi Gallery. He lives in Sag Harbor.

ROBERT LONG (editor) teaches writing at LIU/Southampton. His poems have appeared widely, including *The New Yorker* and *Poetry.* His newest collection, *What Happens,* will appear in 1987. He was born in 1954 in New York City, and now lives in East Hampton.

2/12   "Couple #1"   Josh Dayton